PILGRIM SOULS

PILGRIM SOULS

A Memoir

Jan Murray

Published by Tablo

Table of Contents

ON THE TOSS OF A COIN

PART ONE

The Edge... There is no honest way to explain it because the only people who really know where it is, are the ones who have gone over.
Hunter S. Thompson.

It is often the little things we do that make the biggest difference.

I stopped once at a roundabout in Byron Bay to pick up a hitchhiker and that simple act would change my life forever, change it in a way I could never have imagined.

If a 'junction' is how the dictionary describes a roundabout, then the one I tangled with on that sunny North Coast afternoon in September 1997 was just that; a junction. Metaphorically speaking.

Earlier in the day, something else happened that would also have life-changing consequences. I purchased a property in Suffolk Park, a beachside suburb five kilometres south of the village of Byron Bay. It was a capricious act. I hadn't woken up that morning planning to buy a piece of real estate. Not in Byron Bay or anywhere else.

My spur-of-the-moment decision was done in the manic phase of the bi-polar illness that had plagued my life since childhood, but had only, a couple of years before, been diagnosed, due to a near-fatal psychotic episode.

Life felt large this day. Manic highs leave you no time for quiet contemplation. You feel indomitable. Unstoppable. In the manic phase, you are financially and sexually promiscuous. There is something wildly intoxicating about skimming the high peaks of mania. It's as if the universe is with you all the way. As if you're up there on Mount Olympus partying with the gods. Marian Faithful sang about it. The urge to fly through Paris with the warm wind in her hair—and then in one suicidal leap from a tall building, her wish is fulfilled.

It's no wonder the rise to Olympian heights is exhilarating. And precarious. The fall to earth can be profound.

The painful collapse of my thirty-two-year marriage was the trigger for the psychotic meltdown. What followed was a nightmare, including a serious suicide attempt—the paramedics defibrillating me three times on the way to Emergency; being scheduled twice under the NSW and then the Queensland Mental Health Acts; being locked up in psychiatric wards in both States; experiencing manic episodes that threatened mine and other people's lives; extended periods in and out of clinics; an inability to get even a continuous hour's sleep for nights on end; and the soul-wearying, debilitating effects of living with a malignant depression.

All this, out of the blue, happening to a person used to being on top of her game, in charge of her life, useful to her children and grandchildren, able to run her busy PR consultancy, support her political spouse, and generally cope with life's ups and downs with equanimity.

Then came April 11th, 1995, and boom!

My family was suddenly presented with a wife and parent in free-fall, and with no net to catch her. It was a time before the plethora of memoirs recounting the serious nature of depression had hit the bookshelves, before bi-polar entered the common lexicon, before Beyond Blue, before the Black Dog Institute, before anyone was disseminating professional information and well before politicians were campaigning on funding for mental health issues. In other words, it was a time before the stigma surrounding mental illness had lifted and light was allowed to shine in to illuminate the darkness. And it was a frightening time for all of us.

Had I been hit by a car instead of a psychotic tsunami my children would have called an ambulance. But when suddenly confronted with a mother so 'gone in the head', acting so irrationally, my bewildered and panicking offspring were caught floundering. Unfortunately, what they did next, with all the best intentions, proved disastrous.

Good friends recommended a particular psychiatrist, and my children were able to secure an immediate consultation with him in his Macquarie Street rooms. It soon became evident, however, that the doctor was the problem, not the solution. Without asking if I were taking medication for any existing ailments—and after an interview that seemed uncomfortably fixated on my spouse, the Honourable John Brown, who had been the high-profile Minister for Arts, Sport, Environment and Tourism in the Hawke Government—the Macquarie Street man took out his pad and blithely proceeded to write out a prescription for Prozac.

And so, it began, the nightmare. The medical profession—but obviously not this doctor—had become aware by now that the combination of steroids and SSRIs, in particular, Prozac, was a highly clinically significant one, and such a combination was to be avoided at all cost. The contra-indications were too dangerous, the risks considered not worth the benefits.

On this day of my sudden collapse, the prescription ordered for me, and diligently administered by my adult children, would be a disastrous combo, initiating the phenomenon tagged 'roid rage. Had the man taken the trouble to enquire, he would have learned I'd been taking steroids for the past week, prescribed by a GP for a highly aggravating allergy rash covering my entire body. For days, I had been laying on my bed under a ceiling fan covered in cold wet towels to ease the pain and itch.

The rash was apparent when I presented, and yet the specialist never enquired, but ordered my children to take his prescription for Prozac, get it filled immediately and start dosing me up. Oh, and see the receptionist on the way out.

It was the same treating psychiatrist who would admit me to the Sydney Clinic at Clovelly two weeks later, by which time my condition had deteriorated significantly, there having been serious psychotic episodes within days of commencing the Prozac; one involving my husband and a pair of scissors, the other an attempt to throw myself in front of a speeding car on Ocean Street, Woollahra. But the good doctor would eventually wake up to the problem he had helped create and begin prescribing new types of SSRIs, monitoring me closely as the mania subsided.

Unfortunately, the pendulum soon swung too far to the other extreme. I began sinking into a debilitating depression, compliant when the specialist arranged for my admission into the care of the professionals at Clovelly.

Mistakes would pile on however, and things would go from bad to worse. By the time a week in residence at the Sydney Clinic had passed, and I was almost comatose with drugs, the psychiatrist would be calling in the police and having me locked up and scheduled under Clause 10 of the NSW Mental Health Act. It was a brutal response to what was an insignificant act on the part of a very sick patient. I was in a darkly depressive state, harbouring suicidal thoughts, refusing food, my weight dropping dramatically, and the clinic people so concerned they were considering intravenous feeding.

It was late on the Sunday afternoon. Mothers' Day. Although a special day, my eldest son, Jonathon, was the only one of my family allowed to visit me because I was in such a fragile state of health, physically and mentally. The idea was that this sensible—and sensitive—young man might be able to encourage his mother to eat something. A scone and a cup of coffee was the kindly nurse's short-term goal that afternoon.

Mine was to be left alone. To lay in bed under the sheets and simply fade away.

Although our desires were incompatible, the nurse was always going to win because I was too weak to resist and my son was/is a good talker. The nurse turned me out of bed, tidied me up and congratulated me on my valiant effort to co-operate. I might even enjoy the afternoon tea I was about to have with my son, she said.

Nodding to her, Jon took my arm and helped me down the flight of stairs and in to the canteen.

Our timing was lousy. The canteen was empty and just closing up for the day. However, the woman behind the counter, another kindly soul, generously offered to make us coffees and to retrieve a couple of scones from out in the kitchen. We could sit here while she cleaned up. No worries, love, she said and Jon thanked her and led me to a table. It was then that a man's head emerged from the kitchen, and the scone-maker abruptly ordered us out of his realm.

Meekly, I began to apologize and tried to explain the special circumstance, that it was not my idea but the order of the nurse upstairs.

I have had a significant hearing loss since childhood and did not hear his reply, but he snatched the plate of scones out of the woman's hand and apparently berated her for offering to serve us at this time of day. He turned back to us then, and this time I did hear him. It was an uncompromising order to my son and me to leave the canteen.

His dammed scones had been the last thing I'd wanted, and having had to beg for them, and then been told off by the man? Well, suddenly it seemed to my sick brain that this was the ultimate indignity in what had been weeks of indignities. Despite being so ill, so zombie-like, thanks to the Largactil injections and whatever other drugs the Dispensary were dishing out to me upstairs every time the latch slid open and the little paper cup of pills was presented, I rallied from my torpor just long enough to arc up.

I'm a Scorpio. The sting in the tail, okay? Either that, or my inherently keen highland Scottish sense of injustice, call it as you will, but I snapped. And I still remember how good it felt to let those weeks of pent up, turbulent emotions loose with a heartfelt 'Fuck you!' as I hurled my coffee mug across the room, smashing it against the far wall. As fragile as I was, I ran outside and kept running, back up the stairs to my room. Back under the sheets. Back to the dark place.

But I would be punished. And I did not have long to wait. The temper tantrum would be the immediate trigger for what was to come next, so unexpected and frightening in its rapidity.

The psychiatrist did not appreciate the call he received from the young clinic nurse who had been at the top of the stairs when her patient made it up and collapsed in her arms. After putting me to bed, she rang him, expecting he would wish to visit his highly disturbed patient, talk to her, maybe alter her medication. But he had been somewhat under the weather on this Mothers' Day Sunday afternoon, tired and emotional, according to a senior nurse who knew him well. Irish whiskey was his drink of choice. He had apparently berated the staff for the interruption to his post-prandial siesta.

It happened without warning; the heavy boots on the staircase. Police hurrying down the hall.

The nurse had hardly hung up from her conversation with him and checked my condition when two uniformed policemen burst in and ordered nurses to pack my bag and sign me over. I have no argument with the police. They were simply following orders from a man who wished not to be disturbed, but to be allowed to slip back into his boozy Sunday afternoon oblivion. These days, such a response to attending a mentally ill patient would not be tolerated. At least, I hope it wouldn't. I believe there have been government enquiries into the way mentally ill patients should—and should not—be taken into custody.

All the way down the stairs, Jon fought their attempt to take me away. He knew I was not only very ill, but that for all my life, I had suffered with a pathological claustrophobia. But despite his efforts, I found myself being bundled in to the back of a police paddy wagon. Even during my days of protest, marching in anti-Vietnam moratoria and other acts of subversion, I had squibbed at being carted off in a paddy wagon. And yet, on this Mothers' Day, in my pathetic state of non-resistance, I was being driven off to God knows where in the back of one.

I still recall the terror. In panic, I beat on the doors, on the sides of the wagon and screamed for my son who had been made to sit up front in the cabin.

The police pulled out from the Sydney Clinic's driveway and turned, ironically, onto Murray Street. Not that I knew where we were going—in my state of high anxiety, I was envisaging jail, but in reality, we were on our way to the Prince of Wales Hospital at Randwick where, after further claustrophobic procedures, including being strapped into a wheelchair by a straight-jacket and kept in an air-lock, I would eventually be admitted to the acute psychiatric ward with its high walls, padded cells and the threat of ECT machines. All for smashing a chipped coffee mug and cursing an irritable chef's stale scones.

Happy Mothers' Day.

After two weeks in lock-up, a period in my life in which I was subjected to great indignities, not least by the magistrate brought in to decide on my release or otherwise, I would be discharged and would continue to live another tumultuous year in Sydney, much of it in the loving care of my children and their partners.

There would be periods of sanity where I could almost carry on a normal life but mostly I would swing dramatically between the highs and lows of Bi-polar One, voluntarily admitting myself to clinics when I was down or alternatively, intent on harming people when I was riding high.

It was an *annus horribilis* for our family and one dawn morning, at the end of a volatile period of sleepless nights, I decided I had to escape in order to give my kids a chance to carry on their lives without the burden of dealing with a mother's acute mental illness. I understood deep down in my foggy brain that I would need to find a new way of living my life, of organizing the second half of it, a way that was divorced from the one I had been living up till now. No looking back.

Given that I come from Celtic stock—Irish and

Scottish—this was always going to be a stretch. For me, the past has always been a place I wallpaper prettily with sentimental images; a never-never land in which I spend far too much time. George Bernard Shaw wisely said, *"Talk to me only of the future because that is where I intend to spend the rest of my life."* Shaw was not a real Irishman, not your true Celt. It was always going to be a heartache for me to say goodbye.

I rose at dawn and, leaving a note behind, I departed the Woollahra terrace my family had been renting for me the past few months and drove through the night to our family's Mermaid Beach apartment on the Gold Coast.

It probably wasn't a great idea. Poor darlings then had to handle my madness long-distance for the next couple of years, and I doubt the frequent flyer points they accrued did much to outweigh their distress.

~~~

On the day of the roundabout incident and the property purchase, I rose just as the Mermaid Beach sun was beginning to peak over the horizon. Feeling agitated, I understood this day would be more dramatic than usual. The days, weeks, months, the almost two years of my self-imposed exile on the Gold Coast were over.

It was time to move on. The endogenous depression I had been suffering for months had switched gears overnight, and the mind-revving mechanisms had kicked in, sending me soaring up through the universe. No way could I stay still, stay put.

With no idea where I was going or why on this Gold Coast purple and orange dawn, knowing only that I had to obey an imperative, I jammed everything important to me into the boot of my black turbo Golf and, after a moment's deliberation spent wondering where to now, I decided to toss a coin.

Heads, I go up. Tails, I go down.

North or south?

I flicked the silver coin high, watching as it spun and circled in the air. And then it landed on the paving at my feet.

I let the token sit where it fell, fired up the Golf, and without so much as a glance in the rear-view mirror, left a year and a half of Mermaid Beach life behind me. Once again, I was on the move.

At the corner I made a left, turning south onto the Gold Coast Highway and hit the peddle.

My heartbeat was accelerating. My breath was putrid. My mind was flying off in shards, and the "Voices" had arrived. It would have been obvious to a sensitive onlooker that I was now in the manic phase of my bi-polar condition, but there were no onlookers to witness my madness.

It felt liberating to be free-wheeling down Life's highway. No one could have put the brakes on me anyway.

~~~

A couple of hours later, with the sun still low on the horizon, on a sudden impulse, I would turn in off the Pacific Highway and head down Ewingsdale Road into Byron Bay, where, later in the morning—in thrall to yet another capricious impulse—I would purchase an ugly little run-down beach shack nestled in the dunes of a magnificently wild Byron surf beach.

And still acting on these manic impulses, by the late afternoon I would pull over and pick up a handsome stranger at a roundabout. They say a person's fate can turn on a dime. What happened next would prove it.

A PROPERTY FOR SALE

And I shall have some peace there,
for peace comes dropping slow.
W.B. Yeats

I recall with fondness, but also with some cynicism, the Byron Bay I found waiting for me the morning in September 1997. It was still pretty much the old Byron. Although the genuine locals will give you an argument about that.

In the Nineties, however, it was still Byron; a hokey little village where you could walk down the street and bump into a friend. Still a town centre where you could find a parking spot out front of your bank. The Byron before parking meters. The Byron of old timber houses. The Byron of rainforests and green hills. Byron of the Blues and Roots festivals that still felt small and user-friendly. Byron before over-crowded and expensive writers' festivals. Byron before traffic jams. Byron of the genuine eccentric.

Byron when an impecunious writer could still afford to live there. In other words, it was Byron prior to rampant commercialism.

Byron Bay prior to the invasion.

Back in 1997 Ringo's big friendly cafe in Jonson Street was still the beating heart of the small seaside village of surfers and New Age hippies, serving up its generous helpings of love, peace and harmony to all who felt at home within the faded glory of its walls. But sadly, Melbourne and Sydney money rode in to town one sunny day and tore down the iconic old cafe, leaving Byron Bay the poorer for it.

Ringo's would be replaced by what would become just one more loud sportswear store among a plethora of other clothing stores and over-priced touristy food outlets.

Thanks to rapacious development that even green councilors failed to reign in, today's Byron Bay has lost its unique sense of place, the feeling it once had of a laid-back rural coastal community. The comfortably familiar and quirky now has to fight for its place amid prosaic commercial starkness.

I told you I was a sentimental fool. But, my God, I see Byron today and I weep. Old timber houses that once sat on large blocks hidden behind rampant rainforests have been bulldozed to make way for Five Star holiday resorts owned by vulgar capitalists, the palms growing there now complying with landscaping architecture lining white gravel driveways leading to Reception.

In the centre of the village, on high street and down sequestered lanes, offbeat little timber shops that sold equally offbeat merchandise—hand-made clothing, candles, incense and Balinese Buddhas—were replaced by ubiquitous franchise stores stacked with cheap Chinese sportswear with slogans in windows that try too hard to catch the 'cool vibe' of Byron Bay. There is an obviously desperate attempt to ride the reputation of the rainbow district.

The casual, friendly attitude that was once unique to Byron has given way to a commercial mindset intent on capitalizing on the hordes of holiday visitors who swarm into town, including not only the Gold Coast crowds availing themselves of a freeway that in fifty short minutes of straight highway these days can rockets them into yet another theme park, albeit a quaint one without wet rides, but also the masses of young backpackers, domestic and international, who flock to what is touted on the web, and by word-of-mouth, as the coolest party town in the universe.

It is ironic that these starry-eyed young backpackers, the Gold Coast tourists, and the cashed-up middle class that migrated to Byron Bay in search of its sea change dream have all managed to squeeze the marrow from a once magical little New Age place. Ironic, in so much as what these questers sought is the very thing their numbers and their money were bound to destroy.

But enough of the lamentations.

On the morning in the mid-nineties when I found myself cruising into Byron village with not a clue why I was heading there other than the fact that a coffee and a walk along a beach seemed like a good idea, the iconic Ringo's was still alive and well in all its shabby wonder and I believe it was the friendly embrace of Ringo's Café that sold me on Byron Bay that morning.

I can recall the warmth of its rough old timber floors, a knocked about platform for the mishmash of old tables and chairs. And at Ringo's there were rows and rows of bookshelves lining the walls. From memory, I think the bookshop might have operated on a swap, buy or help-yourself basis but for sure, it seemed an Aladdin's cave of long-forgotten literary treasures.

I took a seat.

It might have been a booth. Not sure. Can't remember. But I know as I looked around and took in the full ambience—the cork board on the far wall where colourful flyers spruiked yoga classes and rebirthing sessions at cut rates, where the art deco counter and hand-written menu stood beckoning, where the gallimaufry of old 1950's crockery and cutlery beamed a message of welcome even to the discombobulated mental case I was that morning—it all felt enticingly homely and today, as you can see, I'm still grieving its passing.

As I sat there, waiting to be served, I noticed a faded floral curtain at the back of the shop and once I'd seen one or two Byronians going through the curtain, I followed and found a hallway lined with even more pre-loved books.

With nothing to do and nowhere to be, I took my time flicking through dozens of yellowing pages of paperbacks, text books and once-fashionable coffee table books.

Dusty. Mouldy.

Tiny red mites scattering as I turned pages. Books smelling of other people's houses, as if they'd had been locked up in an old suitcase in Aunt Myrtle and Uncle Alf's back shed for decades. Romantic melancholy smells reminiscent of the many sweet wet Saturday afternoons I'd spent poking around in fusty second-hand bookshops in places like Paddington, Glebe, Brisbane and Balmain.

Many of the books had underlining and margin notes made by readers long ago who must have seen significance in a word, in a line. I love such books and chose several before I walked back to my seat across timber floors that smelled of beeswax and sandy thongs.

I was checking the menu when a freckle-faced girl with thick auburn braids and eyes the colour of expensive jade appeared at my side, notepad in hand and smiling down on me.

'What'll it be, then?' said the young woman.

I studied the menu for a moment and decided to pass on Ringo's special—a big country breakfast fry-up—delicious as it looked.

This was Byron Bay.

A brand-new day.

'You know what? I'm going to have a stab at that.' I laid down the menu and indicated the blackboard menu. 'Your organic muesli with berries ... and ... ah ... I like the look of your apple, carrot and ginger juice.' So much for the evil fry-up.

Welcome to Mung Bean World. I felt pleased with my choices. Virtuous.

'Coffee?' said the girl, flashing perfect white teeth and smiling green eyes that made even expensive jade seem ordinary by comparison.

'Sure thing. Make it a long latte, could you?'

'Soy?'

'Why not?' It was that kind of morning and I was in that kind of mood. I'd never tasted soy lattes but as I said to this pleasant young local who waited for my answer; why not?

'Decaf?'

'Okay.' I was up for the new. And given my revving brain, it was possibly a wise choice.

There was no sugar pot on the table I had chosen. This, after all, was Byron Bay. Pure honey from the local bees left to graze on lotus blossom was possibly the sweetener of choice around these parts.

'You need the sugar?' The green-eyed one said as she reached for a funny old-fashioned glass and silver sugar dispenser on a nearby table.

'Uh-uh. No sugar. Pure white and deadly!' I had reared my five kids on that mantra.

The young Byronian—or maybe she was a backpacker from Tassie picking up a few holiday dollars—smiled her approval and with a wink, was on her way across the room to place my order and continue spreading the love.

A few minutes later I looked up from a dog-eared and much rubricated copy of *Catcher in the Rye* to see another young likely backpacker setting my decaffeinated soy latte down in front of me with a friendly smile. I thanked the tall, good-looking youth and asked where he suggested I go if I wanted to take a long, uninterrupted beach walk to clear my head.

'You want to get away from the town?' It was said with a European accent, so I guess I was right about the backpacker thing.

'I think so.' I'd had my look around the village, smiled and said hello to a dozen friendly locals.

I knew a little of Byron Bay, firstly, from having come down from the Gold Coast during the previous year to help a colleague, Lionel Midford, with his PR launch of a disco-nightclub. Although it seems my Gold Coast time was defined by my mental state, including a serious suicide attempt, there must have been some reasonably lucid periods, albeit, while still poised on an emotional precipice.

For instance, not long after moving up to the Gold Coast I had received a call one day from Brian Walsh, someone I had known during my PR days in the Eighties. Back then, my public relations business, JMA, was booming, thanks to the various high-profile briefs we successfully—and often flamboyantly—handled. Consequently, we received more assignments than we could take on, and often we would flick some of the smaller accounts—the ones we called the 'rats and mice' accounts—to the more modest PR businesses being run by men such as Max Markson and Brian Walsh. By 1996, however, having graduated to the big league via his work with the NRL's Grand Finals, Brian Walsh was now a powerful Foxtel programming executive.

And here he was, offering *me* a bone, a 'rats and mice' one-off guest appearance on his new program *Beauty and the Beast*.

What Brian was offering was a guest appearance, with fellow panelists Margaret Whitlam, Catherine Greiner and Senator Bronwyn Bishop. It was a parliamentary-type panel to go head-to-head with the host, Stan Zemanek.

Funny, but the thing which sticks most vividly in my memory from my first day on *Beauty and the Beast* is of the four of us women in the dressing room, togging up for the show. Margaret kept making ironic quips. Catherine seemed aloof. Bronwyn wore a corset.

What comes around goes around. Foxtel, said Brian, would cough up for my travel expenses but from memory, I don't believe there was an appearance fee offered. Negotiations of that nature would come later, after the producers realized I was good talent and offered me a binding contract as one of the show's regular panelists.

The salient point here, however is this; I never for one moment let on to Brian that things had happened to my poor brain since our glory days in the Eighties. He knew me not only as a high-profile PR consultant who could handle herself in front of a camera, but also as the lippy wife of a Cabinet Minister who'd gone rogue, shocking the nation back in 1987 with her story of love-making with her ministerial spouse on his ministerial desk. Brian had no account of me as a mentally ill person who had recently been locked up in acute psychiatric wards in both NSW and Queensland, one who'd spent so many months in and out of clinics dealing with a serious bi-polar condition.

I guess he thought the opinionated and often controversial Jan Murray he knew of old would be a good performer on his shiny new agony aunt show.

Poor Mr. Walsh. He went into the thing with blinkers on and would, in the future, have many Jan Murray headaches to deal with.

While my friend Lionel must have believed at the time that I was up to the task he'd asked of me, with hindsight I think he regretted the invitation to help him with his client's nightclub promotion.

And if you asked him today, I think he would admit that the memory of that weekend still pains him because whenever I mention Byron Bay, poor Lionel will rest his hands in his head and sigh deeply. His off-sider had behaved so unpredictably and erratically that weekend, doing the opposite of what a good publicist cozying up to the media is supposed to do.

Several foodie journalists had been flown in to cover the event and been accommodated at Strop's Beach Hotel. I spotted several of them sitting poolside, sipping expensive cocktails on the morning of the Opening and figured they were getting in a little too early on the free ride. I lashed out in words that suggested they better earn their keep with positive reviews.

It wouldn't have happened in my professional PR days, accusing my journalists of exploiting the client's hospitality. Bad, bad me, but perhaps I was letting go of the years of pent up frustrations, the groveling, having to keep schtum so often when I saw free-loading media types hoovering up every last one of my clients' canapés and downing jeroboams of the expensive champagne—and then holding back on the love, holding back on the "ink" as we referred to press coverage in an age before social media.

Long before that disastrous weekend I had known Byron Bay. As a child, I'd been brought to the North Coast by my parents on our regular camping trips. That was a long time ago, in an era when instead of million-dollar acreage properties dotting the hills, you had great herds of black and white cattle roaming that same hinterland and giving up their milk to the Norco Butter Factory. Pigs were sent off to the meat works. And for a few years a whaling station plied its merciless bloody trade.

It's an era that's passed and, thankfully, the meat works became a cinema and backpacker hostel and the whaling slaughterhouse was replaced by the thriving up-market Beach Hotel, owned up until recently by a man known throughout the nation as Strop, John Cornell of Paul Hogan *Crocodile Dundee* fame. These are the kind of displacement no one regrets.

After I'd eaten my Ringo Café breakfast, I started thinking about going off to some quiet place for thinking time before I got back on the highway.

To where, who knew? I hadn't mentioned my morning's decampment from the Gold Coast to any of my children in Sydney. No one would have a clue where I was or know that I had hit the highway at dawn for places unknown.

Despite the decaf, the adrenalin was pumping and the Voices were persistent.

There were always Voices in the manic phase of my bi-polar condition.

I describe it as being like a CD-ROM—remember them? It played inside my skull. No let-up. Just frantic messaging from one Jan to the other Jan. A constant conversation with the self. And boy, did it get exhausting. So, I was up for a long walk on a quiet beach where I might make some attempt to calm my soul and sort out the next phase of my life.

There would be no going back north. I had left Mermaid Beach and the Gold Coast behind.

I had also left behind a relationship with a sweet and gentle man called Robbie, a Vietnam veteran with a head and heart full of heaviness that in our companionable months together—part of which I spent living with him on his sailing boat *Sutra* in Southport harbour—I hadn't been able to lighten. We had both been too emotionally fragile for the relationship to work. Robbie believed his 'Nam' experience hadn't been all that bad. Hello? He had only had to drive the trucks that went out after the bombings and mine explosions to collect the dead, the almost dead and the strewn body parts of his mates! Poor man. If he is alive today I hope he has acknowledged his courage and that the post-traumatic stress arising out of that terrible and unnecessary war he had to endure has abated to some extent.

'Go down Jonson, past the MITRE 10 till you get to the roundabout,' said the green-eyed girl who had overheard my question to the youth and stopped, plate stacks in hand, and joined in. 'Take the Bangalow Road exit out of town. It's the other side of the lighthouse. Suffolk Park. You'll walk forever without bumping into anyone down there. It's just the best beach for some serious mindfulness, if that's what you're looking for. I go there, sometimes. Quite often, in fact.' She shrugged. 'Or there's Main Beach, just up the road, here. Or Clarke's further down.'

She looked deep into my eyes, possibly seeing the mania. 'I'd go to Suffolk Park,' she said, softly as she touched my shoulder with her free hand.

Suffolk Park. Mindfulness? A chance to put a sock in the Voices for a while? Okay, I thought. It sounded like a trip I could use.

I finished off my virtuous breakfast at Ringo's Café and wandered outside, heading for the Golf. Its black bodywork had baked for an hour or so in the north coast morning sunshine and the little lady was a steaming hotbox. I wound down a couple of windows and while I waited for things to cool down, I followed my nose in the direction of the bakery.

Delicious aromas were wafting out of the tiny timber shop across the road. A feast of lovely pastries was displayed in the windows.

I'm not by any means a sweet tooth. Quite the reverse. I go for salty and sour over sweet and sickly every time. But on this odd morning of my flight to nowhere, things were a little topsy-turvy.

Lord make me virtuous, but not right now, said St Augustine, a wily fellow.

Mania feeds on excess.

I opted for not one but two scrumptious-looking big fat almond and cream croissants dowsed in icing sugar, and was devouring the first treat, up to my ears in icing sugar and almond flakes, when I heard a croaky voice behind me.

'G'day, love,' said the tiny crone as she passed me on the pavement, hauling a couple of heavy string shopping bags, plus a pile of books, under each wing.

'Hi, there. Let me help you. Where's your car?' I said.

'Don't have one, love. She's okay. I can manage. This and a whole lot bloody more, I reckon. How y'doin, anyway?' The old lady kept going while looking back over her shoulder at me. 'It's young Gloria, isn't it, Mabel's girl?' she called out.

'No. It's Jan. I'm new around here. Just passing through,' I said as I caught up to the woman I guessed to be well north of her eighties if crocodile skin was a pointer. 'I love your skirt. Did you get it here … in Byron?'

'India,' said the cheerful soul, handing over her load to me then, taking the sides of her hand-embroidered mirrored skirt, doing an agile swirl, flaring the skirt's long hems out with a dainty kick of a sandaled foot. 'You been there?'

'To India?'

'India, yep. Been there?' By now she was relieving me of the bundles and starting to walk off again, expecting, I guess, that I keep up the pace alongside.

'No. But one day I plan to.'

'Good for you, love. Bye, bye for now. Might see y'round at the Rails, okay? Say hello to y' mum for me won't ya?'

'Sure. See you. Bye.' I stood for a moment, my eyes following her as she strode towards a pushbike leaning against a shop front.

She dumped her load in the bike basket, tucked up the hem of her skirt and then this cheery little octogenarian, with all the eagerness of a horny back-seat teenager willing to give pleasure, straddled the bicycle.

She turned to wave at me.

I smiled and waved back as she peddled off, bemused as I drove away, heading for the place the young waitress had advised.

By the time I'd gone a short way I was lost. There were no signposts to Suffolk Park. Only to the Lighthouse. I pulled over. I was at Clarkes Beach.

'A long walk through that rainforest path up there then a steep climb to get to it,' said the elderly, slow-jogging gent who called out to me through the Golf's passenger window.

I hadn't yet asked for directions, although I had leaned out the window and had been about to do so.

'Sounds good,' I said to the wiry old codger who seemed as if he were about to attack the climb himself. 'Thanks.' He had presumed I wanted to walk to the lighthouse. A reasonable presumption I would later learn. It's a favourite nature and fitness trek of locals and tourists, alike.

'That's the lighthouse walk,' he said, doubling back and jogging on the spot. 'But if it's solitude you're after, love, then I'd give Clarkes a miss and keep heading down Bangalow Road. Turn off at the Suffolk Park pub. Clifford Street corner. Camping area at the bottom.... but turn left into Alcorn. You've got a lovely long beach there. No one's gonna bother you. You look the thoughtful type to me.'

'Y'reckon? Thanks.'

Seems Suffolk Park wasn't letting go of me this morning.

After kitting myself up with instructions from the Samaritan on how to proceed to Suffolk Park I took off and within a few short minutes down Bangalow Road I was making the left at the hotel, at the Clifford Street corner, driving almost to the end where I turned the Golf left onto Alcorn Street as directed, and thinking that I should have invited the friendly jogger to join me. Manic people reach out to the world. Depressives retreat.

Alcorn was a street of ordinary-looking homes, some brick, some fibro, some timber, but typically holiday houses on huge flat blocks of land lining both sides of the street. There was the odd vacant block covered in ferns and pandanus trees but mostly the landscape was unexceptional. The beach was hidden by the houses.

At this point, I have to say, Suffolk Park seemed underwhelming. I was tempted to keep going. At the far end of the street I turned in to a shady cull-d-sac, parked the car and took the sandy track and steps down through the bushes to the beach.

Stunning!

The panorama took my breath away.

Laid out before me for as far as the eye could see were

miles and miles of the whitest, purest beach fringed by sand
hills and dune grasses and in all its aquamarine glory, a rolling,
crashing surf. The magnificent Blue Pacific Ocean.

Imagine this in Europe, I thought once I'd caught my
breath. There'd be wall-to-wall deck chairs and touts hitting on
sun bathers like botflies on a carcass, hawking their trays of
kitsch souvenirs and over-priced sticky umbrella cocktails. The
Rivieras, French and Italian, have to suffer over-crowded oily
dirty pebbled stretches of the Mediterranean as an excuse for
their beaches. And don't get me started on California's much
flaunted golden shores. Oil pumps blot the horizon.

'Hi, how y'going?' The young man stopped sprinting and
strolled up to me, his hands on his hips, bending in the middle
and straightening up to gasp hungrily at the air around him.
'Sensational, hey?' he said, straightening up and throwing his
arms out to emphasize his point.

'And what do they call this 'sensational' part of the world?' I
enquired, making sure to keep my eyes modestly focused on
his facial features rather than letting them slip to the Speedos.

'You're at the far end of Tallows Beach. Broken Head's the
next around the headland, and that pile of rocks you can see
out there? That's Julian Rocks. The Bunjalung call it
Nguthungulli.'

'Nguthungulli, hey? Thanks. It's magic.'

'They reckon. See you!'

'Bye.'

Coming upon a jogger in yellow budgies, running along the
lonely strip was one thing but I wasn't prepared for the man in
full business suit and shiny shoes I saw stepping out from the
dunes a little way up from me. He carried a clipboard and had
a camera hanging on his chest.

'G'day,' I said as I came up to him. 'What's happening'

'We've got a property for sale in there.'

'A beachfront, hey? I bet they don't come up all that often.'

'Sell to the first person who walks through the door with the cash. That's the owner's instruction.'

Why not check out what this young pup was selling, I figured?

'He just up and left for good, this time. Shot through. Had enough of the place, I guess,' the salesman informed me as I followed him through thick undergrowth, and he held bracken and bushes out of my way as I ducked the spiky stuff and wondered what I was going to find at the end of this jungle trek.

'Had a bit of trouble of one kind or another, so he decided to sell. Found another wave, I guess. That's what they're like around here.' He seemed embarrassed to be showing me the property before his people had had a chance to tidy it up.

'Can't imagine where he is now could be better than what's out front, there.' I pointed over my shoulder to the beach.

'You won't think much of the property. Be prepared.'

'A magical mystery tour?'

'You wanted to see it, right?'

'Right.' Not a lot of humour there. I took the business card he handed me.

'I warn you, it's a mess. You had surfies twenty, thirty years ago throwing up these shacks all along the best beach frontages,' said the man I now understood hailed from First National Real Estate and who obviously thought he had a potential buyer while, at the same time wishing to make it clear he was not at one with Byron's hippy surfie culture, particularly its impact on local real estate values. At any moment, I expected to be given a spiel about the attractive all mod cons, security lock-up cream brick townhouses he had on his books back at the office.

We broke through the last of the shoreline scrub into the clearing and straight away I knew I was home, knew I was looking at my future. No more than a dilapidated one-room beach shack, but yet a piece of magic nestled behind the dunes on the doorstep of that wild Pacific Ocean out there!

The Voices were clamouring. *Buy it! Buy it! It's ours! It's ours!*

The little shack and its environment were beyond romantic, beyond any of the normal parameters one sets when contemplating a real estate purchase.

It was a keeper.

The agent was right, however. It was a mess. The owner had left behind the detritus of a surfer's life in the rectangular little fibro hut with timber veranda. And, suspiciously, left it behind in a hurry. Apart from the two enormous surfboards I noticed sticking out from under the wide veranda, when I walked inside the shack the first thing I noticed was the old double mattress laying on the wooden floor down the far end. It had a faded pink cotton blanket crumpled across it.

'Feels like he's just gone down to the beach and will be back for breakfast,' I said.

The agent shook his head. 'He's not coming back, I assure you.'

I walked across to the tiny kitchen, no more than a cornered-off section of the rectangle. Doors on the two timber cupboards had come off their hinges a long time ago and hung at an unhealthy angle to the uprights. Their dusty shelves displayed a motley collection of plastic plates and dishes as well as empty jam jars and stoneware coffee mugs, the type I hadn't seen since the early Seventies. Sitting on the chipped green Formica kitchen bench were several more cups and plates haphazardly stacked, and on closer inspection it was clear they had been abandoned before the remains of the owner's last meal had been scraped and rinsed from them. Two battered aluminium saucepans and a dirty fry pan similarly stained languished in the putrid sink.

I shuddered, imagining the cockroach colonies that must be celebrating the abandonment of this hovel.

The place had the look, feel and smell of a squat, of casual visitors coming and going and not bothering to clean up. A pile of dusty mosquito nets Methuselah might have slept under were piled in a corner of the room and all around the walls hung faded surfing posters. Globs of old Blue-tack adhered in some spots, evidence of other posters long discarded.

Outside again, and I noted the few sheets of corrugated iron thrown up at the northern end of the veranda and a net curtain strung across. Someone's ad hoc attempt to accommodate overflow guests, no doubt.

The place was hokey, but it worked, and I was in love with it. Except for the aluminium sliding doors and window frames, which were an affront to any right-thinking person's sensibilities. But none of this mattered. It would be a challenge.

I felt an empathy with the neglected little shack nestled in behind the dunes. It was begging me to love it.

'There's more to see,' said the young agent, stepping down from the veranda and walking me around to the front of the wide, deep property.

We needed to beat through further undergrowth, lush green rainforest rather than the dryer, greyer dune vegetation this time.

We emerged onto a long front yard, overgrown with rapacious blue flowering vines that climbed up through the trees and ran along the fences then climbed back down to strangle a pile of old timber stacked against the fence. Creeper vine overwhelmed anything standing in its path. A huge four-car garage, grey splintery timber walls, a green iron roof and brown double roller doors stood at the side of the property, up front, at street level. Paspalum weeds grew around the base of the garage, and the two narrow windows facing onto the yard were boarded up. Unlike the cozy-but-grubby shack, there was nothing quaint about the garage. Possibly a fairly recent addition, utilitarian at best. It lacked charm but it would be useful for storage.

It would only be later that I learned what had gone on in that huge garage with its boarded-up windows, rows and rows of shelves lining the interior walls and its extraordinary amount of overhead lighting.

'The keys for this are back at the office. I could go get them if you're interested?'

I shook my head. 'Uh-uh. I've found what matters. It's what's back there, the shack and the beachfront.'

I left the young man and walked up the yard to the street. Parking earlier to go down to the beach, I'd tucked the Golf in a sandy cul-de-sac, somewhere along this stretch. Now I realized the car was on the other side of the high ti-tree fence and bushes.

'Serendipity,' I whispered.

'Sorry. What did you say?' The agent had come up behind me.

'Nothing. Just getting a little carried away,' I said with a smile.

DAY ONE - MY NEW LIFE

The fated sky
Gives us free scope, only doth backward pull
Our slow designs when we ourselves are dull.

Shakespeare, *All's Well That Ends Well*, Act 1, Sc 1

Fate, Serendipity, Kismet, Destiny.

Whatever. Here I was. From the moment of packing up and pulling out from the Mermaid Beach house this morning I had been heading for this place. Why else such coincidence; being twice directed to Suffolk Park and then being on the spot the very moment the agent was emerging from behind the dunes.

Eight hundred square meters of land with prime beachfront. Three hundred and sixty-six thousand dollars. Ten per cent deposit. Immediate settlement.

Too easy.

I had some modest savings, mostly from my days running my PR business and, post-divorce I'd had a generous Family Court settlement paid monthly that would amply cover the repayments. Not that my crazy mind was paying much heed to financial practicalities. I had fallen in love. End of story. No nickel-and-diming Mr. Real Estate. I would sign on the dotted line for my enchanted dwelling, aware that had I not been

directed towards Suffolk Park by the angels of Fate I might
have been in the Golf by now and driving aimlessly down the
Pacific Highway to an uncertain future.

Instead, I had found heaven in a homely old café, stepped
onto the beach and serendipitously bumped into a real estate
agent taking pictures of an orphaned property, one for which
he had no heart, one he needed to flog to the first interested
party. It was meant to happen. We were a couple, that little
shack and me.

Too impulsive, perhaps, I hear you ask?

Join my conveyancing lawyer. It seemed my fertile
imagination had thrown a rainbow around everything. At least
that was hinted at by the city slicker from the law firm who
had handled my divorce. To give him his due, he was aware of
my mental condition, thanks to the two AVOs taken out
against me by my estranged spouse during the turbulent early
stages of my illness.

I responded that I didn't believe so. Where better to ring in
the changes than in magical, mystical, legendary Byron Bay.
Parsley, sage, rosemary and thyme; time for Love, Peace and
Harmony. My new life would take shape in a coastal village of
surfers and hippies, where the ambiance of the Nimbin
Aquarius Festival of two decades ago still hung over the
landscape, hung over its hinterland, hung over the lush green
rainforests, over the white crystal sands, the gloriously
unstoppable surf, the golden sunrises that spring up out of
clear aqua seas to kiss the lighthouse up on the headland before
the rest of Australia stirs.

Rainbow-colored country.

Yes.

Take a chance on me, it whispered.

And I was ready to do just that. The maniac does not

entertain the nay-sayer, and that morning in September 1997, I was certainly in the manic phase of my condition.

Easing the Golf into a spot out front of the First National Real Estate office near the bakery where I had earlier scooped up the devilish croissants I dug the second pastry out of my bag and hungrily devoured it. The carbs would centre me, calm the thumping great excitement beginning to manifest itself as sweaty palms and white lights before the eyes. A major adrenalin rush. A grand high. I wanted to dial up the world and tell it what I was doing. Me, buying my first house.

I, me, myself, personally.

Sad really, because there was no world out there waiting on my call. Just me, Jan Murray. Divorced middle-aged woman. Here, alone. *Solista*. About to make her monumental passage from one life into another. About to decide that the dilapidated little beach hut in the dunes, a long way from family and friends, would be her destiny. No going back. All the money I had, or possibly would ever have, going to purchase a wild piece of real estate. Over three decades of marriage and years of abundant motherhood, more years at university as a mature-age student, a working life as a gun public relations executive, my whole life lived around the suburbs of Sydney; all about to be put behind me, all about to be relegated to the past.

With the almond croissant devoured, I wiped the evidence from my face with the back of my arm and looked about. Everything seemed wonderful to me on this glorious morning.

It felt like the first morning of the earth and only for a moment, as I entered the agency, did I stop to consider how all this would play in the years ahead. Woman. Alone. Woman making her own way in life. No fallback position. No husband props. No nearby adult kids or friends to call on. Just me, Jan

Murray, fifty-five years old, by all accounts an emotional basket case, about to sign up for my first ever piece of wholly owned real estate.

Could I manage it?

I took in several deep breaths.

That was when I decided to make a call to a woman I knew who had been living for some years in Byron Bay. One moment of caution, a slight hiatus in the manic high before I signed the cheque.

Di Morrissey, author of several successful books, took my call. She had a mutual friend with her, she said. They were both sitting outside on her verandah enjoying the view. I had visited Di in her home the year before when I'd been down here helping Lionel Midford with his restaurant launch. Di's home was a cute, very pretty feminine abode on a hillside south of Byron which looked down into a rainforest valley.

Di knew Byron. So did advertising and moviemaking man Wayne Young, our mutual friend sitting with Di on her veranda.

Wayne's company, YoungHeart, had been instrumental in getting Rodney Adler to invest in YoungHeart's animated film project, *Fernguly, the Last Rainforest* in the Eighties after Wayne had walked a party of thirty-six Australian and American animators, script writers and potential film financiers through the Byron Bay rainforest, which was, like so much of the beautiful region, coming under threat from rapacious developers.

The rainforest track the movie people would have walked that day would have been much wilder, much closer to nature than it is presently, where the walk leading up to the lighthouse through the rainforest is now serviced by a suspended walkway and is beloved by locals and tourists alike.

Wayne wanted to produce a big budget international film, and funds for environmentally sound children's animated films would not have been easy to come by in those early days of environmental protection. He needed to demonstrate the fragility of the rainforest and the imminent threat. He did, I believe. And the result is a beautiful, poignant children's movie that soon became a favourite electronic babysitter.

Once Adler had invested, I believe it was around $20 million, and the movie was made, Wayne invited me to New York to do the PR launch in the Grand Hall of the United Nations on Earth Day. Diplomats and their prettily dressed children filled the place for the premiere. It was an amazing experience. To top it all off, we camped for the week in Rodney Adler's very posh apartment overlooking Central Park.

Wayne and I had also worked together on the massive First Fleet Re-enactment Voyage project for Australia's 1988 Bicentenary, and not long after that I had secured a $100,000 sponsorship from American Express for YoungHeart to produce a save-the-planet rock concert in Centennial Park starring friends of Wayne's such as environmental crusader Olivier Newton John, et al.

The fact the production, plagued with problems, never got off the ground would be a personal embarrassment for me, having used my reputation for honesty and my friendship with Alberto Modulo, the CEO of American Express, to convince the man to drop in a $100,000 sponsorship—$AU187,000 in 2017 terms—to kick off the concert. I had not had any further dealings with Wayne by the time I encountered him on the end of the line at Di Morrissey's home.

'Suffolk Park?' I enquired. 'What do you reckon, guys?'

'Sufferer's Park!' came the dismissive response from the lean, green Wayne.

I knew Wayne and his family had been, in addition to his much-loved rainforested Wategos Beach, a long-time part of the artsy Belongil community at the other end of Byron Bay. Belongil's coterie of stars included Paul Hogan and John Cornell and was considered the trendy part of Byron. A few years earlier, the friends of Belongil had successfully repelled Club Med's plans to ruin the place with an international Club Med resort.

Suffolk Park, five kilometres south of all this trendiness, was Nowheresville. Sufferers Park.

Not a big rap.

A moment of panic seized me. I had an urge to run back to the car, jump inside its comforting space and head out of Byron Bay at full throttle. Mr. Real Estate Agent would be disappointed that the woman on the beach was a 'no-show' but so what? It would be written down in the annuls of First National Real Estate as just one more crazy female who acted too rashly, who fell in love with Byron and then cooled down and fled the precinct.

I needed time.

My heart was yelling a resounding 'Yes, yes!' but my head was now asking questions, thanks to the negative responses.

And then something happened that smashed all the negatives. Crazy, I know, but just as I was about to turn and do a runner the friendly crone I'd spoken with earlier in the morning came peddling past on her pushbike. I waved but she didn't see me. Yet, I felt it was an omen. A *Somewhere Over the Rainbow* kind of omen, as if I were standing in the middle of the Yellow Brick Road. I can grow old here like her, I thought. I can be a cheerful, healthy octogenarian one day who peddles her bike like a teenager around beautiful Byron Bay, proud to show off her Indian skirt to a stranger—even if the stranger is mistaken for Mabel's daughter, Gloria.

~~~

Sitting in the reception area of the real estate office, waiting for young Mr. First National to call me in, I thought about the prices my few saleable assets back in Sydney would bring at auction should I need to find more cash in order to make the shack habitable. Mentally, I thanked the little Laylas and Fadils, the Dariuses and the Deebas, the ghosts of all the children floating somewhere over old Persia who probably went blind weaving the two antique rugs I could sell to put towards my dream shack.

'Honey?'

'Uh? Oh, no, thanks.' A pretty person in Bali pants and a white Bond's singlet had just set down a cup of steaming chamomile tea in front of me.

'Thanks, that's great.' I brought the cup to my lips, holding it under my nose to savour the aromatic herbs. I wondered about the Ugg boots in this tropical climate. It all felt so special; the shack, the beach, the dunes, this fragrant brew, Ringo's, the G'days, the bicycle lady, the Rainbow shop down the road where I'd purchased some incense and a *Magic Happens* sticker for the Golf. And these cool white timber walls of the First National office, a tiny timber cottage, its exterior painted grey with red trim window frames nestled in the main street. Like Ringo's, another country. For the time being, at least. But don't get me started.

I thought again about my precious rugs back in Sydney. It would hurt to surrender them but I had never been able to appreciate those rugs without pangs of guilt. Oriental carpets are a moral issue, the trade turning on the exploitation of children. The West has had its long love affair with them, a never-ending supply coming out of the Middle East. We tend to ignore the history in favour of the elegance they provide in our homes and offices; ignore the hardships that lie behind the exquisitely woven patterns that must take a terrible toll on the weaver's eyesight, the damage the vegetable dyes must cause, dyes that create the a-brash which the serious collector values; that tiny flaw the weavers still weave into their rugs to remind them—and us—that only God is perfect.

I vowed I'd use the profits of their labours to make my new home a place of mindfulness and good karma.

~~~

Life is never dull for the maniacally high. Two and a half hours after first sighting the little shack, having contacted my bank and the conveyancing lawyer and having soaked up more Ringo's Cafe offerings, I walked out of the First National Real Estate office as the proud new owner of an Alcorn Street, Suffolk Park beach hut.

Who'd have thought?

'Move in anytime,' the young agent said as he handed me the keys. I had the feeling he was glad to have the disreputable property off his books.

'You mean even before—'

'We're different 'round here.' He smiled and clasped my hand with both of his, a genuinely warm handshake. 'May as well, it's empty.'

And waiting for me, I reasoned.

Stepping out into Byron Bay's brilliant morning sunshine, I stared up at the sky, at the universe to which I had just surrendered myself. I looked back over my shoulder. The agent stood in the doorway, waving me off.

'Enjoy!' he called to me.

'I intend to!'

~~~

It was Day One of my new life and I had an ungainly little shack to rescue, meaning that by mid-afternoon I was up to my eye balls in chaos. No waiting for help. Not in my frame of mind that day. Now meant now!

I had been going hard at it for hours, stopping only to dash around to the local shops in Clifford Street to grab a bag of fruit and a mineral water for lunch and then back in to the cleanup, and if occasionally I pinched myself to prove it was all real, this new home of mine, this adventure I had launched myself on this morning, I did so while taking a break from my frantic activities in order to watch the mosquito nets go into the flames, the ancient piles of gauze disintegrating, shriveling to a soft grey film of ash Pompeii-like across what had gone before.

And what had gone before were the faded Billabong and Quicksilver posters I'd yanked off the walls, a heap of fossilized groceries, random bits of lumber, several threadbare beach towels and a crate of surfing magazines, which I regret now having committed to the flames. They would be a treasure trove today. In my frenzy, I considered ripping out the busted kitchen, booting up the flames and hurling it all on the pyre, but then decided against it.

Common sense made a belated appearance.

I would need a handyman, someone with the tools to help me demolish and rebuild the tiny kitchen and bathroom, to pull down the sheets of rusty corrugated iron from the veranda and, above all replace the ugly aluminium windows and door frames with timber ones.

CHILL

I am the master of my fate:
I am the captain of my soul
W.E. Henley

Late afternoon, I decided to go into the village. The occasion called for a bottle of celebratory wine.

Solitary drinking?

Not something I normally did but normal needed to make way for novel.

And I needed to pick up a copy of the *Byron Echo* to check out the Classifieds for a handyman, someone good with timber. I obsessed about replacing the aluminium horrors. The electricity couldn't be reconnected until the official transfer of ownership so there would be no power for a few days and that meant I would also be needing candles, sweet aromatic ones, the kind I had noticed in the *Magic Happens* shop. And I would need mosquito coils.

I stayed in my work clothes but ran a comb through my hair. This wasn't the Eastern Suburbs or Sydney's north shore. Here, the scene was come-as-you-are. Here, you would be valued for how you lived, not how you looked. The Golf waited up the front of the yard in the shade of the big garage. I was ready to head into the village.

I drove up Alcorn and turned right. Already, I felt like a local as I passed the half dozen small stores on Clifford Street.

On seeing the BP Service Station just past the pub corner, I remembered that, in my more rational moments I'd promised the Golf a grease and oil change.

'Hi,' I said to the grey-haired man in overalls as he emerged from the workshop wiping his hands on a grimy oil rag.

'Yeah. What can I do ya for, mate?'

'I need a service.'

The middle-aged man tucked the greasy rag in his back pocket and raised a quizzical eyebrow. 'Y'reckon?' he said with a grin. 'Your desk or mine?'

'Ouch!' I had not seen that coming.

His laugh was a genuine expulsion of joy as he wiped his hands down the backside of his pants then put one out for a shake. 'No offence, hey?'

'None taken.' I shook his hand, aware I had just collected my share of sump oil for the day. 'That's it over there,' I said, pointing. Can I book it in?'

I would later learn that I'd been recognized as a TV face. In addition to my now burgeoning *Beauty and the Beast* career, since the early Seventies I had appeared intermittently as a panelist on the *Midday Show,* and in the Eighties, I was a media-hot PR operator and an opinionated ministerial spouse.

And of course, as my friend the mechanic had just made apparent, I was recognizable from my decade-old *Sixty Minutes* interview. I had created a media storm with that little gem, the segment becoming such a ratings sensation it surpassed even the TV wonder, *Alf,* on the Sunday night in March '87 when both shows went to air.

In passing, I just want to say about that notorious desk story that I had intended it to support my feminist views about a woman's place in the scheme of things, but thanks to Channel Nine's judicious editing of three hours of film into a ten-minute package, my militant message was skewered to imply I was celebrating John's rise to the Ministry. Far from it. I was claiming my conjugal rights at a time they were being seriously denied me by Canberra's political system.

The story that aired had unintentionally titillated the nation's imagination. Such is life and life goes on...but crazily, it seems from the comments I still regularly receive, I'm to carry the notoriety into my crone years.

I don't mind.

I think my story of love on the desk shed a little glow of mirth around our national politics. One newspaper wrote that I should have been made Woman of the Year. The sports journalist Roy Masters had a different take on it. Roy reckoned 'Jan Murray's mouth was John Brown's Achilles heel'!

While the cheeky mechanic went back inside his workshop to check his sheet, I wandered over to where the vehicles for hire were parked on the edge of a gully and dense rainforest patch. A big trailer for the mountain of rubbish was what I'd be needing once I started ripping out kitchens and bathrooms and aluminium frames.

I bent over the side of one of the trailers to look inside and gauge its dimensions.

'Oh, my God!'

I jumped back.

A rush of adrenalin had me grabbing my chest to stop a galloping heart escaping the corral.

A massive reptile lay coiled up in the bottom of the trailer, baking in the sun, a monster! Brownish, with a tawny coloured diamond pattern all the way down its creepy back, heavy, oozy and lethal. Be calm, oh beating heart, be calm!

'Big bastard, isn't he?' said the mechanic as he came up behind me and leant in, tracing, with the tip of his finger, the reptile's languorous curves.

The sleepy creature gave a shudder. It rippled down its length but it continued to doze.

'He's a pet. Lived with us for yonks. Can't hurt you. Only a python.'

'Oh, right. Only a python?' Get this man's blithe spirit.

'Diamond python. Eats mice 'n stuff. Won't poison you.'

'Okay. And it won't strangle me to death?'

'Harmless.'

'Okay, then.' I brushed hair from my eyes and drew in a deep breath, determined not to let this reptilian monster get the better of me. My new neighbour must see me as being at one with God's creatures. A true Byronian wouldn't resile from a mere six-foot long deadly python, and anyway, I was curious. And they're not deadly, anyway, said the man.

'Touch him. Go on.'

'Okay.' I leant in, taking the mechanic at his word that the ductile creature wouldn't rear up and strike me with its forked tongue.

For several moments I gazed down at the reptilian mandala. My chest felt constricted, my heart an electric blender pulsing at full speed. Primal fear. An involuntary reaction. Serpents. Sin. Adam and Eve. The Garden of Eden.

Of course, there would be a serpent in Byron Bay. This, after all, was Paradise.

Finally I took the plunge and traced the creature's shape with the tip of my finger and watched what I imagined were ripples of pleasure run down his back. It seemed in the moment that I had just passed some kind of supernatural test, that I belonged.

'I just moved in this morning,' I said to the mechanic. 'Bought a place round in Alcon Street.'

'Yeah, I heard. You bought the shack. The one on the beach.'

I nodded, perplexed, and then I got it. 'I guess I should open an account with you,' I said. Young Mr. Real Estate Agent had possibly recognized me, and news travels fast in a small town.

'Get used to it, then,' he said, indicating the python. 'Bet y'balls that fella's got family around at your place. They live under the house,' he chuckled.

'You're kidding me!'

'And you got one of those ti-tree fences down the side of your joint, right? That's what they love. Curl up on the top, the bushy part. Same colour as the fence. You'll hardly notice but I betcha you'll have 'em. And smell 'em. They pong a bit.'

This wasn't good.

'They come across the road from the everglades.'

'Everglades?'

'The rainforest, undergrowth, the stuff you've got all around you. That stuff,' he said, indicating the darkness on the edge of the service station.

I stared into the depths of the shadowy undergrowth. Its green stillness appealed. Strange things could happen inside such denseness. Even the word 'everglades' resonated, conjured images of wetlands and alligators, nights on the bayous and Tony Joe White's smoky swamp music. There was a creek in there. I could hear frogs. I also heard a bird, a high-pitched melodious call. Could one hear rustling through there as well, I wondered, still goose-bumped and freaked when I thought of the possibility I might have come face to face with one of these colossal pythons when I was dragging rubbish out from under the shack an hour ago.

'Don't know whether to say this or not,' the mechanic said, interrupting the image of life on the bayou. He looked over his shoulder, scoping the place before continuing.

'Say what?'

He stared into his workshop, then glanced across to the main shop, across at the pumps and then, having done the full scope, back at me. Finally, 'Uh-uh. I can see the snake's shaken you up a bit. Shouldn't go putting me big foot in it about other things that might spook you.'

'Other things?'

The man wasn't smiling any more but creasing his bushy eyebrows and looking uncomfortable.

'What other things?'

He seemed undecided.

'What?'

'That big shed at the front of your property? The huge garage? The windows all boarded up?'

'What about the garage?' I said. The fact I had lowered my voice to ask was probably symptomatic of the fact I felt bad stuff coming down the pike.

He hesitated. 'Nah, don't matter. You'll find out soon enough.'

'Please tell me? What should I know about the garage?'

He seemed to make some kind of compromise with himself. 'Okay, the hydroponics ... for a start.'

'Hydroponics?'

I knew what hydroponics were.

Not good news. Thirty-six poisonous chemicals.

I had smoked grass. Of course, I had smoked grass. And I had inhaled. But not the chemical variety. It had been years ago when the weed we smoked came down from heaven and not via a hydroponic lab.

I'd been a regular visitor to Canberra after Gough Whitlam's victory, having worked hard campaigning for

Gough in those 1972, 1974 and 1975 campaigns.

Thanks mainly to the *Its time* campaign I had become seriously addicted to federal politics, aided and abetted by a neighbour and close friend, the Member for Prospect, Richard Klugman. He and I discussed politics relentlessly; me from a bleeding heart Left perspective and Dick from his long-time Andersonian civil libertarian position. Along the way it seemed he recognized some kind of intelligence lurking within my Stepford Wives persona and in the early Seventies convinced me that although I had left school at fourteen and become a mum by the age of twenty, and now with five little darlings I was knee-deep in motherhood, I could yet matriculate and then go on to university.

Richard guided me all through the years of my Political Science and English Literature Honours degree at Macquarie University and thanks to his friendship—and his parliamentary travel entitlements, which enabled me to barter my research and writing skills with various politicians in return for interviews and information—I came to know several of the Labor Party's luminaries during my frequent trips to Canberra.

This suburban housewife got off on being close to the centre of the action, and action there was aplenty in those turbulent political times. I was able to use my privileged access to the political elites to gain intimate knowledge of Canberra politics, and interesting perspectives on the policies, which helped me in pursuit of my degree.

It was during these heady days of the Whitlam era that I occasionally found myself, late at night after the House had risen, sitting in an outdoor steamy spa in the company of some of Canberra's elite who regularly coalesced around a beltway institution known fondly as a particular staffer's hot tub. *Bliss was it in that dawn to be alive, but to be young was very heaven!*

'But you said, "For a start". What else?' I asked the mechanic.

'Well ... um—' He looked over his shoulder, then back at me. '...a bit of heroin dealing went on, too, I reckon. Plenty of junkies round at that joint. Coming an' going at all hours. Never knew who was living round there. A Yank had it last, I think. Or maybe not.'

'My place, you're talking about? The old beach shack?' I mentioned the street number.

'Your property alright, mate. I know the block, right enough.' He wiped his forehead with his oily cloth. 'Yeah, that big garage up front.'

I shrugged and asked no further questions. I resented the fact my Xanadu was sullied. I had promised myself it would be a place of good karma. I arranged to drop the Golf in the next day for the tune-up and was almost out of the driveway and onto the road, my right-hand flicker on when a teenage girl rushed up to the window and tapped. The girl asked if she and her boyfriend could grab a ride into town.

'To the Great Northern?' said the girl. 'We're supposed to start work at four and our bomb won't start. The man said you'd give us a lift. Is that okay?'

Black pants, white shirts and neat appearances, obviously dressed for bar work, both of them. Almost four o'clock. 'Fine. No worries. Hop in.'

The girl took the back seat and the youth came around and sat in the front. As the doors slammed, I remembered I'd flung my handbag onto the floor at the back. I was about to reach around and grab it when the girl handed it through to me. I felt shame colour my cheeks. I must learn to trust. 'I need these,' I said, digging out my dark glasses and holding them up before passing the bag back to the girl.

'It's got a bit or a bad repo, your joint. Drugs 'n that,' said the youth as we travelled along Bangalow Road into Byron. I had just finished answering the young man's friendly interrogations about what part of the world I hailed from, how long I'd lived in Byron and what I thought of the place, of my own piece of the Bay, in particular.

'What do you know? Or is it just rumour?' I said, looking across at the boy and into the rear vision mirror to catch the girl's eye.

The youth hesitated, turning to look behind to his girlfriend. I couldn't see, but I felt they were exchanging cautious looks. 'A bit of heavy stuff used to go on there, that's all,' he said.

'Junkies 'n that,' the girl volunteered. 'That big garage you got up the front? Grew hydroponics in there. Lots.'

'Bit of heroin dealing went on, too,' said the boy.

'Where's the best place to catch some good music?' I wanted out of this conversation with these strangers. This sure ain't Kansas, Toto. If I'd landed in Oz then I wanted rainbows. I didn't want to hear any more about bad things that might or might not have happened around at my new home. Especially not if the bad thing was heroin. Dirty, lay-about heroin addicts didn't do it for me. I was in the zero-tolerance camp at the time of landing in Byron Bay. Sydney had had a spate of house break-and-enters. I felt the scourge had been around long enough for even the dumbest kid to know the perils of starting down the heroin highway. There had been stories of young nurses and police being stuck with dirty syringes, having to wait to know if they were HIV-positive and likely to die from AIDS some day.

'The Rails Friendly Bar,' the pair chorused. 'Best music.' They seemed relieved themselves to have made it out of the quicksand and onto safer ground.

'Y'know why they call it the 'Friendly' bar?' asked the girl, who went on to answer her own question. 'It's because, up till a few years ago ... according to my Mum, that is, when the trains still used the railway and holiday makers got off there at the station ... well, like, the part of the station that was the pub had a band that would come out onto the platform and play music to greet everyone. How cool's that? The band from the pub welcomes you as you get off the train!'

'Best music's at the Rails, for sure. No cover charge, either.' The youth checked his watch. 'Not like at ours. And Cornie's pub's always too crowded. Too many tourists.'

'Everyone gets up and dances at the Rails. That's what's so great about it,' said the girl.

'Don't matter if you're on your own, even.' The boy was looking my way as he spoke. 'Or old,' he added before the girl leaned though and jabbed him in his ribs to shut him up.

I pulled the car up across the road from the Great Northern on Jonson Street and thanked them both for their company. 'I'll save it for another day if that's okay,' I said when the girl offered to fix a drink for me if I cared to park and come inside.

'See you, then. Toodle pop,' said the girl as she took her boyfriend's hand.

Halfway across the road, the boy doubled back. He came up to the car window and leaned in. 'Don't worry about your garage. It's gonna be okay. It's gonna be great. Welcome to the Bay.'

He straightened up, looked to where his girlfriend now stood in front of the hotel—pointing frantically at her watch—then back at me. He took something from his pocket and put his hand through the window.

'Chill,' he said, opening the Golf's glove box and placing

something in it. Then the youth, as he crossed the road, gave me a wave over his shoulder.

By the time I discovered the fat joint, my passenger had already caught up with his girlfriend and the pair had disappeared indoors.

I shut the glove box on my illegal bounty, took a deep breath and counted to ten as I came to grips with the fact that a Byron Bay welcome seemed not to be the usual polite knock on the door by a friendly neighbour carrying a tray of scones.

'Chill,' the youth had said and that's exactly what I intended to do.

THE ROUNDABOUT

Fate slowly builds her mute countenance ...
and the soon-to-be lovers smile on each other ...
                                    Rainer Maria Rilke

The Hunter Valley shiraz in its brown paper bag rolled
around on the passenger side floor, the *Byron Echo*sat on the
seat beside me. Bob Dylan was filling the cabin with *Girl from
the North Country.*

After dropping off my two young passengers I'd spent a
lazy hour in the village, poking around. Now the setting sun
was taking some of the heat out of the sweltering day and I
was beginning to think about the night ahead, about sleeping
on a stranger's mattress on the floor with only the same
stranger's pink rug for cover. It was crazy! I should have
booked in to a motel. But the agent had given me the keys and
permission to move in. And in my present state of mind
impatience went with the territory.

What did it matter that I'd be spending the night in a run-
down hut, all on my own, in a lonely part of the dunes. In the
dark. No electricity. No one knowing where I was. What was I
thinking!

I passed the MITRE 10 hardware store on the corner of
Jonson Street and turned into Browning. I was approaching the
roundabout when I saw him.

Beware, beware! His flashing eyes, his floating hair! Except for
the black hair blowing around his face, the hitchhiker up

ahead, trapped in the glow of a violent late-afternoon sunset, could have been mistaken for a civic monument, a piece of zany street art. My first thought: He looked handsome. My second: He looked dangerous. Even from this distance, the man's aura troubled me, but what did I know about auras? One day, my first, in Byron Bay? Please.

Under the old linoleum I'd ripped up this morning in my frenzy I'd found sheets of yellowed newspaper. An article on hitchhiking had caught my eye. *Seventy-five per cent of all rapes committed in the United States were as a result of hitchhiking*, the article had screamed at its 1974 readers. The FBI had issued a poster, a warning guaranteed to scare the Bejeezus out of any woman considering hitching or giving a lift to a male hitchhiker. *Is he a happy vacationer or an escaping criminal, a pleasant companion or a sex maniac, a friendly traveler or a vicious murderer?* it had asked the American population of the day.

Not a soul back in Sydney knew of my whereabouts. The disconnectedness felt liberating but it posed challenges; self-preservation being one of them.

To pull up and invite the stranger into my car, or be just one more uncaring driver who speeds past and doesn't give a damn? An ethical dilemma wrapped in a roundabout. What was my moral obligation to a stranger in need of a lift?

I checked the SUV cruising ahead of me. Hard not to be cynical. Its back windscreen was papered with stickers campaigning for love of trees and whales and urging the world to save the planet from pollution. Another faded 1991 bumper sticker screamed *No Blood for Oil*, reminding me of my own protest activity at the time of the Gulf War when my son, Jonathon, and I had taken part in an all-night sit-down in front of the US Embassy in Sydney.

I had also staged a second protest at the time when I

refused to attend with my ministerial spouse, the official Prime Ministerial welcome to President George H. Bush at the National Maritime Museum where, on behalf of the American people, Bush was presenting the Museum with a fat cheque. The gas guzzler ahead of me pulled out and overtook the small green rust bucket in front. I watched this Master of the Universe head his mighty gas-guzzler towards the traffic circle and made a small bet with myself.

And I was on the money. No way did he stop for the hitchhiker. No sense of a moral obligation there.

The driver of the old green car in front, short of the roundabout, tooted a pedestrian, a girl with bum-length dreadlocks, wearing a long skirt, a quilted top and Jesus sandals. She ambled across the road to the driver, tossed an apologetic wave to me then stuck her head in the driver's window. A good rainbow country citizen wouldn't let herself get too upset about such a minor delay, I cautioned myself. This wasn't Sydney. We didn't sit on the horn in Byron Bay or rudely overtake just to make our point. Instead, I bade my time and spent it reflecting on how most of the streets in Byron Bay were named after literary legends. Jonson Street led into Browning, which converged with Tennyson at the roundabout where the hitchhiker stood with his thumb out.

Ruskin, Byron, Keats, Milton, Wordsworth and Shelley, I'd spotted them all during the day, and as well, my map showed a Marvell, Carlyle, Cowper, Burns, Kipling, and Scott. I'd even noted a tilt at the Aussies with Wright, Lawson, Kendall and Patterson Streets. The city fathers must have thought they could expunge the district's savage history as a whaling station and abattoir with all their poesy. But one of my favourites, Samuel Taylor Coleridge, seemed to have missed out on his eponymous street. I thought of the books I'd purchased this morning at Ringo's Café, a 1921 edition of Coleridge's Literary Criticism.

No car had come up behind me. I was chilling, waiting for the two hippies in front to finish their conversation. Another friendly wave to me as the girl finished chatting and strolled back to the pavement. Now the little green car would stop for the hitchhiker, I figured, and I would be relieved of the duty to be kind and considerate to a stranger.

But I was wrong. The little green car took the first exit on the left out of the roundabout and headed up Tennyson, going in the opposite direction from the hitchhiker's intention. That left yours truly as the next car into the circle.

I now entered the force field of the stranger. *Weave a circle round him thrice.*

The hitchhiker made eye contact with me. *And close your eyes with holy dread.* His look was an appeal to my humanity. A challenge. Compassion or disregard for a fellow traveler. I felt half annoyed that he could turn this chance meeting into a personal issue between the two of us, two people who were strangers to each other.

The Golf was almost stationary inside the circle and I could see he was no civic monument but a real life, flesh and blood virile male with a tanned and muscular body that showed up well against the stark white cargo shorts and the dark blue and white floral Hawaiian shirt. The boat shoes weren't doing the casual chic look any harm either. And the hair I'd seen from way back blowing around his face was very straight, very black and very shiny.

I brought the Golf to a stop a short way past him and rolled down the window, watching in the side mirror as he picked up his bag and stood for a moment, looking around. Tall. Muscular. Broad shoulders. And, surprisingly, a Dr. Zhivago moustache. He began walking towards me. I spotted the gold earring. A gypsy!

When he came up to my window it was as if Omar Sharif himself was standing there, and how often had I'd drooled over Doctor Zhivago's dreamy, come-to-bed eyes.

For he on honey-dew hath fed.

The man at my window had the features of a mogul warrior. High chiseled cheekbones, scaffolding for the olive skin. This is ridiculous. I had better things to do than mess with handsome strangers who wore gold earrings.

What if he had a switchblade under that Hawaiian shirt? A dagger stuck in his white cargo shorts? The FBI weren't stupid. They knew things. He could be a serial killer. No one was accounting for my whereabouts and on reflection, it wasn't Omar Sharif, at all. There was something more powerful in his bearing; something darker in his aura that warned me the man was trouble.

I shrugged, and before he could speak, I'd rolled the window back up, put my foot on the pedal and accelerated away from him. The sensible thing to do, of course.

I was looking back over my shoulder, embarrassed and trying to send some kind of lame apology but, in doing so, I managed to miss my exit. Now I would need to full circle the roundabout and that would mean having nowhere to go but towards the Hawaiian shirt again if I were to get out of the circle and onto Bangalow Road.

His thumb was still out but there was no stepping forward this time as the Golf approached him. He simply raised a quizzical eyebrow and grinned, a cheeky do-you-want-me-or-don't-you-want-me kind of grin.

I kept my eyes straight ahead, making certain I'd catch the southbound exit this time. My intention in coming into the village had been to pick up a bottle of wine, the *Echo* and a few candles, not a stranger with God knows what mischief on his mind. Let someone else take their chances with him, I needed to ease myself carefully into the life of the Bay, get to know people.

I had my local rag and all I wanted was to get back to the shack and check out the Classifieds for a carpenter, someone good with timber. Once I had the place up to scratch I figured I would start inviting people around, create a bit of a salon of interesting Byron Bay types. I could forgive Wayne Young. And Di Morrissey might be up for teaching me something about novel writing. I would join a yoga class, maybe an outdoor painting group, a book club, bush walking, the local branch of the Labor Party. There were so many ways I planned on bringing myself up to speed as a fully-fledged Byronian woman.

As I was about to leave the roundabout, I glanced in the rear vision mirror. With the setting sun illuminating the hitchhiker's physique and having just seen the man up close, staring him down for a second or two, but enough to have caught the sexy smile, my impulse was to reassess the whole aura thing. It wasn't disturbing, it was just unusually powerful. In fact, I felt sympathy for the poor man and annoyed at my own rudeness and timidity. J. Edgar Hoover? What would that vicious old closet queen know about Aussie hitchhikers, anyway? Keats Street was up ahead. Keats reminded me again of Coleridge, the rich poetry. Opium-fueled. High on laudanum and magic phrasing. *In Xanadu did ...*

Kublai Kahn.

That was it! That was the image the man back there had brought to mind. Not Doctor Zhivago, but Kublai Khan. *In Xanadu did Kublai Kahn...* Xanadu. Caves of ice. Abyssinian maids strumming dulcimers. I slowed and let a cyclist overtake me, myself still overtaken by indecision.

And drunk the milk of Paradise.

The last line came to me as I pulled over onto the side of the road, reversed along the curb then leant over and threw the passenger door open.

I watched through the side mirror as he took his time sauntering up to the Golf. Rather than go straight to the open passenger door he strolled past on my side and around in front of the car, all the time keeping his gaze locked on me through the windscreen. Was he daring me to take off again? He stuck his head in the open door and smiled, one eyebrow raised and flashing the half-smart grin he had just given back at the roundabout. I got what it implied; recognition of a moment shared, a moral dilemma settled.

'You're sure about this?' he said, tilting his head to the side, smiling with his whole face.

The American accent! Unexpected. I smiled back at him and shrugged. 'Sure, I'm sure. Why not? You're not an axe murderer, are you?'

'No, lady, I'm not.' Grinning, he tossed in his bag and without further discussion settled it on the floor at his feet then buckled his seat belt, and only then did he look my way. 'You're not a local,' he said. A statement, not a question.

'That's an offence round here?' Already, I regretted stopping for him. He was too masculine. Too cheeky. Too something. Too present beside me, that was it. 'Suffolk Park,' I said. 'Any good to you?'

'Suffolk Park?' He sounded disappointed. 'That's fine. I'll get out on the pub corner, okay?'

'Sure thing.'

'Pardon?'

I took my hands away from my mouth. I had been leaning forward while he settled in, resting my elbows on the wheel, breathing in recycled air between my cupped palms, something I did when anxious, when I needed to buy thinking time. 'Sure,' I said with what was intended as an insouciant shrug.

'Thanks a lot. Its real kind of you. The pub corner at Suffolk will do just fine. I can pick up another lift from there, hey?'

His voice pitched soft and low. A man more used to intimacy than authority. Clutching at the wheel, I stared ahead through the windscreen and took in deep breaths. I could feel him observing me. Finally I put the Golf into gear and shot back on the road.

'How long have you lived in Byron?' he asked after we'd had gone a short way.

'Since this morning.'

'This morning?'

'I bought a house here this morning. Doesn't qualify me as a local, I know.'

No reaction to this. Instead, he turned his gaze and stared out his window. I compared him to the young kids who'd chatted to me the whole way in to the Great Northern. 'You'd have to have lived here since its hippie heyday to qualify as a fair-dinkum Byron local?' I said, turning to cast him an enquiring glance. 'Since the '73 Aquarius Festival, I reckon. I get the feeling this place only hands out brownie points if you've lived here for yonks, right?'

'I don't mix much. I just hang in there and kinda do my own thing, y'know.'

'California?'

'I grew up around Los Angeles and San Francisco. Thousand Oaks, mostly.'

'Nice place, huh?'

'Small place. Good, though. Plenty of trees and open space back then. Where they filmed all those cowboy movies actually. Back then. Not now.'

'Just visiting Byron?'

'I guess so,' he said as he stared out the window, then added softly, almost to himself, 'But its been a long one.'

'Oh, yes, how long?'

He spoke to a distant point outside his window. 'Since '74.'

That came as a surprise. I kept looking across at him, admiring his strong profile, the baby-smooth skin of his suntanned neck and the hair that fell like black silk to his shoulders. Yes, he could trace his ancestors back to the plains of Mongolia, this one.

I returned my eyes to the road but kept the image of him alive in my mind's eye. He wasn't ordinary, this Genghis Khan, Kublai Khan of a man. No, he wasn't ordinary. Neither was his musky scent ordinary. It had me imaging him in exotic places. I would put him in a desert, most likely. Corrugated sand hills stretching to a purple horizon. A turbaned head, a bejeweled scimitar tucked into his belt. Riding a camel at full tilt towards his Bedouin tent beside a palm-fringed oasis. Belly-dancers circling him, offering up their platters of dates and other desert delights.

I checked my mania, reigned in my too-fertile imagination, but understood the pull his physicality had on me and why he had attracted my attention back at the roundabout. He had secret places in him. His presence spoke of adventure.

While he had his face turned away, I made a further appraisal, admired how the sun caught the dark curly hairs glistening along the length of his strong forearms. A tattoo. An anchor. A man who lifted heavy objects. He looked fit. I

guessed at early forties. Worked hard for a living. And from his
tan, an outdoors guy. What was happening? His thighs were so
close we were almost touching each other. When he turned
from the window and smiled, I felt caught out.

'I've got some of those brownie points I can share if you'd
like them,' he said with a grin.

'I'll manage on rations, thanks.' I accelerated to get away
from where that remark seemed headed. I had just enough
smarts about me by now to know my head was not behaving.

When he lifted his left arm to pull down the sun visor, I
noticed the scars buried in the hollow of his elbow. Strange. A
couple of angry looking raised lines, a couple of inches long,
purplish against the fairer skin of his inside arm. Some kind of
accident, I figured.

'Don't suppose you need any work done around your
home, timber work, carpentry?' he said.

'Oh, my god!' I reached for the *Echo* and waved it at him.
'Believe it or not, I came into the village to pick up the
Classifieds. I'm desperate for a handyman!' I looked out the
window then back at him, shaking my head. 'I knew there was
a reason I stopped for you back there!'

'Eventually,' he said with a grin. He put his hand out. 'Yuri.
Yuri O'Byrne.'

'O'Byrne? A touch of the Irish, hey?' So much for Kublai
Khan. That one had just ridden off into the sunset.

'I guess. And Russian. On my mother's side.'

We were back on the steppes. Kublai Khan lives!

'Got it here, somewhere,' he said, busily patting his shirt
and shorts pockets, unfolding and refolding odd scraps of
paper. 'I'm a shipwright. Timber boats. He shot me a look that
came with a raised eyebrow. 'And a qualified carpenter.'

I waited while he continued to search the bag at his feet.

Not the organized type. Finally he presented me with the business card. There was a phone number, but no address other than a post office box in Yamba. I studied the buff-coloured card, ragged and frayed at the edges with green writing and an attractive line drawing of a yacht in the right-hand corner. *Yuri O'Byrne, Shipwright. Specialist in timber boats. Design. Building. Repairs. Maintenance.*

'I could cut you a good hourly rate. For cash. I've got no overheads.'

'So, it seems.' I placed his card on the dashboard. 'The house is just around the corner. Well, it's a shack, actually. Want to take a look?'

'Sure thing. Why not?'

Why not, indeed?

THE HITCHHIKER

Then a mile of warm sea-scented beach...
Robert Browning

We left the car parked beside the garage at the front of the yard and made our way through the rainforest patch, around the side path to the veranda. 'Da, dum!' I said, throwing my arms out to announce my humble abode.

'I know this property,' he said, looking around.

'Of course. Byron's a small town.'

'Nearly bought it ... about fifteen years ago.'

'The place needs work. I need all these doors and window frames replaced for a start. Can't bear aluminium.'

'Yeah, timber's the go. Nothing classy about al-oo-min-um.'

His mellifluous accent was ear candy, tubs of creamy caramel sentences pouring out of his mouth. His 'al-oo-min-um' tickled my fancy.

I stepped up onto the veranda and opened the double doors to the inside.

'Unless you were doing a PhD on the history of the disappearing 1950's Australian coastal holiday shack you'd write this place off,' I said. 'It's pretty ugly.'

The building was no more than a rectangle with a small corner hived off for a dog of a bathroom, made even uglier by a broken concrete floor and exposed pipes. And then there was the sorry-arse third world kitchenette.

'If nothing else, the locality deserves better,' he said, sizing the place up, bending to look under the house, tapping on the fibro sheeting of the walls. 'It's been built well enough.'

As he walked around the building checking it out he picked leaves from the shrubs and held them to his nose.

'This long timber veranda is sure something, hey?' he said when finally, he came back and took the veranda steps. 'And y'gotta love the position ... what you've got out there ... the doons and the beach. The guy who owned this went back to the States, y'know. Shot through.'

'And it seems he's decided to stay over there. Anyway, the agent told me the owner needed to sell in a hurry, so lucky me.' I saw him nod in agreement. 'You knew the previous owner. Byron really is a small place,' I said.

'Sometimes too small.'

With permission, he pulled a small broken, hanging piece of fibro away from the side wall to examine the timber frame beneath and noted they had used good timber for the frames. He found a piece of flattened cardboard and slid himself in under the house to check it out while I worried about his white shorts and the lovely dark blue and white Hawaiian shirt.

'There's some decent work been done,' he said as he climbed out from under the house and dusted the sand from his legs. 'It's well-built.' He grinned at me. 'What there is of it.'

'But like you say, the location's the hero, isn't it? The Pacific Ocean at my front door?'

'I reckon. This part of Tallows Beach is pretty much deserted. Surf gets a bit wild, too. It's terrific. Worth fixing up. With a little imagination, of course.' He smiled. 'It really is all about what you've got out there.' He pointed, again to the sea. 'And up here.'

Now he was pointing to his head. I didn't get it. But I would before this day was out.

'The view stretches for miles in either direction,' I said. 'You want to walk through the bushes and see my beach.' Then I corrected myself. 'The beach,' I laughed. 'It's not all mine. Just feels that way. But then, you already know the place.'

'Broken Head's the next beach south around the point,' he said. 'I built a house on the peak round there. Years ago.' He shrugged, 'Or started to.' He added the rejoinder in a way that suggested the memory hurt.

He left me standing on the veranda and started through the undergrowth, bending over in order to climb under the bushes and bracken overgrowing the pathway. As I hastened to catch up I could feel the grit in my sandals but it felt good.

Finally, we broke out onto the windswept beach and together, surveyed the scene. I took in a lung full of the coastal air and relished every bit of it.

'Cape Byron lighthouse. Magnificent, isn't it? Get up early enough and you'll be the first on land to see the sun rise,' he said, staring off to the left. 'And down there, that's Broken Head. And way out?' Now he was pointing to the craggy outcrop jagging the horizon. 'Julian Rocks. A favorite with divers.'

I was beginning to understand this was a man of few words. Short sentences. But I was hanging on every one of them. This was my new home he was describing with such abbreviated enthusiasm, and it was having the effect of banishing the last remnants of doubt I'd had when my hand had signed the deal this morning.

He walked off a short way and stood on another sand hill scanning the horizon, a hand to his forehead to shield his eyes. 'One day,' he said when I came up behind him. 'One day I'll be out there again.'

'Sailing?'

'Cruising, yeah.' He seemed to disappear into another place for a minute or two before shaking his head and moving further down the sloping sand. 'This southern end of Byron's my favourite part of the Bay,' he said. 'This, and around at Broken Head.'

He went on then to tell me that years ago he had bought ponies for his small son and daughter. He and his wife, and the children, would gallop flat out along this stretch of beach at low tide.

'Seven miles of flat, hard sand. Bare-chested,' he said with a laugh. 'Crazy! The wind in our faces, the four of us eating up the sea air all the way up and down this long stretch of beach.'

Deep in his own thoughts, I think he almost forgot I was standing alongside him. 'A good life,' he said to himself.

'By the way, what do you reckon about my trees back inside, there. Are they're worth saving?'

'They're fine. Burrawong palms. Or Bangalow palms. Whichever. They're native to these parts. They're in good shape, actually. A bit of work clearing away the rubbish trying to strangle them. And this coastal banksia, too, it's worth saving.' He broke off a twig from the tree and handed it to me.

'Is that what they're called? Bangalow palms?'

'*Banksia Integrefolia* if you want the botanical name.'

'You know your onions.'

He squatted down and tugged at a different type of bright green foliage growing in the sand around him, pulling out a large clump and holding it out for my inspection. 'South African weed. It flourishes all along the beachfront. Bitou bush,' he said, showing his disgust for the sticky leaves in the way he crushed them and tossed them away. '*Chrysanthemoides monilifera*. There's a bit more botany for you to remember.'

'I'm a fast learner. Keep going.'

'The mining companies started planting the stuff way back. Their answer to the erosion problems their mining caused. Digging the sand for their rutile.' He shook his head. 'The way those mining companies savaged this beach ... and around at Belongil ... man, it was ugly stuff! Massive equipment down there, ripping up the beach. Huge dredging machines up and down the length of this place. And their sheds. Would have been something to see, I reckon. Horrendous. Then they went and planted this South African weed to cover their tracks. It grew wild. Kills everything in its path. See.'

He pointed to some stunted native saplings being strangled by the bitou. 'The native dune stuff can't survive. It didn't stand a chance. Some good people got the mining stopped back in '68 but a bit too late by then. It'd got away from them, the bitou.'

'And here's me telling the agent this morning how lush I thought it was,' I said. 'Waxing lyrical over it. Said I liked the way all that lovely bright limey green creeper protected the dunes!'

'You weren't to know.'

'Feel pretty dammed stupid now, though.'

'Don't sweat it. Bet your life the guy didn't have a clue, either. Was he wearing a suit?'

'Yes.'

'Shiny shoes?'

'Yes.'

'Well, there you go.'

'I've got a lot to learn about Byron Bay, haven't I? Local lore, the kind of inside info that gets you those brownie points?'

'Y'know something?' he said, turning to me and grinning,

an echo of the cheeky grin I'd got from him back at the roundabout an hour ago. 'The penny has just dropped. What do y'know, you're the politician's wife. The desk story, John Brown's wife.'

'John Brown's body.'

'... *lies a moulding in the grave.*' He laughed. I was pleased it was a gentle laugh and not the kind of smirk I sometimes attracted.

'No. The body's alive and well, thank you.' And then came a total *non-sequitur.*' I'm divorced.'

He gave a shrug. 'Hey, who isn't?' Turning from me, he again scanned the horizon. 'See it?' He pointed to the north horizon.

'See what? Whales?' I was too busy worrying about my silly remarks to care about whales. Promiscuity, it had been explained to me by the various psychiatrists who'd had a go at trying to fix my head in the past couple of years, is a hallmark of the bi-polar condition, financial and sexual promiscuity when in the manic phase. And here I was, having already purchased a property on a whim this morning, about to go all haywire around the gypsy. The man was a good decade younger than me, and a stranger, albeit a handsome and interesting stranger, but a stranger.

He put one hand on my shoulder and with his other hand, turned my face in the direction he was pointing.

'Out there, look. A yacht. Coming down the coast. Way out. Just a speck coming around the headland. See it?'

'No. I don't see it.' I squinted, trying to spot the illusive vessel, but the hand and the man's closeness was seriously distracting me from acknowledging distant sailing boats.

'No?' He twisted me by my shoulders in the direction of the yacht and standing behind me, his cheek close to mine, took my arm and held it straight out, using my hand to point out the yacht. 'See, look straight along your arm,' he said. 'Way out there.'

Resisting the intimacy took an effort. He smelt good, smelt musky, and the man had his guiding hand on my shoulder. When I turned my head, our lips were within kissing distance of each other. Cue Hollywood violins. Doctor Zhivago bought a second of it then let go of my arm and turned back to look for his yacht out at sea. Be still, my beating heart!

'Oh, wait!' I called out. 'Wait! Okay, yes, now I do see it!' I turned back to him. 'Just,' I said. 'A beautiful, lonely kind of thing isn't it; a tiny sailing boat, all the way out there?'

'Sure is. She'll have a strong nor'easter behind her, that one,' he said, as much to himself as anyone else. 'There's nothing in the world like it. Nothing like the freedom of being out there, driving through the waves.'

'Away from all formulas.' I smiled across at him. 'A poem. I quote poetry. Endlessly. It's my shtick, my weakness. I drive people mad doing it,' I laughed.

'The rest of it? How does it go?'

'It's a long one. Your very own Walt Whitman. Guess they taught you Whitman in school. You might know it. Just a few lines are all I can quote, though.'

'Go on.'

'*We will sail pathless and wild seas. We will go where winds blow, waves dash, and the Yankee clipper speeds by under full sail.*' I hesitated then went on. '*Away from all formulas!*'

'Away from all formulas.' He repeated it, *sotto voce*, seeming to commit the phrase to memory. 'Sounds good. I like it. I'll remember that one. Walt Whitman, hey? *Oh, Captain. My Captain*.... Yeah, I used to like his stuff.' He turned and trudged up the sand hill. 'Anyway, forget the bitou,' he said when I caught up. 'You're real lucky you've got all those tuckeroos back in there as well as the palms.'

'Tuckeroos?'

'I'll show you.'

Ducking through the undergrowth and holding pandanus branches out of the way for me, he led me back inside the property and pointed.

'Tuckeroos. See? Those over there. And here. They're natives. Lovely things.'

He walked across to a stand of spindly trees growing in a hollow part of the sandy ground near the veranda. I noticed other similar trees were spread around the place, growing in clusters among the rest of the coastal shrubbery. The foliage was a dusty grey green, the leaves elongated and spike-edged, dark on the top side and a paler silvery grey underneath. The trunks were mostly rough textured but some were smooth with a mottled effect.

'A bit like birch trees, with those variegated trunks,' I said. 'Only thinner. And the leaves are different.' I pulled a leaf from a tree and held it to my nose.

He smiled and shook his head. 'Uh-uh. It's not fragrant. But it's a great tree.' He pointed across to another stand of tuckeroos near the ti-tree fence running down the north side of the property. 'This many in one place is rare nowadays. They're a feature of this area. Or were. Once upon a time.' He patted the trunk as though it were an old friend. 'I love 'em,' he said, looking around. 'The suburban sprawl's gonna kill them off, though.' He walked over to the edge of the veranda and plonked his frame down then patted the spot beside him, signaling me to join him.

Once I was seated—a safe way along the veranda from him—he turned to me. 'This location warrants something special, y'know that?'

'Tell me about it.'

'If you're serious, I will,' he said. 'Tell you about it, that is. I'll tell you what I reckon you could do with it. An undeveloped piece of beach front's sure something.'

'Except for that ugly big garage up front. You saw that when we drove in, right?'

'The guy built the garage. He did some music recordings in there at one time. Among other things.'

'The cannabis? Yes, I've been told about that already.'

A perky little brush turkey—black feathers, red head and a yellow necklace—strutted out of the dunes, scratched about for a bit then, when I tried to move towards it for a closer look—not yet appreciating what pest they are—the creature darted back in among the undergrowth and disappeared.

I came back to the veranda, sat down, wondering if the man had checked out my backside while I was leaning over and tussling with the turkey. I broke the silence.

'What I've got here is nothing more or less than a very run-down property, isn't it? Really?' I was looking at the mess of embers from my morning's labours, at the rusting corrugated iron wall down at the veranda's edge, at the ugly fibro, at the aluminium window and door frames. With a sigh, I pictured the monumental task ahead of me if I were to make the ugly little hut even half presentable. 'Just a dilapidated hippy hang-out, I guess.'

Before he answered, and as if to confirm my assumptions, he reached down and picked a syringe out of the grey sand at his feet and held it out to show me. I was horrified.

'You should get someone to do a sweep of this place. Under the house, too. It's not just a rumour. Surf documentaries weren't the guys only trick.'

'God, don't you hate them? Some dirty junkie,' I said, putting my hand out to take the needle from him.

'Uh-uh.'

He pulled his hand away and went across and retrieved a plastic water bottle from his canvas shoulder bag. After tipping out the remaining water, he pushed the needle against the step, bending it back on itself then dropped the syringe into the bottle and screwed the lid back on.

'I saw a skip out the front of that house they're renovating down the road. I'll drop it in there as I go by.'

He collected his canvas bag and slung it over his shoulder.

'You're going? So soon? But what about—'

'Yeah. I'm going,' he said, flatly.

His mood had changed, as if I the yellow brick road we had started down together moments ago had vanished. I watched as he walked towards the side of the house, trailing the bottle in his hand. When he stopped and looked around, I was standing, stunned, where he had left me. He looked down at the bottle for a moment then walked back and indicated the scope of the property with a wave of the bottle. 'Look, you've got a nice place lady, okay?'

He might as well have slapped my face. I recoiled from his words.

'A really nice place.'

'Thanks,' I said. 'It could be.'

He had just checked me out of la-la land. A thick, empty silence reigned in which I had time to regret my harsh outburst. Coming down like a tonne of bricks on heroin addicts didn't play well in Byron Bay, apparently.

Uncool.

No brownie points awarded for a new arrival so conservative she was repelled by Byron's famous junkies. My comment had reflected poorly on a place this local man loved. I had been insensitive. He was holding his gaze on me, unblinking.

'You'll find someone,' he said more gently as he turned from me and headed off.

'I thought I had,' I called out as he beat through the rainforest to the front yard.

He stopped walking, cast his eyes down at the bottle in his hand then around at the property. He looked back at me and seemed about to say something.

'Well?' I asked.

He looked down at the bottle again, rolling the syringe around in the plastic barrel, watching the way it tumbled. Finally he turned and walked up the yard to the street and without turning to look back, waved the bottle in the air above his head to bid me a final goodbye.

'Russian-Irish? Is that right?' I called out.

'You got it.' He didn't stop or look back but waved again with the loaded bottle.

'I hear they like a drink, those guys? Right?'

He turned and eyeballed me as I came closer, holding the stare for several seconds, challenging me to be the first to look away. But neither of us blinked. Not till he broke out in a smile and shrugged. 'Yeah. They'll take a sherry or two at Christmas.'

'If you're up for it, then how about a glass of Christmas cheer?' I was offering to buy him a drink. A hitchhiker I had just picked up. So, what? I was invincible. Still trawling Mt Olympus.

He looked puzzled. 'It's only September. A little early for Christmas, don't you reckon?'

'It's one of the 'er' months,' I said. 'It's Christmas once you hit the 'er' months. That's the rule.'

'Er months?'

'September. October. November. December. The 'er' months.' I was challenging him to question my logic. 'September? It's a down-hill run from here.'

'Life's a downhill run.' He said it and it seemed that straight away, he regretted the bitter tone.

'C'mon. Hear those sleigh bells?'

'You're crazy, y'know that?'

'And I like you, too. Mr Builder of Fine Timber Boats. A Christmas drink around the corner at my local? Please?'

I retrieved my bag from the Golf and slung it over my shoulder. 'I've been here a whole day,' I said as I came back to him. 'It's time I got acquainted with my local watering hole. Don't want to walk in there on my own if I can help it. It's a lovely day so what say we walk around?'

'Okay by me.'

I fell in beside him. We reached the front of the yard and turned left.

When I began walking ahead of him to pick frangipani off the ground I imagined I could feel his eyes on me.

But they weren't.

He was back at the skip bin in front of the renovation site, moving aside cardboard boxes and pieces of broken plasterboard. I watched him bury the plastic bottle deep down beneath the refuse.

Good man, I thought as I started walking backwards, dodging the branches of an overhanging hibiscus.

He plucked a red blossom from the tree and handed it to me. A romantic gesture? It landed on me as such.

We were soon strolling through the back door of the Suffolk Park Hotel and it wasn't until I let him guide me to the bar, where he ordered a gin and tonic for me and a White Russian for himself, that I stuck the hibiscus flower behind my ear. Left or right?

THE DREAMER

I'd not give way for an emperor.
I'd hold my road for a king.
To the triple crown I would not bow down
But this is a different thing.
Drawbridge let fall! T'is the Lord of as all!
The dreamer whose dreams come true.

Rudyard Kipling

The temple bells above the screen door tinkled as we entered the unpretentious little café squeezed in between Suffolk Park's organic greengrocer and the hardware shop-come-local post office.

We were greeted by a traditionally dressed young woman, her head bowed, her palms pressed together who showed us across the room to a corner table.

Around the café's walls Tibet's political sorrows, hand-written by the owners on A4 coloured sheets hung on string, there for the benefit of a sympathetic clientele. The young Tibetan couple had set up their venture with pine tables, cane chairs and a glass take-away counter with a white lace curtain strung across the back.

Through the archway, beneath a Buddhist shrine was a minuscule kitchen with a two-wok burner. Crates stacked high against the wall competed for space with a toddler's pusher and small dinky.

The Buddha had his presence everywhere in the room, no

more so than in the ornate Tibetan sacred shrine adorning the wall above the blackboard menu boasting Specials of the Day.

Wok smells. Incense. I inhaled the aromas of the East as we took our seats.

There were other perfumes just as pleasing. A trail of night jasmine and frangipani was arranged across our table. I liked this place, liked it a lot.

'You're the expert. You order,' I said after taking a look at the handwritten menu. During a couple of hours next door in the hotel bar, I'd learned of his life growing up as a little boy in Hong Kong; speaking Cantonese, but no English, his mother, a party girl outsourcing his childhood to an amah whom he'd cherished.

'Thukpa, please. Two bowls,' he said with a smile to the Tibetan woman.

'Thukpa?' I repeated.

'Tibetan noodles with meat and vegetables in a kind of broth.' He looked back up at the hostess. 'And we'll have the Sha Phaley, thanks.' He explained it to me. 'They're little buns stuffed with seasoned beef and cabbage then deep fried. Is meat okay?'

'Meat's fine. The deep fry's a worry,' I laughed.

'And one mango and one cucumber lassi, please,' he said. 'That okay? We try both lassis? Yak's milk?'

'You're kidding me? Yak's milk? I don't believe you but it sounds good.'

The food ordered, I felt keen to continue the conversation we'd had next door at the pub. 'So, tell me more. It must have been wild; a teenager in LA and San Francisco in the late Sixties. And you really did know Kurt Russell? You're not pulling my leg? And David Crosby?'

'I went to school with Kurt. We fought over the same girl.'

'And?'

'And who got the girl?'

'Yes. Which one of you?'

'I think I did. I must have. He was dirty on me after that. He had a party going on at his place one night. We're all high school kids. I wasn't invited. So, my buddies and me, we go around the side of his house and I climb in through the bathroom window. The beers are piled up in ice in the bath tub. It's right under the window. I'm standing in the tub and lobbing the cans out the window to the guys as fast as I could. Next thing, Kurt's coming through the door. Not happy. He lunges at me and lobs one on my jaw.'

The Tibetan princess placed bamboo chopsticks and napkins in front of us and retreated.

'Shouldn't we be discussing the work you need done around at your house?' he said.

It seemed that in the past couple of hours in the pub next door we had covered just about everything from Aborigines to Zen, as well as enjoyed a game of pool. I had already given the gods silent thanks for my small act of recklessness this afternoon at the roundabout.

'I loved what you were saying earlier about the timbers,' I said. 'Such lovely names; Jarrah. Hoop pine. Camphor Laurel. What were some of the others?'

'Silver Ash, Alaskan cedar, rosewood, quila, turpentine, black butt, ironbark. Mahogany's a nice one. Lots of streets in Byron are named after timbers. Used to be a timber district. You noticed the names of the streets. Timber names?'

'Not really. But I've got to say I did notice the poets' names. Seems yesterday's city fathers accommodated both our passions.'

'I work with a kinda vision,' he said. 'I kinda go for the

clean lines of Japanese design. How about you?'

'The Balinese look.'

'That's okay. By mixing your timbers with other materials ... things like, well, for instance, bamboo and shoji screens ... you'll get perfect harmony. It's all in the way you do it.'

Perfect harmony.

All in the way you do it.

I let his words fall gently, his lovely American drawl flooding my senses. 'I'm fifty-four,' I blurted out, apropos of nothing.

'And you'd make your kitchen bench from a polished rosewood slab. And I reckon then that you'd ...,' He stopped talking and smiled.

'You?' I said. 'How old?'

'Who's counting? As I was saying, we'd—'

'Really, how old?'

'Roughly? Forty-two. And we'd make the kitchen benches from—'

'A rosewood slab. See, I have been listening.'

'Cross-cuts of the trunk,' he said, with a two-handed slicing of the air above the table to demonstrate the saw mill's action in cutting through a tree trunk to create a slab. 'I've got them in storage up north. Great rosewood slabs, camphor laurels and long pieces of mahogany and beech. Heaps of it that we could use. Fantastic, the rosewood with its natural edge left on. You get your dark red and then a thin layer of yellow at the edges and then the raw husky bark.'

His hands were expressive, his passion for his subject obvious in the way he threw his whole being into what he was telling me.

'Great contrast in textures and shades,' he said, adding that if it were his property around there in the dunes, then he would be replacing the ugly fibro sheeting on the outside with vertical rough-sawn timber planking and giving it a light forest green wash so the hut blended in and meshed with the tuckeroos. 'Your green-grey walls would be a great foil for the stained natural timbers on the sliding doors and windows. Part of the forest.'

While he explained how he would put a shingled roof up to replace the rusted corrugated iron one, I drained the last dregs of the mango lassi and scraped my middle finger around the inside of the glass to scoop up the delicious froth. The amount of alcohol I had taken aboard as the sun had been setting over Byron Bay had brought me to the point of idiotic coquettishness.

I licked my fingers of the lassi froth. Slowly. Deliberately. I was behaving like a middle-aged fool. Blame the crazy serotonin roller coaster ride I was on.

'It probably leaks, anyway,' he said of the roof. 'It should be shingled. And I'd use some turpentine logs, natural tree trunks, to replace those ugly four-by-four hardwood posts holding up your veranda roof. It's a great veranda. Best part of the shack at the moment. And I'd make louvers out of Australian red cedar for the small bathroom window. I've got some good cedar put aside up north too. See how you're starting to get the Asian feeling going now?'

'Sure am.' I was smiling, feeling the good vibrations.

'A bit of work, but you'd have a sensational little place. A real Balinese hut,' he said.

'All this is presuming I forget about building the main house. Not utilizing all that yard fronting the road.'

'Call me crazy, but a house on a main road, directly under a street lamp? At a bus stop? Or a Balinese beach hut accessed through a rainforest and hidden down among the dunes ...

with the Pacific Ocean at its front door? What? You go to sleep at night to the sound of the sea or the 10.45pm to Ballina?'

'A no-brainer?'

'What do you reckon?'

'Keep going. What's happening inside? What are we doing in there, in the kitchen? Apart from our polished rosewood bench tops with their natural edging and the bathroom's timber louvers? Red cedar.'

'So, you were listening.'

'Been with you all the way, genius.'

'Y'see, I'd also use some red cedar planking on the walls.'

Grabbing my napkin and taking a stubby carpenter's pencil from the pocket of his Hawaiian shirt, he started to draw.

'Like this. Get it? I'd slant the planks on the two tiny walls in the corner to define the kitchen area. Then I'd put bamboo ply on the rest of the walls, on what'll be your living area. We cover the bamboo joins with darker, contrasting beading. Makes lovely walls. Then we'd install sliding shoji screens to close off enough of the north end of the rectangle for your bedroom. Make the screens out of pale silky ash and rice paper. I've got some good ash up north, too ... across this part, see?'

He had reached for another napkin and was scribbling away like crazy.

'We'd render the bedroom walls with a creamy coloured plaster to give the space a different feel from the living area.' His pencil raced across the page. 'This way your one long space is starting to flow into three distinct areas; your kitchen, living area and bedroom. You could polish those turpentine floorboards, too. They'd come up, great. You'll never get termites ... great flooring ... termites hate turpentine. It's gummy and sticks to their teeth. They can't get it off.'

'Eeeek!' I bought both hands up under my chin like tiny

paws, curled my face up into a ball and became one of his termites attempting to rub its teeth clean of the gooey turpentine. 'Eeeek!'

'You're really crazy, you know that?' he laughed.

'I try to be. Please go on, sir.' With the fingers of both hands, I mimed the stretching signal a TV director gives the talent when he or she wants them to extend their performance.

He smiled, shrugged. 'Well, then you'd line the ceiling with hoop pine ... and then we'd lime-wash the hoop pine. And by the way, we'd put a heavy beam of Brazilian mahogany above where the shoji screen goes. Here, like this.' He described it with his pencil. 'That'd strengthen the ceiling and add contrast, define the bedroom area even more so.'

Unstoppable, but I was lapping it up. The Californian accent, the man's romantic vision of my ugly little shack, his obvious knowledge of timbers and his flair for design. And his contagious enthusiasm.

He was a dream weaver.

'You want some more poetry?' I asked once our plates had been cleared away.

'Sure.'

'It's Kipling, okay? Here goes: *"Hand him the keys! Down on your knees / 'Tis the dreamer whose dreams come true."*

He stretched his arm across, leant in and laid his hand on my shoulder. 'You know something? I reckon if I'd had you for a teacher I might have stood half a chance.'

He hadn't meant it but it made me aware of our age difference. I looked around the room and noticed the other patrons had departed and the Tibetan couple seemed shyly anxious to close up shop. 'It's late,' I said as I stood up. 'We'd better let them close up.' I excused myself and walked across to the counter.

When I looked around, Yuri O'Byrne had vanished.

For a moment, I had the impression I'd dreamed him up.

I bid the young Tibetan couple goodnight, responding to them with palms joined, and left the café, the temple bells tinkling above my head as I walked out the screen door into the warm summer night. At once, the jasmine fragrance hit my senses, reminding me, if I needed reminding, that I was no longer in Sydney or even up on the Gold Coast. I had docked by chance in Byron Bay, and Kublai Khan was standing on the footpath near a parked car waiting for me.

'Thanks for dinner.' He pushed a ten dollar note into my hand. 'I'll be going.'

Suddenly I realized that by taking control of the bill I had offended him, implied that because he was a hitchhiker he wouldn't have the means to pay for dinner. 'So, you've got all these lovely timbers stored up north, right?' I said.

'Ah, you can pick up some good stuff around Mullum or Billinugel, no problem.' He tossed his canvas satchel over his shoulder.

'About the alu ... the al-oo-min-um windows?' I said, believing that if I could get him thinking of those timber frames again I might be in with a chance.

'Yeah, the windows.' He dug into his pocket and produced the stubby carpenter's pencil again and took the napkin I handed him, the one I had just pocketed from the table as a souvenir; my first night in Byron. But I could see that his earlier enthusiasm had evaporated. His voice was flat.

'Anyone can knock up some replacement windows for you.' He started to rough out a set of window frames. 'A few days' work,' he said. 'Should cost you around ... let's see.'

I studied him as he stood beside me, resting the paper on the car bonnet while he did his calculations, no longer the dream weaver but a tradesman now, nominating a ball-park figure which, he said, included materials and labour.

'But they would just be run-of-the-mill window frames, right?' I said, aware a portal had opened somewhere and the stardust I'd been gathering all evening was floating away. I moved further under the lamp light and pretended to study his figures. Eventually, I looked up at him. 'It all seemed so exotic,' I said. 'So ... so not ordinary ... the way you told it back in there. What happened? Where did it go?'

He took the napkin from me and quickly drew a series of straight lines just in from the edge of a rectangle. Three vertical lines crossed by three horizontal lines near one corner of his drawing and, with just those few strokes, an economy of line, he had conjured up a distinct Japanese-style window.

Magic does happen.

'So, when do we start?' I said.

He turned his sights towards the main road. I put my hand on his arm. 'When do we start, Yuri?'

He turned his eyes from the road and looked back at me, then down at his drawings. It was a long time before he spoke. 'We could sure create something special, couldn't we?'

'We sure could.'

'And we could top these windows with tiny shingled awnings.' He started racing his pencil over the paper again. Above his Japanese windows he drew thatched awnings in detail, shading the shingles, emphasizing the supports. All with a carpenter's stubby pencil. A work of art. Never had windows felt more important to me. And then it was over.

'Look, forget it,' he said. 'I gotta go, okay?' He had his palms held up to me as he backed off. 'I get carried away. Sometimes.' He was walking backwards, away from me, shaking his head, his arm out behind him, his thumb already up as he turned and headed for the Bangalow Road corner.

'Thank you,' I called out to him.

'For what? You paid,' he called over his shoulder and kept walking.

'For inspiring me, Mr Yuri O'Byrne, shipwright of Yamba.'

I saw the lights of a car coming down Bangalow towards him, saw him move onto the road and stand in the car's headlights, attempting to thumb it down.

'No', I whispered. It was meant as an incantation, a spell to make the car and its driver vanish into the night. No, I said, again as the white sedan slowed down. It would stop for him, carry him away. I held my breath. At the last moment, the car swerved and accelerated, speeding away from him.

Make him stay, I pleaded with the gods. 'Stay.'

He looked up and down the highway then turned around, surprised to see I was still there.

'If you want to, that is,' I said, walking up to him.

'Say again?'

'Stay the night, why don't you?' I indicated the empty road. 'You could be here till morning. Why not stay?'

He hesitated. Looked up the highway again then back at me.

'Stay. Please?' I said more softly this time.

His steady gaze held mine. It took him moments to respond. 'You're sure?'

'Very sure,' I said, and as I took the hand he held out to me and felt a quiver of excitement, I knew I meant it with every part of my being.

We walked home hand-in-hand, down a road lit by moonlight and alive with the sweet tropical fragrances of an enchanted evening.

Live dangerously, whispered a voice carried on the gentle breeze. A voice, or the Voices?

SEDUCTION

Now glowed the firmament
With living sapphires.
John Milton, Evening in Paradise

Like Eve leading Adam to the forbidden fruit, she takes him by
the hand and leads him down the garden path.

~ ~ ~

Having grabbed my tartan rug from the boot we beat
through the pandanus bushes, over the dunes and down to the
sand, where I laid out the rug, produced the six large scented
candles I'd bought earlier in the day and positioned them
around the perimeter.

I lit the candles and inhaled their exotic eastern perfume
before pouring two glasses of red wine into plastic cups and
looking up at the man standing above me. What he was
thinking, who can say?

Two strangers.

This woman making the moves on him.

I was up for this, an important point I want you to
remember as the story unfolds.

The breeze wasn't enough to bother the flames or to chase
the drift of clouds from the moon but sufficient to waft
fragrances of the summer night past us; frangipani, clematis
and night jasmine blended with the bergamot and patchouli
perfumes of the candles to create an intoxicating mix—at least

for me, whose brain chemicals had been performing high-wire tricks since dawn.

As if I needed props to enhance my sense of the night's erotic possibilities.

Our fingers touched when he reached down and took the bottle shop's plastic cup of wine from my hand, then, as we sat sipping the fruit of the vine, watching waves crashing onto the shore and me babbling on in lyrical terms of how Art had got it right; the whiteness of the foaming peaks capturing the moonlight, majestic white stallions charging for the beach and vanishing into fantasy, his contribution was to wonder at the constellations above us and to begin describing the separate parts by name.

This shut me up. He impressed me with his sailor's knowledge of the skies. But I was only up for so much stargazing and eventually I took the initiative that would complete Fate's intention.

I leant over and kissed the curve of his tanned and silky Californian neck and when he didn't recoil, the manic Voices cried Hallelujah! I had arrived at where I'd yearned to be since I'd spied him at the roundabout this afternoon. If I were honest. But instead, I was manic. There is a difference.

But two decades later I still recall with a thrill how wonderful and right it felt when my fingers slid up into that mass of blacker-than-black shiny hair and I pulled him close, so close that all there was left was for him to find my lips and return my hunger with a hunger of his own.

Never a thought that it was a bad idea to seduce this fascinating gypsy man, and by the time the tip of my tongue had found the loop of his gold earring desire was crashing against my consciousness like the waves out on Julian Rocks.

'Is this a good idea?' he asked, leaning back a little to search my face.

'A wonderful idea,' I said, believing it a thousand times over.

'I don't have—'

'Shhhhh. Let's make it a night to remember.'

~ ~ ~

'A night to remember?' he whispered, reaching for my hand as we lay, sated, alongside each other on the rug.

'A night to remember,' I sighed, content now to lay in his arms, sharing in the sweet, unwinding moments and contemplating the mysteries, not of life, but of sensational sex. What could compare with what had just happened to me? This beautiful, sensitive lover had shown me I could find the far side of Heaven in his arms.

A revelation.

Laying naked and spent, we began to tell each other the stories we were prepared to share.

'I almost didn't say this afternoon that I recognized you,' he said.

'Why? Why wouldn't you?'

'Too shy.'

'Shy! You?' I laughed, sitting up to pour more wine and admire his body, his flat, tanned belly and the line of dark silky hair running down his middle and into his groin, as straight and sharp as the blade of a scimitar.

'You want to hear the sad story about my boat?'

'Of course,' I said, refilling his cup with the shiraz.

He took a generous sip then set it in the sand beside the rug. His hands were still folded behind his head as he studied the stars. 'She was nothing fancy. Just a cramped, seventeen-foot Stella. But it was my home. She was cozy. I followed the work up and down the coast, from Yamba up to the

Whitsundays.'

'The beautiful Whitsundays,' I said, remembering how in the previous decade, as the wife of the Minister for Tourism I'd had a dress-circle view of Queensland's magnificent Great Barrier Reef.

'Sure is. I spent a fair few years up there, living on the Stella after my divorce.'

'Your divorce? Tell me about it.'

'Nah, it's ancient history. I worked up on the islands, building resorts. Keith Williams' Hamilton Island, mostly. I did a lot of work for him. And I was restoring the Stella. People said she was the best cared-for yacht on the Reef. She was my calling card, that boat.'

'I restore things too. Nothings as big as boats, though. I've always loved trawling the op shops. Finding old furniture, picture frames, candle sticks, old clothes, all kinds of knick-knacks and bringing them back to life. I can never understand why people are so quick to junk things. Just for the sake of a little effort ... and a belief in their goodness.'

'They don't see what you see, I guess.'

'Perhaps you're right, but some things are precious if you take the time and trouble to bring out their true essence. Their inscape, that's what the poets call it.'

'Inscape?'

'There's an inscape to everything. I guess it's another name for the soul, a deep inner essence that's unique to that ... that thing ... that object or that person.'

I sat up and looked at him. 'Think about when you stare deep into burning coals. Really deep into the centre of the glow, the hot red embers of burning logs. It takes you to another place. It's fascinating, right? Not just your eyes, but your mind penetrates that fiery inner glow. You understand the thing that makes it a burning log. It just seems to be an endless mystery to me. And to Gerald Manly Hopkins.'

'Gerald who?'

'He was a priestly poet who nailed it a long time ago. *Each mortal thing does one thing and the same/myself it speaks and spells...*

In the silence between us I could see I had given him something to think about. He nodded, as if consolidating a certainty.

'Yeah, I kinda get it ... I think. Say, the ocean. It's got that ... that ... what did you call it?'

'Inscape.'

'Yeah, inscape. The ocean has it for me. It's got a soul ... no, not a soul but something ... I don't know ... something so unique about it that it kinda grabs you and doesn't let go ... something you can't touch but you know it's there.' He paused. 'I'm not doing a great job of this, am I? But you get the picture? It's all its own, the thing that's the ocean. And a wooden boat, it's got your inscape, too, for sure. If you love her enough. A part of nature but a special thing, a way of being what it is.'

I placed a platonic kiss on his forehead. 'That, my moon river friend, is the very inscape the poet wrote about. But, whoa, I'm getting a bit carried away with the metaphysics. Let's get back to this actual boat of yours.'

'Wait on. I'm interested in *my* inscape. How do you read me?'

'Stop taking the piss. I'll tell you about your inscape one day. Not now, though. I want to hear about your boat.'

'Okay. I was living aboard her ... in Yamba. Then came the accident. The night my guardian angel jumped ship.'

'You believe in angels?' Earlier in the day he had mentioned the awful road accident he'd suffered the previous April; how the paramedics had scraped him off the bitumen when his new Ford utility crashed late at night on the highway down at Karuah on the mid north coast. Nine broken ribs.

He shrugged. 'You gotta believe in 'em, don't you? Angels? On your shoulder?'

'I guess so.' I had the feeling I might have hooked one myself today.

'The morning I got out of Taree Base Hospital I hitched back up to Yamba and that's when I found the repo men crawling all over my boat. Just throwing everything, all my gear, onto the jetty. The finance company was repossessing her.'

'Tell me it was insured, the ute?'

He sat up and drained the wine from his cup.

'I remember completing all their forms, the finance company's forms. Why wouldn't I insure it? Just a small premium added to the repayment plan. And the guy whose boat I was gonna restore had put money up for me to kick off with the work. I reckon they stole my papers, the policy ... along with a lot of other stuff. But I couldn't prove anything. They did some bad things, those insurance guys. A local north coast crowd. Small time ... shonky as Hell.'

He explained how, with his chest strapped and his back killing him, he had been too ill to do anything other than gather up his few belongings off the jetty and walk away from his cherished boat, his home.

'On walking sticks. And not a cent to my name and my family nowhere in sight. My ex-wife had been notified but she didn't bother to enquire if I'd lived or died, not during the two weeks I was in intensive care and then in a ward. And wouldn't let the kids call me, either.'

'That's awful.'

He shook his head and stared off into the distance. 'It was tough, being in there with the other guys. They had visitors.'

'You don't have any family'

'A mother in the States. And a step brother over there, too. I think. If he's still alive.'

'Where do you live now?'

'After they sealed off my boat I wandered into this café in Yamba, a place I sometimes went to for coffee and burgers. The lady who owns it felt sorry for me. Took me in.'

'The comfort of strangers.' I should have known there would be a woman.

He caught my drift. 'Accommodation only. She's my landlady. In fact, her boyfriend wants me gone.'

'Is that why you were in Byron this afternoon? Checking out digs?'

'No, to be with my daughter. She had a baby at Byron Hospital this morning.'

'You became a grandfather, today! Why didn't you say something around at the pub? We'd have had champagne! Oh, God! A grandfather, Yuri!' I took his face in my hands and planted a kiss on his lips. At least we had that in common, we were grandparents. The age gap had just diminished a little. When I pulled away, I saw sadness where I had expected to see joy.

'I thought I could make things right between us now that she was having this baby,' he said. 'But she's dark on me, my daughter. Long story. They wouldn't let me see her. She's nineteen. I've been told nothing about the father, except my son said the guy was only twenty and in the Army.' He shrugged. 'My ex did well for herself. Married one of Byron's top businessmen. The kids grew up in a better house than I could've given them. He gave them smarter gifts for birthdays. I did a bike up for my son's twelfth birthday.

I was pretty proud of it. But the guy had already given the kid a super-duper one earlier in the day. He took them on overseas skiing holidays. I could only manage to fly them up to join me in the Whitsundays where I was working. Live on the boat. Although we did have some good times on the couple of occasions she let then fly up.'

He sat up and reached for the bottle of wine but saw we'd emptied it.

'I'm just a bum to my kids these days.' It was a flat statement. As though he were doing no more than echoing a universal opinion of himself.

You are no bum, I thought. You are a gentleman. 'They honestly wouldn't let you in to see your own daughter?'

'Uh-uh. "It would upset her", the young nurse said. "You're to leave. That's what she told me to tell you, Mr. O'Byrne? Please? I'm really sorry, I really am." Yeah, and so I left. Feeling like a mongrel dog chased from the yard.'

I reached over and laid the back of my hand across his cheek. 'Yuri, I'm sorry. That's an awful story.'

'I waited outside on the veranda. Okay that the whole gang from Central Casting was allowed in for the birth. But not me. Not her own father. I'd been palmed. Yuri O'Byrne, the pariah, the guy no one wanted to know about.' He stood up and started slipping on his shorts. 'Just gotta go for a ... you know. Won't be a minute, okay?'

'Sure. Go for it.' I reached into my bag and produced the joint my young passenger had put in my glove box this afternoon.

'I've got this. Should I light it? A celebration?'

'Suit yourself,' he said with a shrug, shaking his head as he left me and I watched him walk back up to the shack.

~~~

'So, after all that? What did she have? Boy or girl?' I asked when he eventually returned to the beach, having been gone so long I'd been sure he had crashed out on the mattress inside.

'A boy.'

I noticed him rubbing the tip of his nose, as if a butterfly were tormenting it.

'Be careful. That stuff's got a decent kick.' He lent across and retrieved the joint I was holding and stubbed it out between his fingers. 'Reckon you've had enough.'

'It's not doing anything for me. Honestly.' I took it back and lit it again, inhaling deeply.

'Bad move.'

I lay back on the rug and watched him out the corner of my eye.

His nose was still itchy, apparently. Except, now, as he sat staring out to sea, it seemed he had trouble finding it. He kept bringing his hand up slowly, near to the tip of his nose, but then couldn't quite make the connection. When his head dropped forward, he jerked it back up suddenly and looked around, startled. 'Baby boy? Ummm, yeah, lovely baby boy,' he said.

It's the wine, I concluded and left him as I went for a stroll down to the water's edge. The man didn't handle his wine well.

I danced naked on the sand, twirling my sarong behind me like Isadora Duncan, a sea nymph down by the shore flitting about in high spirits, showing off and only slightly aware that it might not have been such a great idea to have smoked the "Welcome to Byron" gift.

The next thing I can recall is being in the shack, flat on my back on the mattress on the floor and trying to stop the pasted stars scattered on the ceiling from spinning crazily towards me.

To dodge the million shards of bright meteors raining down on me I tried keeping my eyes closed, but when I did, the nausea hit me in massive waves. I was in trouble. I couldn't stare at the phosphorescent stars without a giddy attack, but neither could I shut my eyes or the nausea would swamp me.

I was aware that someone had a cloth of some kind at the ready for a possible barf. Even a hearty vomit would have been better than the awful queasiness. It was morning sickness magnified ten times over.

Mullum Madness!

I would later learn just how potent the home-grown variety of cannabis was in Byron Bay. Pure, but deadly. The devotees would rhapsodize about the 'big purple heads' produced up in the hinterland around Mullumbimby.

The stoners are probably still singing its praises today, for all I know. And taken in moderation, I am sure it's harmless enough. But I binged and paid the price. Later consideration would convince me that the anti-depressant medication, Aropax, the serotonin re-uptake inhibitors I had been taking for the past two years, had a significant cumulative effect on the way my brain metabolized the psychoactive THC.

Whatever, it was mad, bad and stupid and I would only repeat the stupidity once more when Foxtel colleagues from Sydney visited me months later and coaxed me to try their hash cookies.

While my world spun in crazy circles, wave after hideous wave of sickening visions bombarding me and wild things leaping off the walls and racing across the ceiling, a tropical downpour was turning the iron roof into a cacophony of kettle drum sounds.

And I cursed that someone, some hippie, some surfer some time had pasted those stars and moons all over the ceiling.

They glowed.

They were glowing now, and violent giddiness kept assaulting me and all I wanted was to escape my head. Had hours passed since I'd come up from the beach? I tried to make sense of time and place. Maybe only minutes, maybe a decade. I was beyond clocks, only spasms of this awful giddy sickness each time I shut my eyes.

And a fiend, a monster, something vile was out there somewhere and coming for me. I couldn't remember getting from beach to mattress.

I had let him in. A stranger ... a deserted shack ... the dunes ... a lonely beach ... middle of the night ... no one knows where I am ... happy vacationer ... Hoover was right ... escaping criminal ... sex maniac ... vicious murderer ... Keep your eyes open! Nausea.

Writhing pythons. Pythons. Everywhere. Inside and outside my head. What's happening? Where am I?

You're okay. You're okay, Jan. It's me. Yuri. It's okay.

Never felt this sick. Help me. I'm dying.

No, you're not. It won't last. You'll be okay, someone was saying. Who was saying? I'll walk you around. Come on, pal, on your feet, let's go for a walk.

No ... no... sick ... too sick ... where are you taking me?

'Letting you smoke so much of that 'J' was my mistake. I'm sorry. But you'll be fine. Let's walk,' he said with authority.

'Go!' I screamed.

I was a crouching tiger in the darkened corner, a death grip on a pair of scissors aimed at the heart of the man who, in my delusional state, I figured must be a rapist killer. On any reckoning, I had been the sexual aggressor, but that was before the mule had booted me in the head and kicked off *Carnivàle*. Now I was facing the devil himself in the form of this big powerfully built man, this stranger who keeps trying to touch me.

'Go! Get away from me!'

Gently—and I guess without wanting to excite a new round of agitation—he opened my palm and took the scissors from me and tossed them across the floor. 'C'mon, back on the bed. You're tired. Lay down a while, then. I'll lay beside you. It'll pass.'

I collapsed onto the mattress.

He covered me with the pink blanket and lay down alongside me, cuddling into my back with his arm resting across my body. A pair of spoons. How long we lay like that I don't know, but when I turned over, throwing him off, I suddenly sat up, squatted on my knees, as if to spring.

'Go!' I growled. 'Get out! Just go! I want you to go!'

'It's alright. It's alright.' He tried to sooth me. 'Just lay down. It'll pass. You'll sleep it off. Nothing's gonna hurt you. Nothing. I'm here for you. Just let go.'

I crawled off the mattress and foraged about on the floor in the dark, searching for those scissors.

'Alright. I'll go, okay? What is it about me and crazy women?' He reached across the floor for his clothes. 'I was going when the sun came up, anyway. '

I fell back onto the mattress, groaning. Later, I would recall that old Khayyam had nailed it when he wrote "*...this delightful Herb ... Ah, lean upon it lightly*"!

I lay prone for how long I haven't a clue, but when I sat up again I puked the contents of my stomach—red wine and Tibetan noodles, washed down with mango lassi—onto the floor and watched my carer going to my bag where he grabbed a t-shirt and blotted my mouth then wiped up the patch of vomit.

'Sorry, but I'm still here. It's been raining and it's still pretty dark out there.' He was pulling on his shorts and buttoning up his shirt. 'Don't suppose you'd have an old towel or something I could put over my head. I guess I'll be waiting up the corner a fair while.'

I grunted and pointed to the pink cotton blanket, then collapsed back onto the mattress in a foetal position. I wanted to die. God, let me die. It would be hours before I woke again and when I did, my head would be clear and the paranoia gone.

I wasn't surprised to see that he was asleep beside me. As I lay staring up at the ceiling, I noted that the pasted stars no longer swirled in their malignant and chaotic galaxy, but simply sat up there, as faded as the glories of the hippy-trippy Seventies that had welcomed them.

I lay beside Yuri O'Byrne, imagining that when he woke we would laugh at how crazy I'd been to drink so much wine, and to smoke marihuana just to impress him. And I'd be embarrassed and I'd tell him I regretted having tried to turn him out in the cold and rain last night.

We would probably make love again and I would say something about my new life in Byron Bay being launched.

The sun would shine. The world would feel good again. The balance would be restored.

Or so I thought as I closed my eyes and drifted back into easeful oblivion.

GREEN ICING

I have the sense of falling light.
Stephen Spender

I open my eyes and look towards the window. There is the hint of a brand-new day about to break through out there. Then I smell the vomit somewhere in the room and a morning-after feeling swamps my spirit. Like the slow ooze of a mudslide after monsoonal rains, heavy shame threatens to subsume me.

I turn back to the wall and discover that he is still lying beside me. And despite the hangover headache and the shame, I feel a rush of joy. I stroke the gypsy cheek so close to me and wrap my arm around him. Snuggle into his chest. Life is good. I am where I am meant to be.

'We have to talk,' he said, softly, not turning to look at me.

That tone. Here it comes. There's a woman.

I cursed my promiscuity. Hitchhikers with golden earrings should come with a warning. I'd been right to fear his aura. I rolled from him, turning my head away.

'Yes? About what?'

'Feel that?'

He reached out for my hand and moved my fingers until I was tracing those scars I'd first noticed in the crook of his elbow yesterday afternoon.

'What am I feeling?'

'Tracks.'

I turned back to him, puzzled. 'Tracks?'

'Heroin,' he said. 'They're scars from the needle ... from shooting heroin into my veins.'

He stepped off the mattress and reached for my Bali sarong and wrapped it around his waist, native-style, rolling the top edge down over his hips. 'I'm sorry.' He was moving from the room, out to the veranda.

I stayed put. Immobile. Paralyzed.

He came back to the door. 'I thought you'd have noticed them, known what they were. I'd been waiting the whole time for you to say something. It's why I asked if you were sure ... last night, down on the beach'

Breathe!

He came across to the mattress and knelt down beside me, taking me by the shoulders and making me sit up and look at him. 'You had no idea, did you?'

I shook my head but no words came out. No, I hadn't had an iota of an idea and it was taking time for the one he had just planted in my sore head to take shape. His accident? After he had told me about the road smash down at Karuah I'd been sure they were scars from his accident.

I attempted to recapture wild fragments of my brain and bring them back into alignment. Pull yourself together! But too late. I'd had unprotected sex with this man. A junkie!

AIDS! The Grim Reaper was grinning, writing his headlines even as I tried to come to grips with this thing. *Death From AIDS!*

I cupped my palms and dragged in the carbon monoxide. Monoxide or dioxide? Never mind. Think straight! No condom! I had never in my life used a condom, didn't know how to use one! Adolescents in high school are shown how to slide them onto bananas. Safe sex! What was happening to me?

I leapt from the bed and reached for my clothes. Fight or flight; the adrenalin rush.

I had to get away!

Now!

He was no visionary. Not a boat builder, not at all. Not my dream weaver. Not my beautiful gypsy lover. He was a heroin junkie! I stood clutching a handful of clothes to my chest, glaring across the room at him.

'It was all a lie, all that ... that stuff about timbers ... about building boats and things. All a lie. You're not a builder of boats, are you? Well, are you?' I screamed at him.

'No,' he said, quietly. 'I'm just a bum.'

'What?'

'If you say so, lady.'

'You can't build boats, can you? Answer me!' I spat the words at him. It seemed vital to know if he built boats, as if having that skill would validate him, render him no danger to me.

'No, I can't build boats. I know nothing about timber, either. Can't hold a hammer. What do you reckon?'

His bitter irony had me confused. Why wasn't he rushing in with words to comfort me, take me in his arms and tell me I had nothing to worry about, that he was free of AIDS, free of the means to destroy my life? This was the Nineties and we were in the vortex of the HIV horror, death the only way out.

I threw the clothes I'd been holding to my chest into the case on top of my other gear and tried to shut the lid, shoving him away when he tried to help me. I put my hands to my ears and turned my head when he came close. I was beyond letting him try soothing me with his empty words. I didn't need them. Too little, too late! My body and mind were going into some kind of wild spasm.

Sheer panic.

A meltdown like I'd never experienced.

My lips felt numb.

I was sweating, feeling light-headed and feint, irrational fear a red blaze in front of my eyes. Disorientation had me stumbling as I dragged clothes from my bag and dressed. This rotten place. Rotten to the core with drugs. The man had tried to warn me, the mechanic around at the BP. He had tried to warn me about this place. The hotel kids, too. But I hadn't listened, had I?

He gathered up his few things laying scattered over the floor and shoved them in his canvas bag. I turned from him when he attempted to kiss me goodbye. 'It's still pretty wet out there,' he said. 'I don't suppose—'

'Take it!' I shoved the pink blanket at him, almost knocking him off his feet.

With the blanket draped over his shoulders and his head bent into the rain, he stepped off the veranda and headed around to the front of the shack. I ran to the kitchen sink and poured myself a glass of water, cupping the glass with both shaking hands. My whole body trembled. My heart raced. This was a panic attack of major proportions. My future had just turned ugly, turned frightening. I cursed that I'd ever met the man. Cursed my stupidity.

Despite the rain, the morning was warm, a beautiful Byron Bay dawn. I stayed at the kitchen window and watched as Yuri O'Byrne, hitchhiker, sailor, wooden boat builder and a man who had shared his dream of creating a Xanadu for me from my little ugly duckling of a shack trudged up the long yard past the garage towards the street and disappeared.

The junkyard dog chased from the yard twice this day.

~~~

I found him standing on the verge of the road with his thumb out, the dopey pink blanket still draped over his shoulders and the nor'easter blowing his drenched hair about his face. A lonely figure, the raggle-taggle gypsy with the Dr. Zhivago eyes.

For the second time in less than twenty-four hours, I pulled over and offered the hitchhiker a lift.

The only difference being that this time he was no stranger to me.

~~~

The Sunday morning ride down the coast as far as Ballina, through wind and rain, was uncomfortable but illuminating. Until I helped him score the heroin, he'd been all-but mute. Only the drugs would switch his mood and loosen his tongue. Ballina was not only my first experience of scoring drugs but my first experience of a pawn broker's establishment. We had earlier pulled in off the road at a service station, one favoured by long-haul truck drivers. I had tilted my seat back and closed my eyes. He had curled up on the back seat. A couple of hours must have passed and all the time, I was aware of his restlessness.

Sick, he said. Aching everywhere. His broken ribs. His knees. His back. He was sick, sick, sick. There was a man down in Ballina who ran a pawnshop, a Sunday early opener if you knew the owner who lived out the back.

We hit the highway again. In Ballina, I gave him my wristwatch, my ex-husband's to be exact, and while he negotiated with the drowsy bruiser behind the counter I wandered around the bleak establishment picking up items and picturing the stories that lay behind each of them, belongings that desperate people had traded for emergency cash, just as we were doing on this wet, bleak early Sunday morning.

After the exchange, I cooled my heels for another hour, parked out front of an old blue weatherboard house, a sullen little house perched behind a forest of dark gloomy pine trees.

I waited while he did whatever it was he did inside the blue cottage.

He had used up all his prescribed medication, Physeptone, in his efforts to present well at the hospital yesterday, he had explained on the way down the highway. He would get his next prescription at his scheduled appointment on Tuesday and then he wouldn't need the heroin.

We would both be seeing doctors come Tuesday.

'The Catalina ferry,' he said once we were back on the road and he was high; relaxed and talkative. 'My nerdy cousins goofing off,' he continued. 'Mom had thrown a party for my birthday. My seventeenth. Over to Catalina. Everyone jazzed about the bourbon they were smuggling to the party to lace their Cokes. And there's me, birthday boy, standing apart from them. Clinging to the rails. Sweating. Feeling like death. My nerves strung out and sick as a dog that'd swallowed a bait.' At that moment, he said, he had understood what was wrong: He was hanging out.

Seventeen and he realized that night how different he was from his cousins. He had a habit. He was a junkie. Happy Birthday! 'Following year, my Mom dragged me out of the gutter to get me on a plane to Europe for a couple of months. To clean me up.'

'How did it start? The heroin business?'

'Lots of older guys around us doing drugs back then. Coming back from 'Nam. They taught us how to do it.'

'Do you hate them, now?'

'Don't hate anybody. It's life.' He was staring out his window. 'At first, I was sent away, over to Hawaii to my

Mom's brother and sister-in-law. New school. New start.'

'And?'

He grinned. 'Didn't work, did it?'

'Seems not.'

'Poor old guys, they ran up the white flag. I was a pretty out of control kid. Came back to LA and got a job. No one seemed to notice I'd even left school, so two of my buddies and me, we bought an old van and hit the blacktop, up to Big Sur to surf and hang out on a commune. That was a blast!'

'Drugs, sex and rock 'n roll?'

I copped another of his bad boy grins as my answer and proceeded to listen to a snapshot of a wildly precocious sixteen-year-old's life on a Californian commune during the Summer of Love era. These postcards from L.A., delivered in his smooth Californian drawl, shot it home to me just what a suburban life I'd lived during those same years, my mothering years when I'd been knee-deep in shitty nappies.

'Yeah, well Mom took charge, didn't she?' he said. 'The flighty Katia became the caring Mom. We went abroad and for a while I was pretty well-behaved ... churches, monuments, recital halls. The grand tour. And then we hit swinging London! Mom returned to the States. I partied hard for six weeks; girls and drugs. Not good.' He shot a glance at me and grinned. 'Well, it wasn't all that bad, either.'

'Go on.' I was lost in his charms, forgetting for the moment, my anxiety. 'When you got back to the States?'

'I woke up one day and realized I was a loser. If I was ever to get it together and go to sea, I had to clean up.'

'And so, did you?'

'The dream made me strong. Living back in LA. Clean for a year. But just as things were going okay and I was learning the boat-building trade from Mom's husband—her sixth one—and doing good, the sky kinda fell in.'

'What happened?'

'This waitress rang, someone from the life. Begged me to score some dope for her. I tried every excuse in the book. Told her I'd cleaned up. And I really had. One hundred per cent. But she pulled a cry baby act, said she was sick, said for old times' sake and I fell for it. Got busted. Two FBI guys jumped me. She'd set me up. It was entrapment.'

We were coming up to his drop-off point, Yamba.

'If you could pull over just past the bridge?' he said.

My heart lurched. This was it, then.

I slowed down and drove the Golf onto the rough verge and switched off the ignition. I watched him bend down and gather up his bag. He looked out the window, beyond the green paddock to the coastal track leading in to Yamba, and then he looked back at me.

'Aloha,' he said, trying to keep it light as he patted my thigh. 'Give us a smile.' And then he said the word I'd known was coming. 'Goodbye.'

'Why?'

'Why, goodbye?'

'Why did it have to be like this?'

'Because that's life.'

He reached out and drew me towards him, holding me tight against his chest. I could feel the warmth of his cheek resting against the top of my head, smell the now familiar smell of him and I wished for the moment never to end.

'I'd have been good for you, once,' he whispered, his fingers playing with my hair until he tilted my head back and I had nowhere to go but to look up at him, let him see the tears.

His kiss, when he wiped the tears away, was tender, but it was a kiss that held an ending, not a future.

'Goodbye,' he said again as he released me and opened the car door, one foot already on the ground.

'Yuri?'

'I have to go.' He bent in and kissed my cheek, his hand resting against it. 'We had a good time, didn't we, pal? We were something!'

'Yes,' I sighed. 'We were something.'

'C'mon, a smile ... and a wave when I get down there,' he said, pointing to the paddock he had to cross to reach the dirt track into Yamba. 'Okay, a smile? It's all good. It's gonna be okay. You're gonna be okay. Don't worry. I promise you.'

'Sure, it's going to be okay.'

'Some pit-stop though, huh?'

'Some pit-stop, you're right.'

'Watch out for that Mullum Madness. It'll get you every time. Promise?'

'I promise.' I reached over for his hand but he was already backing away.

Two fingers to his forehead, he saluted me. 'Have a good life. I know you will. You've landed in Paradise up there. Just avoid guys like me and you'll be doin' real fine.'

The door slammed and he was gone, ducking under the railing, skating down the side of the grassy verge until he was standing in the paddock at the bottom. With his bag slung over his shoulder, and without looking back, he started walking across the field towards the coastal track.

Green was the colour I saw all around him, what I remember so clearly about that morning.

And his distinct walk; he had a ponderous way of walking. Legs bowed. Shipwright's knees, he'd said with a laugh on the beach last night.

But it was more than that. He was a man walking with a

heavy heart. I had let him down. Chased him away. His habit was more important than the man himself. That was what my panicked reaction had implied. He seemed the loneliest of men. And the most complicated. A man isolated by his demons. A good man doing bad things.

Conrad's phrase came to mind. *The acute consciousness of lost honour.*

Watching him walk away it dawned on me; I shared something in common with Yuri O'Byrne. I understood the pain of withdrawal. I was going cold turkey and, already, it hurt.

What a mystery, the intimacy of sex.

With every step I watched him take across that Yamba field he became more and more a stranger to me. And yet he had done things with my body so intimate that the thought of it made me blush. Six billion people on the planet, just two coupled in that kind of tenderness. So how was it possible he was about to disappear into another life, become the stranger again? Was the meaning of it all that there really was no meaning to it?

No there, there when you got there?

I stepped out of the car and put my hand up to my eyes. He had stopped at the edge of the grassy paddock, a distant figure in white cargo shorts and a navy blue and white hibiscus Hawaiian shirt set against the brilliant green of the paddock. The morning sun coming up behind him.

I saw him raise his hand and wave. Slowly, with no heart for it I returned the gesture and whispered goodbye.

The stranger, come and gone.

He had crossed his heart, sworn I had nothing to fear, but both of us understood a trust had been broken, truth the casualty and no amount of foreswearing on his part could cancel my anxiety. I contemplated the awkward medical consultations coming up, the months, possibly two years of waiting for the final word on whether or not I would prove to be HIV-positive. I thought of Byron. Lord Byron, mad, bad and dangerous to know. How dangerous had it been to know Yuri O'Byrne?

By the time I pulled away from the Yamba lay-by and was on the road again, my path set for Sydney and a scarily uncertain future, Richard Harris was taking the high notes of *MacArthur's Park* on the car's stereo.

It was a favorite, even though I'd always thought the lyrics obscure; all those poetic images of leaving cakes out in the rain, of green icing flowing down, but this time it was different. The lyrics resonated, the sweet green icing being all around me.

And after all the loves of my life—as the song goes—after all the loves of my life I knew I would still be thinking of him. And wondering what became of him.

THE MURDERED MODEL

The death of a beautiful woman is, unquestionably,
the most poetical topic in the world.
                                        Edgar Allan Poe

It had been only a little over twenty-four hours since I'd broken camp on the Gold Coast.

In that time things had moved fast: I had decided I would park my new life in Byron Bay; bought a beach house at Suffolk Park; picked up a stranger at a roundabout; made crazy love with him; had my heart broken; and along the way got stoned, paranoid and fearful of the consequences of unprotected sex.

The universe had had its fun with me. *As flies to wanton boys are we to the gods. They kill us for their sport.*

Since leaving Yamba behind a couple of hours ago I was trying to process the twin emotions of panic and sadness, a high-octane mix, especially in my present volatile mental state.

I continued to drive south, and after some hours felt the mania coming off and a more moderate mood beginning to prevail, one in which I could process my feelings with some degree of equanimity.

The gods had declared that the partying on Olympus was over and the Voices were stilled. If I'd learned anything about my bi-polar condition, thanks to the mind mechanics who had been trying to sort me out for the past couple of years, it was that I cannot control my moods. I can, however, control my thoughts.

It goes like this: the thoughts affect the emotions and the emotions affect the moods and the moods affect the levels of the brain chemical, serotonin. Ergo: my thoughts must not be allowed to trip the serotonin mechanism because that disruption can fling me so high I do irresponsible and promiscuous things, or they plummet me so low I've viewed death as a friend. Cognitive Therapy 101.

So, on my flight down the Pacific Highway I began to distract myself from darker thoughts by mulling over some interesting and unfinished business I'd had going for me up at the Gold Coast before I'd decided so capriciously to make a run for the border.

Not long after I'd fled Sydney and moved in to my Mermaid Beach home a compelling offer had been dropped in my lap. It came by way of a phone call from a long-time Sydney mate who had moved up to Surfers Paradise. He had a couple of people he was keen for me to meet, people who had information he thought would interest me—as a scriptwriter and as someone familiar with the Canberra political scene. Phil Avalon has been a filmmaker since the Sixties when he first discovered a bright young actor, Mel Gibson, fresh out of NIDA and starred him in his break-out movie, *Summer City*. He has always been a hands-on film man, often running the full gamut of writing, producing, directing and sometimes appearing in his own movies. He dropped himself into *Summer City* as a typically good-looking tanned Aussie surfer.

During the early Nineties I had traveled a long and expensive road trying to fund my film projects, mostly in company with Phil Avalon as producer. The major project, *Sweet Surrender*, was a story set over two time periods, tying in the adoption secrecy of the 1950s with the Vietnam Birthday lottery nineteen years later.

Although I'd been backed by Village Roadshow with an impressive quarter million dollars Heads of Agreement to kick off my five million dollars fund-raising efforts—an advance that executive Alan Finney claimed was their biggest to date—and had Claudia Karvan, Loene Carmen and Kiefer Sutherland attached, even Geoff Goldblum at one stage, the project struck a serious roadblock when I proudly, and confidently, presented it to the Film Finance Corporation for its entitled component of Australian government FFC funding.

The top honchos at the FFC resented my connection to the Hon John Brown, my husband having been, among his other portfolios, Minister for the Arts in the Hawke cabinet up until a couple of years prior to my putting in my submission to the FFC.

Apparently, I was too hot to handle. I got the palm, their doors slammed firmly in my face. Avalon, a favourite of the FFC because of his films consistently returning them a profit, claimed he had never encountered the kind of hostility lobbed at me by those industry bureaucrats, public servants who had total autonomy over allocating tens of millions of tax-payer dollars to their favourites. Phil Avalon was stumped that even with him on board as the producer the FFC would not consider our project; not while ever my name was on it.

By the time of my psychotic meltdown in April 1995 I had all but given up trying to raise funds. To jump forward; many years later I would dig the script out of my bottom drawer and rewrite it as the novel, *Goodbye Lullaby,* and in the process, create a successful piece of commercial fiction published by Harlequin under their MIRA imprint. It is, however, a fact that my film producer efforts had cost me a small fortune, not only in production costs of promotional materials and air travel but also in disappointments and heartache. A folly, for sure.

Understandably it was with some reluctance that I agreed to meet with Avalon's friends and hear their story. Did I really need to embark on another heartache, another folly? Phil claimed he was keen to write the script himself, or could source any number of keen scriptwriters, but given my background in federal politics, he believed I was the 'girl' for the job. Both he, and the man and woman he brought to my Mermaid Beach home to meet with me were clueless about politics.

'Jan, I'd like you to meet Cheryl,' said Phil. 'And this is Gavin.'

Gavin, in his early thirties, was a tall, angular man with a shyness about him I wouldn't have expected in someone who ran a restaurant nightclub on the Glitter Strip. He looked smart in white jeans and a short-sleeved pale blue linen shirt. Cheryl, younger than her man, was drop-dead gorgeous. Tall, tanned, coltish and with sun-tipped Jean Shrimpton hair; long, straight and heavily fringed.

The young Gold Coast model was a picture straight out of Vogue in her snug-fitting cream mini skirt, red and white striped top and espadrilles. Phil, the surfer, was also looking the part in colourful Okanui shorts, a smart white tee and casual loafers. The moment I opened the door to the Gold Coast trio I cursed my daggy blue jeans and cotton shirt.

There was the usual small talk over white wine and nibbles out on the patio overlooking the ocean as we chatted, the visitors saying how much they loved my apartment, how brilliant life was on the Gold Coast, how they loved Phil's movie, *Exchange Lifeguards,* and how they hoped I'd be their guest at Gavin's Orchard Street restaurant soon.

They had bumped into Phil one night at Gavin's

establishment and had downloaded their story on him. Phil had immediately thought of me. He believed I could use the information I was about to be told to write the screenplay, information that did not come out a couple of years ago during the 1995 Criminal Justice Commission's investigation into Gold Coast crime and the police's Operations Wallah targeting links between politics and prostitution on the Coast.

This was now 1997 as we sat talking on the patio. As the story unfolded, I learned that back in December 1991 Gavin had been the boyfriend of Cheryl's best friend, Christine Petersen—perhaps not her boyfriend, more her protector, because at that time, the young Gold Coast model feared for her life and Gavin was allowing her to hide out at his townhouse in suburban Benowa.

It was the afternoon of her 25th birthday, December 13th, a black Friday. Christine received a phone call. It was her estranged lover, Lawrence Stehlik, the person she feared and from whom she was hiding. He had a big beautiful surprise for her birthday. A new car.

Christine loved her couturier clothes, loved her baubles and she certainly coveted a smart car of her own, not simply just one more rental from her ex's car lot. The gift was downstairs waiting for her, tied off with a bow. He wanted to take her for a ride in it. Cheryl pleaded with her not to go, begged her to resist the enticement. Cheryl knew the man to be dangerous. But her words fell on deaf ears, and with a heavy heart, she watched her friend leave the house.

Christine Petersen would never return. The beautiful Gold Coast model went missing, triggering a massive nine-day police hunt in which the estranged de facto husband, Lawrence Stehlik, would be the chief suspect. Stehlik was well-known on the Coast as the proprietor of Topless Car Rentals. His and

Christine's turbulent, often physically punishing relationship was well-known, their public arguments legendary, according to Cheryl. The relationship had been over for the past two months but the jealous lover had problems accepting the breakup.

Christine was a missing person and Stehlik was on the run. It was learned that he had purchased a large fishing knife a couple of days before Petersen's disappearance. The police would soon discover a bloodstained mattress in the bedroom of Stehlik's Pottsville farm and a burnt-out Holden on the Queensland property the couple had shared.

Meanwhile, three days into the Gold Coast search for Christine Petersen, Stehlik's body turned up down on the NSW south coast, a gun in his hand and a bullet in his brain. With his death, the Broadbeach detectives wrapped the case up as murder/suicide, even though it would be another six days before the model's body turned up in an abandoned industrial site, a lonely part of the Gold Coast hinterland not far from the recently opened Warner Brothers MovieWorld theme park. The crime scene was discovered by two young men road-testing a new SUV.

Avalon was right. All the elements for a ripping yarn were there. Cheryl and Gavin's story had me hooked and Phil Avalon and I could see there was a movie in fictionalizing it. Given that I then learned that Christine and Laurie were the parents of two-year-old twin girls, there was that extra element that excites a writer. I was hooked; locked and loaded and ready to go.

Like childbirth, trying to fund your film project is painful, but you forget the pain all too quickly and you back up for more of the same. By now I was ready to go through with it one more time; ready for the months of research and writing;

for the rewritings; the compromises; the submissions to funding bodies; the years of knocking on doors with a begging bowl; the insults; the rejections; the head-butting; the big spend on promotional materials; the costly trips to the LA and Cannes film markets; the "I'll get my people to talk to your people, we'll do lunch" routine; the kissing out the door brush-offs from big and small studios with promises forgotten even as you're walking out and the perky assistant is ushering in the next starry-eyed writer to meet the guy sitting behind his big sexy desk who has the power over your dreams.

~~~

There is more to tell of Cheryl and Gavin's story, as told to me that day.

Background: Duringthe Eighties, which flowed into the Nineties—and is possibly still going for all I know—the Gold Coast played host to international tourists and out-of-town VIPs who knew who to dial up when they had an urge to enjoy Surfers Paradise's night life and avail themselves of some away-from-home benefits.

Spargo's was a fashionable seafood restaurant owned by a couple of nefarious businessmen (Wilkinson, "The Fixer", 1996), a place where glamorous escorts mixed it with the powerful, where one of the restaurant's owners, Nick Karlos, a Gold Cost businessman whose core business it seemed was to curry favour with politicians on behalf of developers and others of the white shoe brigade was accused by the 1995 Queensland Crime and Justice Commission of arranging escorts for his influential VIP pals. Karlos, according to the published records, would have his driver deliver the women to the assignation.

Sarah Gee, a young sex worker who later turned police informer and gave evidence to the QCJC enquiry was one such escort familiar with the Karlos routine.

Gee would testify to how she and her girlfriend had been picked up one night at Spargo's and delivered to the Hyatt Hotel at Sanctuary Cove.

A 'tubby man in his fifties with grey hair and grey eyebrows' (Wilkinson, p-363) had come out of the hotel and put his head through the car window to check them over before giving the nod to the driver delivering them.

Sarah Gee had not known the identity of the man she and her girlfriend were selling their favours to that night. She would soon learn. As would the rest of Australia because the police's Operation Wallah investigators had their man and would serve him up to the Crimes and Justice Commission. Prostitutes for political favours.

The evidence was in. Ultimately, the accusations aired during the CJC enquiry did not end with any politician being convicted but a light had been shone on a dark side of Gold Coast society, a society of favours done and bribes received, and where beautiful women were currency in the deals.

Senator Graham Richardson, to the surprise of a stunned nation, resigned, not only from his ministry but from politics all together, just days before he was hauled before the Commission to answer charges. It is all there on the record, and intelligently written down in Marion Wilkinson's book.

But as my guest's personal story unfolded during the afternoon on my patio, I learned that Gee's story of sex served up in a limo to certain high-fliers had an earlier iteration.

Cheryl told of hers and Christine's own experience at the Sanctuary Cove Resort a couple of years prior to the Gee episode. When I questioned her, I found that Cheryl had never heard of the Queensland Crimes and Justice Commission or Sarah Gee. Nor could she name even one Australian politician.

The way my visitor told it, she and Christine had been a couple of young models fresh from New Zealand who occasionally made the rent between modeling gigs by working as glamorous escorts.

They had arrived by appointment this night in 1991 at Spargo's and were then driven by limousine to the Hyatt Hotel at Sanctuary Cove where they said goodnight to their ride and knocked on the VIP's hotel room door.

As Cheryl related it, the door was cracked by a youth wearing a white hotel towel around his hips. The youth turned to the naked man on the bed behind him and waited while the older man dug out cash from his wallet. The young man at the door pushed the cash at Christine. There had been a mistake, said the youth, relaying the man's message. They wouldn't be needed tonight.

The Queensland Crimes and Justice enquiry investigating politicians and their use of prostitutes was still four years into the future. Cheryl described the man she and Christine glimpsed on the bed at the Hyatt Hotel that night, but had no idea who he was, other than what they had been told; a VIP.

I kept quiet.

A Gold Coast escort agency, Elite Escorts was run by the madam, Jacquie Leyland, a woman who, like Sarah Gee had been called to give evidence against Senator Richardson at the QCJC enquiry. Leyland came from Sydney's famous Touch of Class brothel. In the ensuing court case, she testified she was paid $4000 by a Gold Coast restaurateur to supply prostitutes for a 'sex romp' with the (by then) former Labor Cabinet Minister, Senator Graham Richardson.

As a sad footnote; Jacquie Leyland would turn up in 1999 just as dead as Christine Petersen, having bled to death on the pavement outside a trendy restaurant in Tedder Avenue after being viciously stabbed multiple times, following a party at her home where the white shoe brigade and politicians had been present. Her alleged killer was her obsessed ex-boyfriend, and SP bookie Neil Morrison. The man who was also slain along with Leyland that day was her drug dealer friend John Ski.

In researching Cheryl and Gavin's story, I would meet up with Dawn Leyland, Jacquie Leyland's mother. Dawn had a stall out at the Carrara Markets and it was there I was introduced to her by a mutual friend.

The mother was heartbroken. She was also angry. Dawn Leyland dumped a truckload of her own files in my lap following that day, telling me, with tears in her eyes, that she believed the wrong man was in jail for her daughter's murder. Someone had ordered her daughter murdered, she claimed. It was a savage place, the Gold Coast, in those days. Drugs, sex, money, murder, politics and beautiful women. A lot of it around.

In a Courier Mail story dated September 9th, 2016, journalist Greg Stolz wrote "Leyland may simply have been murdered out of obsessive jealousy. Or was she killed, as her family believe, for more sinister reasons? Not by Morrison but by someone else? ... In his closing address in Brisbane Supreme Court, Mr Hunter said the pair's involvement in the sex and drugs industry could have meant they had other enemies who wanted them dead."

Drugs, sex, money, murder, politics and beautiful women. A lot of it around.

In June 1995 the body of another beautiful model, Carolyn Byrne, was found at the foot of the Watsons Bay Gap in Sydney.

Eric Wood, a chauffeur to high-profile businessman Rene Rivkin was charged with her murder but later acquitted.

Evidence was sworn at two subsequent inquests; "...Wood claimed that he was asked by Rivkin to chauffeur prominent lobbyist and ex-federal minister Graham Richardson to an appointment. The Richardson alibi was compromised by Richardson when he was interviewed by police in 2001..." (Wikipedia), by which time one of Australia's most notorious financial scandals concerning the Offset Alpine 1993 fire and insurance claim was under investigation. Father of the murdered woman, Tony Byrne, claimed that it had been indicated to his daughter that the fire was a set-up for insurance purposes. "Tony Byrne has always disputed that his daughter took her own life." (Daily Telegraph 25/2/17)

Drugs, sex, money, murder, politics and beautiful women. A lot of it around.

With all this—and as we would later come to understand, the possibility of rogue Gold Coast cops in the mix—Phil Avalon was certain I had enough material for a screenplay and I couldn't agree more. I was on the starting blocks.

Later, once I'd begun researching the alleged 'murder/suicide' of Christine Petersen and Laurie Stehlik and sat down to plot the story, my imagination would run off in wild directions. Something seemed fishy in the state of Denmark, as the saying goes. Some bits of the official story I couldn't line up. For one thing, I believed the Broadbeach detectives were preemptive—with only one body available to them—in writing the two deaths off as a 'murder/suicide'. The now-dead couple allegedly cultivated marihuana crops in the hinterland. Was the harvest protected?

Did it suit someone's purpose to have the messy business of Petersen and Stehlik done and dusted, murder/suicide and on with the show?

It's a fiction writer's right-brain prerogative to get down in the weeds for their stories. I try to tell here, only what I was told and what I learned through research. Yet, like my guests that day on the patio, I can't help but wonder if there is a different truth somewhere out there that's now lost to history.

On the morning of Monday 16th, as the search for her missing daughter entered its third day—and before the body of her ex-lover had turned up—Christine Petersen's mother, a New Zealand woman, made a televised appeal to the public to help find her daughter.

According to Cheryl, who had been at the mother's side during the press conference, what the woman revealed shocked the media pack: Stehlik was the father of Claudia's twin girls and the woman was adamant that Stehlik, who adored his baby daughters, Chloe and Chanel, would never harm them or their mother.

Cheryl, despite her poor opinion of Stehlik, agreed. While the few in their circle who were aware of the twins' existence had believed the toddlers to be Christine's baby sisters, Cheryl knew the real story and believed that the frantic grandmother would have had no reason to make such a claim had she not believed it. No sooner had her appeal and assertions gone public, however, than something happened to cast doubt on the mother's judgement.

A senior Gold Coast CIB detective announced to the media that they had received a breakthrough. Laurie Stehlik, their chief suspect, had confessed to a friend in Sydney that, in a fit of rage, he had murdered his former mistress, stabbing her through the heart multiple times—dumping her body in the hinterland woods, covering it over with leaves, returning to his Pottsville home to burn the murder vehicle—and then fleeing down to Sydney.

Contrary to what he claimed in his confession, the body,

when it finally turned up, was found in a deserted industrial site. No burial in the woods. No stab wounds, either, apparently. The Broadbeach detective was able to report to the media conference that Petersen's body showed no obvious cause of death. *No obvious cause of death.* No multiple stab wounds to the heart, as per the supposed killer's confession?

How, if the body had been exposed for nine days in scorching Queensland summer conditions?

Nine days in summer heat, laying exposed in an abandoned industrial site. The body would have been almost skeletal by then, even if it hadn't already been ravaged by feral animals. There would have been bloating and putrefaction, seepage from every orifice and the ground beneath the body would have been greasy with melted flesh and body fluids. Had the remains been as decomposed as they logically ought to have been after such a weathering, how was it that the body showed no obvious cause of death?

Was it possible that Christine had been alive for most of the time the search for her whereabouts was going on? Could it be—and here comes the fiction writer—that she had been either in hiding, or had been captured and was being held for several days by a person or persons unknown before being murdered and her body dumped in the lonely industrial site?

John Marsden was the Sydney friend who radioed in Stehlik's confession, on Stehlik's orders. Marsden was a wealthy high-profile Sydney/Campbelltown solicitor, a civil liberties and gay rights activist and a member of the NSW Police Board. He was also a former president of the NSW Law Society and friend of the politically powerful. In researching my story, I contacted him. As the Minister's wife, I had met him several years before and considered, for the purpose of getting the down-low, that I knew him well enough to make the call. Even so, it had been a long time since we had spoken to each other, so I was thrilled when he took my call, given his reluctance back in 1991 to speak with the press.

As he told me over the phone from his Campbelltown home, he had been not only Stehlik's life-long friend—almost a brother—but also his lawyer, and as his lawyer he had been bound to follow his client's orders. Marsden emphasized to me that the distraught man could not be persuaded otherwise. He wanted the Broadbeach detectives to know Christine was dead.

According to reports, (Candace Sutton, Sun-Herald, Dec 15th 1991) Stehlik had been acting in what was believed to be a frantic cocaine-induced state for a couple of weeks prior to the murder/suicide. Why? Was he, like Christine, also afraid for his life? Was he running for his life when he high-tailed it down to the NSW south coast after radioing in his "confession"?

Years later, reports of drug crimes on the Gold Coast and police involvement during this period would surface via various investigations, including the long-term investigations by the Criminal Justice Commission (Operation Shield) and the Carter inquiry into police corruption. As the Gold Coast Bulletin, April 9, 1997, reported, "Several search warrants, issued by a Supreme Court judge, were executed at Gold Coast premises ... including the police station ... and a number of police were interviewed."

More of that, later.

Marsden told me how he and Laurie Stehlik had grown up together as brothers in Campbelltown, the Marsdens having taken the neglected boy into their home after Stehlik's mother had committed suicide. He claimed to have a brotherly affection for Laurie. Marsden was obviously the person to whom the terrified man would run if he feared for his life.

When turning up at John's Campbelltown home on the

Sunday morning after Christine's disappearance, according to what John told the Courier Mail and the Gold Coast Bulletin, Stehlik had been highly disturbed and incoherent, insisting on his confession getting through to the Broadbeach detectives.

But was it all a lie, a public lie told for the benefit of someone who might have wanted him and Christine dead? How weird, an unforced confession from a man on the run, a confession to killing the woman he loved, right down to the specific details of the grizzly act—which, incidentally, turned out to be wrong in some details. He had already been given a free pass by Christine's mother declaring on the Monday that she believed it unlikely he would harm her daughter. And then he contradicts her!

Could it be that the confession had been simply a red herring, a means to pull the wool over someone's eyes? Maybe that someone in the drug cartel both he and Christine were mixed up in, maybe the same person, or persons, who would soon eliminate him with a bullet to the head?

What if Stehlik knew Christine wasn't really missing during the hunt for her, but instead was in hiding? Might the pair have planned her 'murder'?

The knife, purchased locally by a man well-known on the Coast? The bloodied mattress? The burnt-out car on their property?

Staged? Meant to convince someone she was dead? Did he 'confess' in order to take the heat off her?

The writer asks, imagines.

Petersen was due in court on drug charges. She knew too much. She could name names. Did she and Stehlik want the bad guys to think she was already out of the equation? Finito? No problemo?

If Stehlik's confession was a ruse—an attempt to buy time

for Christine by lying to distract unsavoury characters who would feel more comfortable if she were out of the way—it tends to explain why she felt safe leaving the safety of Gavin's Benowa home to take a ride with her former de-facto. Would she, if she were so terrified of him? Was it not Stehlik, but the bad guys who terrified her? Was it when she went downstairs and out to Stehlik's car that the pair decided to plot their escape? Did the bad guys follow him down to that south coast motel and did they manage to drag the truth from Stehlik? Did he disclose Christine's hideaway?

Did these bad guys kill Christine Petersen?

Did they kill Laurie Stehlik?

The writer asks, imagines.

When I asked John Marsden if he believed Laurie Stehlik had shot himself he said he believed he had been murdered—to shut him up.

The clincher, according to John, was that Laurie had been left-handed. 'Couldn't wipe his backside with his right hand.' And yet the dead man had been found with the gun in his right. Murder/suicide. So tidy. Even without the other body. Nothing like a little intrigue to get a writer's imagination going.

There would be a further angle to Christine's story, a romantic one. I could write into the script, an intriguing memory of Christine Petersen that would linger long after her passing.

This was a story I would learn from Deb King, a Sydney friend of mine who had moved to the Gold Coast some years before the murder and had worked as a waitress manager at Spargo's in Surfers Paradise during the time when Christine was a regular at the well-known haunt of the high-flyers. Deb told me about one of Christine's adoring clients, a man so besotted that he had created a shrine to her memory. Even six years after her death, according to Deb telling me the story in 1997, the flamboyantly wealthy elderly Greek man was still so infatuated that he kept a room in his Sydney Eastern Suburbs home dedicated to Christine's glamorous outfits.

A high-class escort. A glamorous model. A loving mother to twin babies. A goddess.

In my writer's imagination, I saw Christine Petersen as a beautiful enigma. For the woman to go missing for nine days before her body turned up would have made big news on the Gold Coast in December 1991. And yet, this day on my patio in 1997 was the first I learned of it, despite realizing I had been holidaying at our Mermaid Beach home at the exact time of the disappearance and murders.

Why hadn't I taken notice of the drama?

Because there was a different kind of drama going on in my own life to distract me, one that involved a certain senator and a soon-to-be Prime Minister.

TO THE HINTERLAND

The night is darkening around me,
The wild winds coldly blow;
But a tyrant spell has bound me
And I cannot, cannot go.
                                    Emily Bronte

It was a long, nine-hour drive down to Sydney on the day of these reflections, giving me plenty of time to try and parse the puzzle.

Pulling off the highway to fill my tank, grab a coffee and one of the abysmal sandwiches in a plastic triangular coffin that are the basic fare on offer at roadside service stations, was when it struck me that I had actually been at the Mermaid Beach house in December 1991 when all the drama was unfolding.

I was staying at our beach house during Christmas holidays at the time Christine went missing. Why hadn't I read anything about the murder or caught the television reports?

And then I remembered who else had been holidaying with us, and what had been going on at the time. I must have been so distracted by the more immediate drama that I had failed to notice the kerfuffle over a missing Gold Coast model.

Paul and Anita Keating and their children had been holidaying with us at our Mermaid Beach home and by long distance, Keating was manoeuvring to unseat Prime Minister Bob Hawke. By the 19th December Paul would be Prime

Minister of Australia. Graham Richardson was the powerbroker behind the caucus coup, having switched his allegiances to Keating.

With Paul kicking back and enjoying our Gold Coast sunshine, and Richardson in Canberra gathering the vital numbers for him, our phone and fax machine ran hot for days. Constantly, I would take off down to the beach out front to give Paul another of Richardson's frantic messages, his numbers tallies. It was all about the numbers. It was Paul's second assault on Hawke's position and this time, thanks to his diligent lieutenant, Richardson, he would win. Our house guest became Prime Minister of Australia.

As Christine Petersen's body lay decomposing in a desolate part of the Gold Coast hinterland I was nearby, getting up close and personal with history, a witness to an historic episode in Australian political life. No wonder I was distracted.

I wondered if the yet-to-be-disgraced senator took time out from the frenetic numbers game he played in Canberra so effectively to catch the Gold Coast news item about the missing model.

I carried my coffee and white-bread sludge back to the Golf and kept driving south towards doctors' appointments, blood tests and uncertainty.

~~~

Arch McDonald, chief of the Gold Coast CIB in 1997, a man I had met through the Gold Coast friend, Bonnie—the same friend who introduced me to Dawn Leyland—was the man who suggested I interview the detectives at the Broadbeach Police station. Arch was one of the good guys but, given the smell of corruption permeating the Gold Coast at the time it was hard for him not to despair.

I recall a conversation one night at a Surfers Paradise

nightclub where a group of us—including McDonald and his wife—had dropped in to enjoy the DJ music and a cocktail or two. Arch McDonald's major concern that night seemed to be the youth drug scene.

I can't recall whether or not he specifically nominated the three detectives at the Broadbeach Police station I would ultimately interview or whether they simply happened to be the ones who were in the detectives' room when I arrived, but I remember the three men initially being happy to speak with me.

The opening gambits were general. We all agreed Arch was a great cop. The Gold Coast Chargers were a great team. John Brown had done a great job as Minister for Tourism in the Eighties. Everything and everyone were great. Hawkie? What was he like? A fair-dinkum bloke? Was it true he was back on the piss? It was only once they knew what I had come for that the shutters went down.

Months after I interviewed those three detectives, I saw on the Gold Coast evening news the three of them being taken into custody and escorted from the station. I instantly recognized them as the ones who had, after all the small talk, then tried to dissuade me from taking an interest in Christine Petersen and Laurie Stehlik's 'suicide/murder' case. They had laughingly assured me they could give me stories much more exciting than the one I was thinking of writing about.

'Better than NYPD Blues, mate. A whole TV series,' one had guffawed.

'Forget this other stuff. The guy was a mad Yugoslav. He killed her. Murder/suicide. End of story,' said his colleague.

To my persistent questioning, they had denied any knowledge of Petersen being due in court on drug charges at the time of her murder, a fact I'd learned from Cheryl and

Gavin.

'No, no. We never heard anything about drug charges, did we, boys?' they said with wide eyes and much head shaking.

Give me a break, fellas! You three are investigating a woman's murder—a woman who is the ex-lover of a convicted drug dealer—and you tell me you're unaware she was due in court at the time she was bumped off? Hardly credible that the detectives investigating her disappearance and murder would not have known about the drug charges.

No wonder I was keen to pursue the story. Now I not only had the Gold Coast's seamy side as the setting and two dead witnesses, but I also had what might be three crooked cops and a whole script load of unanswered questions to be explored.

Drugs, sex, money, murder, politics, beautiful women and rogue cops. A lot of it around.

One thing was for certain, however; the young mother had been mixing with dangerous types. No wonder she feared for her life and took the Benowa safe-house option Gavin offered her. On a lighter note, Gavin had us smiling when he recounted how Christine had sent him out late one night while she was in hiding to buy formula and disposable nappies for her two-year-old toddlers at an all-night pharmacy. Gavin, as a restaurant/nightclub owner, was a well-known identity around town, a bachelor.

I didn't ask how he had come to know the murdered woman. Surfers Paradise was a small metropolis and after all, they were both in the hospitality business.

I would leave the meeting with the three Broadbeach detectives that afternoon even more confused than when I arrived, not knowing at that stage what to make of their feigned ignorance of Christine's drug charges, or why they had tried so hard to deflect my interest in the December 1991 murder/suicide story. I had a quiet chuckle to myself on the way back to my Mermaid Beach home about their suggestion I should write a TV cop show based on the dozens of yarns they could spin me, and how they could see themselves as heroes in the series.

Living alone in the apartment, I had no need to prepare dinner or make conversation with anybody that night, and so I took my wine and a note pad out onto the patio overlooking the darkened beach and listened to the roar of the high-tide surf and admired the way the moonlight played on the water. Mentally, I was processing the afternoon's interesting and thought-provoking visit to the Broadbeach cops, reflecting on how little and yet how much it had revealed.

I began to come up with a theme. Men and their dangerous appetites. Sex, drugs, money and power. I scribbled a few notes and started breaking my story up into scenes. There was dialogue filtering into my imagination and taking hold on the page. I had a story coming together. Phil Avalon would be pleased with my efforts. But I wasn't writing a documentary, I reminded myself. I was writing for commercial cinema.

The story was intended as fiction, not fact. I needed to put flesh on my make-believe characters. My beautiful enigmatic victim was going to be *Claudia Christiana*. Her jealous, devoted lover, the man who had taken the rap for her murder and allegedly topped himself, I had already named *Stefan Bojanic*. Cheryl would be *Lizzie Parsons*. Gavin, *Jess Carmody*. John Marsden would be *Adam Teresak*.

By my second glass of shiraz I was well into it. This was the fun part of working in the creative arts, naming your characters and giving them life.

I must have been in fantasy land for hours. When I came to and looked up and around me, I noticed the moon had ridden a great distance across the night sky while I'd been off with the pixies. I knew what I wanted to do. I had my characters. Now I needed my settings, starting with the scene of the crime.

I ran inside and turned on the kettle, made a thermos of Irish coffee, threw a handful of wheatmeal biscuits into a bag and grabbed my car keys. I was off to the hinterland, the dark, lonely, deserted no-man's land beyond the Glitter Strip's sparkle. It was almost midnight and that seemed appropriate.

~~~

The Golf sat in the lonely industrial park, its interior littered with Cheryl's copies of Gold Coast Bulletins, Courier Mails and my own pages of notes. I took a swig from the thermos. It was past the midnight hour by now. A warm tropical evening but I felt chilled. This would be a long night's vigil. My intention was to just sit here in this abandoned industrial estate in the hinterland of the Gold Coast and try to get a feel for the crime that had put an end to the life of my beautiful *Claudia Christiana*.

I turned on the cabin light and by the dim glow, studied the photo of Christine Petersen that I had brought with me. *Never forget me,* was what the eyes had first said to me when Cheryl had handed over a series of photographs. And here, tonight, in this desolate place, a place where her screams might have pierced the air before she gasped her last breath, that plea felt even more urgent.

'Then help me, *Claudia*,' I whispered to the image staring back at me, the image of one who had been a real flesh and blood woman, Christine Petersen, but who was now the tragic victim in my story. Help me write your story, whoever you are, I pleaded, confusing fact with fiction before checking myself.

Resting the photograph on my lap, I leaned my head

against the window, closed my eyes and with my writer's imagination, tried once more to imagine that Black Friday in December 1991 when a frantic *Liz Parsons* reports to the Broadbeach police that her girlfriend, *Claudia Christiana*, has left the Atlantis apartments at around 3.30pm, gone off with her jealous ex-lover, *Stefan Bojanic*, and hasn't returned.

The Atlantis had sprung into my mind as the setting for this scene. A Benowa safe-house was too suburban, too boring. I could make the towering Atlantis apartments work for me. Might even open on that scene. It's mid-afternoon in Surfers Paradise. The front door of a glamorous apartment stands open. Two beautiful women are in the hallway. *Claudi*a is impatiently waiting for the lift. *Lizzie* is begging her not to go. CUT TO *Bojanic* and the car waiting below...CREDITS ROLL....

There was an unearthly quiet in the deserted industrial estate, an eeriness that gave me goose bumps.

Whoever the murderer, and however it had been done, I hoped death had come quickly to poor Christine Petersen and that it had been as painless as murder could be. I stared out the window into the darkness. I needed to line up my thoughts. At the moment, they were scattering like a handful of tossed marbles. I needed to gather in my marbles before I lost them. I flipped to a clean page of my notebook and began to write down my impressions of this crime scene of six years ago.

I thought I heard a rustling noise somewhere outside the car. Quickly, I wound up the windows, slipped the locks and reached for the torch I kept in the glove box.

I waited, the torch gripped tightly in my fist as I listened for footsteps. It was dark. This was a bad place to be alone. I related to the victim's terror. Did Christine try to escape, run before she was caught and brought down? Did she know her killer or killers? It felt eerie, as though I weren't actually alone out here.

It was time to go. I fired up the Golf and made a hasty exit. I was not to know it then, but something weird was about to happen back at the house. And it would be no coincidence it happened on the heels of my visit to those cops at Broadbeach earlier in the day.

~~~

I arrived back home, tossed my files on the desk and plodded upstairs to bed.

Our Mermaid Beach apartment was a luxury job, the centre apartment of four others. It had a tiny rooftop pool and three levels of living space with a cathedral ceiling up through the middle. A long winding staircase connected the various living and sleeping areas. My bedroom was way up at the top. As I noted before; something strange happened when I returned home that night, something so weird that to this day it still freaks me a little.

I was in the en-suite cleaning my teeth when I heard the front door bell ring downstairs. It was almost 2am. It was a long way down. I hurried as fast as I could, almost tripping as I took the stairs, and opened the door.

There was no sign of anyone. I heard a car take off out front beyond the thicket of palm trees. I stood there for some moments, puzzling, and then came inside and locked the door.

It was not until I had made myself a cup of tea and was about to head back upstairs that I noticed the black business card that had been slipped under the door.

Detective Sergeant Mick Niland, Gold Coast CIB was the name on the front of the card and on the back, in blue biro, another name had been scribbled; Senior Sergeant Mike Sparke, Mudgereeba Police Station. I had read of the latter's name in one of the newspaper reports. It had been Detective Sparke who had reported the Stehlik confession to a media conference during the drama (Candace Sutton, SMH, 15/12/91).

I can't recall whether I phoned Detective Niland or Detective Sparke, but I do remember that when later in the morning I made the call, the detective wasn't up for small talk. He got straight to the point.

'Mrs. Brown?'

'Jan.' I dispensed with the 'Murray' and my usual sermon on feminism. It wasn't the right time to proselytize.

'Listen, I don't want to frighten you, Mrs. Brown, but I'd advise you not to pull that stunt again, going out to that place so late at night. On your own. Be careful. There are people who don't want you poking around. We're looking after you, don't worry. But just be careful.'

And with that, the man hung up. And I still, to this day, have Detective Sergeant Mick Niland, Gold Coast CIB's, black business card. It's tucked away safe in my Petersen file, otherwise it would seem unreal, something my too fertile imagination had dreamt up.

While watching the ABC's *7.30 Report* recently a middle-aged detective appeared on the screen in relation to the disturbing Gold Coast biker crimes. It was none other than the man who had had my back all those years ago, the man whose calling card I still had tucked away.

Today Detective Superintendent Mick Niland is Head of Taskforce Maxima and is the outlawed Queensland bikie gangs' worst nightmare. Mick Niland, still one of the good guys and still fighting crime. If he should ever read this, I want him to know I appreciated his efforts back then to warn me I had put myself in danger by going out to the hinterland alone.

His advice was noted but I had a story that had grabbed my imagination. I wanted to turn it in a screenplay, and like a terrier, I would go at it for years to come. In vain, as it turned out.

It was cloak and dagger stuff. I could only conclude that my visit to the Broadbeach detectives earlier in the day seeking information about a six-year-old murder/suicide case involving drug deals must have rung serious alarm bells among men I didn't yet know were allegedly corrupt, as well as men who were not—such as Detectives Sparkes and Niland who had my back.

I probably hadn't imagined the rustling noise outside the Golf as I'd sat gripping the torch, alone out there in the creepy hinterland, a writer trying to get a feeling for her story. I had been followed. By the good men of the Queensland Police Force who had apparently been protecting me. Arch McDonald's men.

I contemplated all this as I sped down the Pacific Highway, bound for Sydney and what would be not only these rounds of HIV blood tests, but the yearning for a man I hardly knew and yet in the last twenty-four hours had known so intimately.

Phil Avalon and I would once again sink significant resources into trying to get *Savage Love* into production in the years ahead, but despite some exciting, nail-biting close calls, despite visits to Cannes and LA's film markets armed with our big glossy cardboard poster headed 'Picture This!', and despite some good marquee attachments, we were never able to get our project off the ground.

Not unusual. It's a tough industry and only fools participate. Take the great Oliver Stone; it took Stone twelve years of shopping his project around the studios to get his double Oscar-winning *Platoon* onto the screen. When I complained once to a legendary Australian film producer he said to me; "If it was easy, love, they'd let girls do it." And I do believe the man was serious.

Today, I notch up my *Savage Love* film project as another expensive failure, another folly. But I know there is a story there. I've already begun the novel, *The Milk of Paradise.* Drugs, a la Surfers Paradise, the stuff of murder and intrigue. *Remember me,* said those eyes of Christine Petersen.

I shook myself out of my reverie. I was approaching Newcastle, meaning three more hours of driving, providing I didn't strike peak hour on the Bridge. I would be back in Sydney by dinner time. I wondered how I was going to explain things to my family. Would I tell them about the hitchhiker, or not?

Probably not.

RETURNING TO BYRON

When the lamp is shattered,
The light in the dust lies dead;
When the cloud is scattered,
The rainbow's glory is shed...
Percy Bysshe Shelley

It had been a long drive back up north after three weeks in Sydney but here I was; Suffolk Park, at last. The sun was beginning to set on the village by the time I turned off Alcorn Street and bumped the car over the uneven lawn, pulling up alongside my garage.

In passing, I noticed the boards had come down off the garage windows. And someone had tidied up the yard. Tidied up inside the garage too, I noticed when I peered through the window. Mr. First National Real Estate, I presumed. We're different around here, he'd said.

It was a homecoming, but a sad home-coming. The emptiness hit me. I had missed the place so much, romanticized it and what it signified in my search for a new life. But now, as I wound down from the arduous drive and looked about, reality began to dawn.

The ordinariness was plain to see. The folly of what I had done was obvious. Spontaneously and irresponsibly, in my manic phase, I had purchased a property that I could see now was nothing more than a dilapidated old fibro hut with ugly aluminium window and door frames, a tumble down one-room shack stuck on the edge of the dunes.

I knew now that those beautifully evocative Japanese-style windows would never be built. The bamboo walls and rosewood kitchen bench tops would be no more than a dream, a memory of another time. My black lacquer antique Chinese Coromandel screen with the ivory ladies and their parasols forever crossing willow-fringed arched bridges that he had planned to cut up and use for the front of the kitchen cupboards would stay uncut.

The magic was all in the past now, because the dream weaver was gone, leaving me to find myself a carpenter of lesser imagination.

I dragged my bags out of the car, kicked the Golf's door shut behind me and beat through the rainforest passageway, still wondering as I came around the side of the shack if a time would ever come when I didn't associate this place with that unique and solitary man.

~~~

The thick army socks and clunky work boots at the end of a pair of long, tanned and muscular legs was the first I saw of him.

He was sitting on the veranda boards with his back against the wall, asleep, his dark hair fallen around his face.

A paperback rested across his lap. A guitar sat at his left side and an open sketch book, three HB pencils and an art gum eraser on the boards to the right of him near his old canvas shoulder bag.

I've loved the smell of art gum rubber since I was a four-year-old gifted her very own pencil case. Art gum rubber. And those sticks of coloured plasticine joined together in their clear wrapper, natural plasticine, not the synthetic variety that replaced them. And Perkins paste with it funny little brush as part of the lid. But I digress. Literature, music and art was here, represented in the props laying around him.

For a romantic like me, could the set-up be more perfect?

There was also a bedroll, a large duffle bag and a carved nautical-looking sea chest sitting just inside the glass door. Were I a film director wanting to 'hang a lantern' on the romantic hero's entrance, I could not have dressed my set more descriptively.

I dropped down onto the edge of the veranda and sat there for a moment staring at him, taking in the vision. If anything, he was even more handsome than I remembered. I gave a slight cough, enough to bring him back into the world.

'Uh? Oh.' He shook his head, and then, cocking it sideways, smiled. 'Hi, there.'

'Hi.' I was in shock. Couldn't say much.

'Been waiting for this guy to come around,' he said sleepily. 'He's gonna give me a lift down the coast.' He looked up at the sun. 'Or said he was. Maybe not.' He looked at me. 'Anyways ... .'

He shrugged and, putting aside the book, dived into his bag and retrieved a large manila envelope. 'Here. For you. You can read it.' He leant across and handed it to me. 'I was gonna leave it inside on the bench.'

'It was you, wasn't it?' I said as I took the envelope and laid it aside. 'You took the boards down from the garage windows and cleaned it up in there. And tidied the yard. You've been busy.'

He looked uncertain. 'I conned the real estate guys into letting me in. Margaret in at First National knows me. Told her I was your handyman.'

'My handyman. Is that what you are?'

'I just thought ... well ... it kinda needed someone here to keep an eye on the place. People, y'know. They wander in ... and some of them aren't all that savoury.'

I pulled the sketch book towards me and examined the sketch he had done of the beach out front, of Julian Rocks and a distant sailing boat on the horizon. Flipping other pages, I saw quick charcoal sketches of timber boats, trawlers, yachts, little dinghies. To my untrained eye they looked shipwright perfect, if just a little idiosyncratic, as if they were a one-off, unique thing. Inscape?

'You never said you were an artist.'

'A few months at Brisbane's College of the Arts, that's all.'

I studied him for a few moments longer. Now that he was fully awake he looked alert and bright-eyed and that pleased me. No dozy nodding off or garrulous chatter, as had been the case the morning three weeks ago when I'd helped him score dope. 'When?' I said.

'When we got back to Australia after our honeymoon. I cleaned office tower windows and went to art school in Brisbane.'

'I meant when did you get here ... to the house?'

'Oh. A while back.' He paused. 'Couple of weeks ago, okay?' he said it with a cheeky grin, the kind that had won me when he'd flashed it at the roundabout, the kind that by-passes a woman's eyes and goes straight to her uterus. 'Yeah. I quit the Yamba place. Been camping on your mattress. Kinda care-taking. Hope you don't mind.' He shrugged. 'Anyways, I'm ready to push off.'

I laughed, then shut my eyes for a moment, needing time to take it all in. 'Thank you for looking after the place.' I noticed that the paperback was Joseph Conrad's *Heart of Darkness*. I nodded towards it. 'Any man who reads Conrad to pass the time of day is welcome around here.' I tossed my car keys at him. 'Let's go, sailor boy. I need a coffee. And then a swim. It's been a long day.'

'I'm not licensed.'

'We'll fix that. Let's go.'

'Aren't you going to read what's in that?' he said, pointing to the envelope.

'What's in it?'

'What do you reckon?'

'I've no idea.'

'My hospital records. From the accident, down in Karuah last April. Doctors' reports, blood tests. Pathology. I sent off for it. It's all there. Read it.'

The sense of impending doom, a threnody that had sat heavy in my gut these past three weeks, my constant companion since the morning I left this house in a blind panic, seemed to take a walk. Without opening the envelope, I realized I was in the clear, finished with all the drama, the anxiety associated with years of needing those problematic blood tests.

'A clean bill of health,' he said. '"Except for the patient's extreme tolerance levels to morphine" it says in there, somewhere.

He took up his guitar and strummed a few cords. 'I've seen fire, and I've seen ...' He put down the guitar and looked across at me. 'I could take all they could dish up and more. The ambos who scraped me off the road that night reckon I broke all records. Gave me three separate shots of morphine on the way to Emergency. Never done that before, they reckoned. The hospital's intensive care unit said the same. I'm some kind of a legend to those guys down there in Taree Base.' His eyes were twinkling with mischief.

'Yuri O'Byrne, what's a woman to do with you?'

'Do you need to ask?' He reached out for my hand and pulled me over to him.

'Uh-uh, come on. Let's go into town. I need provisions now you're here, fella. We can sit and talk over a coffee at Ringo's.' Nine hours sitting behind the wheel in the same pair of sweaty jeans was no prelude to love.

He set his guitar against the wall. 'Howz about you let me decide the order of things, Ms. Bossy Boots. Come!' He jumped to his feet, scooped me up in his arms and carried me down through the jungle of pandanus trees and rough terrain that was the path out to our beach.

'Put me down, you idiot!' I clung to him with one arm and used my free arm to batter him around the head. I felt my Dr. Scholl's fall to the ground. Just as we broke through onto the beach he set me down. We stood close, face-to-face.

'I've missed you,' he said.

'I don't believe you.'

'Okay, then, I didn't miss you. Happy?'

'Yeah, I'm happy. Now let's go get that coffee. Or a beer, maybe. Yes, a beer at the Suffolk.'

'Take a look at that!' he said, pointing to the surf through the dune bushes. 'C'mon, let's enjoy it.'

And we did. Naked as babies. And we swam way out from the shore and made love to the rhythm of the waves, two people the universe had flung together, celebrating life and their basic nature.

~~~

I was still enjoying the after-glow of our surf romp when we entered Ringo's Café a half hour later and chose a table in the corner furthest from the door.

'Say, what'll you have?' he enquired as I sat down.

'Froffy coffee, a la nutmeg. Not with coco, thank you my

love. And make that soy.'

'That'd be a soy cap, right?'

'Well ... kind of. It starts out as an ordinary cap but instead of powdered chocolate on top—which I loathe—I like it dusted with freshly grated nutmeg. Ask them. I bet they can do it. Freshly grated, don't forget, but if they can't do that, I'll just have a latte, okay? A soy latte in a long glass. But a nutmeg cappuccino's my first choice.'

He looked at me as if I were a loon then, shaking his head, walked over to the counter and spoke to the man waiting to take the order. Both shot a glance my way and chuckled, but the man gave me a thumbs-up and set about making the coffees. Trust Byron Bay to come through, I thought, so happy to be back here.

I looked around the room, empty save for a woman in the opposite corner doing battle with a couple of fractious little golden-skinned girls. Twins. Identical. I guessed their age at maybe three-years-old. Maybe four. One twin was sulky, looking up from her milkshake and sticking her tongue out at her mother. The other was wilder, kicking her mother's shin under the table. The woman leant across and ruffled their hair and patted their tear-stained cheek. I thought of the two little motherless girls of Christine Petersen and Laurie Stehlik. While in Sydney, I'd made great advances on my screenplay, having taken an all-day Saturday writing course at the NSW Writers Centre and contacted a tutor who, after reading the script, said he was keen to help me progress it.

I watched sailor boy at the counter. He had noticed the woman with the twins and was walking towards them.

From their greeting, it was obvious they knew each other. A twang of jealousy spiked me. He started kidding around with the two little girls, distracting them from their naughtiness as he kept up a conversation with the woman. He tickled the kids' tummies with the tips of his ten fingers, the giggling pair repeatedly hitting his legs and, when they had his attention, daring him to tickle them again. They seemed to love it, poking their tongues out at him.

A huge joke. And when he caught each little girl and tossed her into the air with his strong arms, their happiness seemed complete. Here was a man who was fond of children and comfortable around them, I thought. I made a note to ask him more about his own when they were little, before his divorce.

'She's great with those kids,' he said as he came walking back to our table and took his seat. 'She's a New Zealander.'

'You don't say, hey? Land of the Wrong White Crowd, hey? How come you know her, but, hey?' I looked at him teasingly. 'Hey, lover boy?'

He shook his head. 'Last summer. They were toddlers. I saw this frantic lady running along the beach with one kid under her arm and screaming out the other one's name. I found the missing one with a bunch of older kids aways down the beach. They'd dug a hole and had her sitting in it. She was giggling while they poured buckets of water over her head. I brought her back to her mother.'

'And I reckon mummy thanked you most kindly?' I pinched his knee under the table but he gave me only an enigmatic smile, one which gave nothing away. He looked across to where the twins had begun amusing themselves by tearing up paper napkins and tossing them in the air and at each other. 'Great kids. You are such a softie, Mr. O'Byrne. Such a softie.'

'She's proud of her heritage. She's some kind of Maori princess, first-born of a family with rank. Or at least her forebears had rank. Anyways, she knows parts of New Zealand, Bay of Islands where we used to sail. I owned a piece

of land over there for a while. My mom was going to come out
and join us from the States but it all kind of fell through.
Anyway, forget that. Here we are.'

My coffee and his hot chocolate had arrived. He piled
spoonfuls of sugar into his mug.

'Happy?' he asked.

'Very,' I said, bringing the brew up to my nose and inhaling
its spicy pungent aroma. 'Ah, freshly grated. I love this place.
Bet it racks up plenty of Byron brownie points.'

He took a long draft of his chili-laced hot chocolate, a
legacy I would later learn of him having grown up with a
Mexican housekeeper when he was a boy in California. He
eyeballed me.

'So, when do you we start?' he said.

I reached for his hand. 'I thought we had.'

He had been referring to the renovations, of course. I was
thinking more along the lines of our wonderful life together.

TEAHOUSE OF THE SPLENDID MOON

PART TWO

What care I for my goose feather bed
Wi' blankets strewn so comely-o?
Tonight, I lie in a wide-open field
In the arms of my raggle-taggle gypsy-o"
                                        A traditional Scottish Border ballad

The Teahouse of the Splendid Moon we named it one moonlit night of wayward lyricism.

Yuri, and the off-siders he employed, had spent the past few months turning the shack from a neglected surfer's relic into a charismatic little Balinese hut tucked away down among the dunes, within hearing distance of the ocean.

He had worked his magic in creating our exotic Xanadu from the dreams spun for me at the Tibetan cafe on our first night together.

Inside the teahouse the walls were lined with golden bamboo, the woven texture contrasting with the smooth beadings of rich dark timber he used to cover the joins and blend the panels into continuous walls. The sliding door into the bathroom was exotic, Yuri having set a full-length panel of my black Chinese Coromandel screen into the golden wood. Weeping willows and elegant kimonoed ladies with ivory parasols, endlessly crossing tiny arched bridges beneath which floated carpets of water lilies.

Aaah, so pretty.

In contrast to the bamboo walls, he created the tiny kitchen nook by placing red cedar planks on an angle of 45degrees running from ceiling to the floor. The rest of the Coromandel screen was chopped up and inset as panels on the front of the cupboard doors, a stunning feature in such a miniature kitchen.

The bench was one huge cross-cut slab of rosewood, a rich dark red, smooth all over except at its outer edges where a thin striation of yellow and then a rough textured fringe of gnarled wood followed the contours of the slab. The contrast in textures and colour was highlighted thanks to the many, many hours Yuri spent polishing the rosewood surface. It had gladdened me to see someone who loved his timbers immersed in this task, seeing the pride he took in bringing his ideas into being.

One of his special Japanese-style windows was set into the wall above the sink, giving a view out onto a Balinese archway separating our hut from the front yard. From the world. The windows, the one in the kitchen and one at either end of the hut, were elegant in their simplicity, built exactly to the design Yuri had sketched for me with his carpenter's pencil outside the Tibetan cafe.

The high cross-beam defining our bedroom at the north end was a massive length of pale beech. The sliding screen which hung from the beam was made from dark timber with stretched rice paper panels, a light and elegant oriental contrast. Throughout, the ceiling had been lime-washed, to give height inside the tiny teahouse.

And yes, gone were the ugly aluminium sliding doors onto the veranda.

Lovely timber-framed doors now stood in their place.

Outside, beneath the veranda, we had stripped the native flora of the invasive bitou bush so that the palms, the ferns, the tuckeroos and other native shrubs could grow and prosper. The fibro walls were now clad with rough-sawn raw timber, which we washed with a forest green to give a faded, natural look, blending our teahouses into its surroundings.

The veranda, the epicentre of our existence most days and nights, was brought into the overall scheme by banishing the ugly hardware 4x4 timber poles holding up the sloping roof and replacing them with slim polished tree trunks which Yuri lightly adzed.

He taught me that adzing was a technique where you used a special type of small adzing axe to chip the surface of the timber, creating a special roughed-up natural effect. The new poles appeared to be growing out of the ground, up through the veranda floorboards, giving an organic effect. Like the lozmans in Bali.

Between the veranda and the beginning of the pandanus and ferns forest that lead down to the sea, I had draped a hammock from the sturdy branches of a tuckeroo. I had also hung wind chimes and temple bells from the palm trees, and tucked an antique statue of Ganesh, the Hindu god of education and bacchanalian feasts, among the lush greenery.

To top it all off, a big fat stone Buddha sat at the foot of the veranda steps to remind us every day to meditate on the Enlightened Path and Four Noble Truths.

There was more work to be done but we were getting there and the 'getting there' was more fun than I had ever had in my fifty something years. Every day I blessed the universe for having turned me off the highway and into Byron Bay. Gertrude Stein might claim there is no there, there but I beg to differ. I found my 'There' there in Xanadu.

Yuri's Russian mother occasionally phoned me from the States to chat about her 'boy'. We had also become pen pals, Yuri being disgracefully negligent in the letter-writing department, a lapse that caused the elderly woman cut off from her adored son much heartache. She would say to me, in her attractive Russian-American accent, that she simply needed to know that her darling was still alive. And she was comforted by the fact she believed I was doing a good job of caring for her precious child.

~~~

Only Yuri's heroin habit shadowed our blissful Byron days. Heroin, and his spasmodic but challenging dependency on it.

This was the gorilla sitting in the corner. Heroin was at the crux of those long absences that I failed to challenge. Likewise, the numbers of bent spoons. The nodding off. Chasing the tip of his nose. The cash that disappeared from fruit bowls, from underwear draws, from my personal accounts. The tools lost—hocked. And needing to be replaced. His insistence that he wasn't using even when I found the hidden syringes and the pharmacy packs—the sterile wipes, the cotton buds and other appurtenances of the injecting business.

This was the story of our lives, and I understand now that my refusal to call him on it was wrong-headed. But I wanted him to have his dignity, to be able to play the man for me. So, I tolerated his habit. I funded it.

'It doesn't feel right,' he said, a week into the work, when he' was unable to make love. 'You're the paymaster. The boss lady. I'm a man. It doesn't work for me.'

'That's crazy. What you're creating here is for both of us. Everything I've got, I want to share with you. We're building more than a house, aren't we? Our boat? Our tiki bar? Haven't we got all these plans for our future?'

By now, we had come up with the idea of buying a cruising boat one day and setting off to far flung parts of the South Pacific where we would build our tiki bar and it would become the must-do, drop-in place for adventurous cruising Yachties. We spent countless hours dreaming about the adventure. Admittedly, I was aware, like Keats with his laudanum muse, that our dream was an opium-fueled dream, coloured-in gloriously for me by Yuri when he was high.

At the time, it seemed the decent thing to do; to trust Yuri with paying for everything to do with the renovation work. It removed me from the role of paymaster. Yuri knew so many of the local traders and could wrangle deals. It seemed sensible that he had the means at hand to make the purchases and pay his off-siders their wages.

That is not to say I wasn't aware of the various scams he pulled. New to heroin and ignorant of its crippling effects as I was, I still knew enough to know he was skimming funds. For instance, he would purchase hardware items on my Mitre 10 account and then return them and keep the cash refund. He would spin credible yarns about how his tools came to end up in hock. He could spin a yarn, alright. He was an expert.

At great expense, I kept reclaiming his tools, mostly the tools and machinery I had purchased for the job in the first place and given to him. The two surfboards that came with the house, my good Minolta camera, a video camera, a pair of designer sunglasses and several pieces of jewelry, as well as cash, all found their way to the hock shops around Byron and Ballina.

All for the heroin he denied he was using. Money was ebbing from my account, draining away like the surf out front. Only it didn't flow back in on the returning tide.

It would all sort itself out later. That was my mantra, the con job I did on myself. And in the meantime, life was beautiful. I loved being around the building project. Loved being around Yuri all day and every day. Loved the wonderful days we had together in Mullumbimby and beyond as we trampled over stacks of timber in lumber yards, Yuri showing me how to appreciate the smell of the wood, to know the different strengths and qualities of various timbers, learn what heartwood was, what a burl was, how wonderful it was to find a few really long planks of white beech that we could use for our boat, come the day we found one to restore.

I had become as passionate about timbers as Yuri, raking through stacks of beech and Australian teak, climbing over giant slabs of camphor wood and rosewood, sniffing, comparing, imagining.

Later, on these lovely days, as we sat in the Mullum pub or a roadside cafe up in the hills, we would spread out our dreams and work on the details.

We travelled often to Lismore for the necessities such as plumbing hardware and the like, but we preferred the adventure of scrounging around the weird and wonderful old barn down in Bangalow, an Aladdin's cave of iconic old tools, old bits and pieces of copper and brass, taps and electrical fittings, and especially nautical paraphernalia—old world things that had graced the yachts of yesteryear. The small china hand basin, the brass towel wrack and the 'gentleman's' toothbrush and soap holder we found to enhance our Asian-style bathroom.

Anything but the ordinary and mundane commercial product off the shelf. We were souls in unison on this quest.

Hard to find the inscape in a set of Mitre 10 taps, we figured.

For all the joy my life with Yuri gave me—and there were mountains of it—I could not help but acknowledged there were also those lies, the thieving, the connivances. And yet, only to myself did I admit how much his habit was costing me. He was working so hard, putting in such long, arduous days building the teahouse, so I kept on believing I was allowing him his dignity, showing my faith in him. There would come a time soon enough for us to work things out.

In truth, and with hindsight, I realize I was stalling, enjoying the ride too much to slow down and straighten up. I was taking the corners at break-neck speed. A wild ride.

The spectacular work he was doing each day as he brought the Balinese shack into being would be the source of great pride for him, I reasoned. His 15-year-old son, Cedar, unbeknown to his mother—because she would have barred it—had taken to dropping in on us now that I was around to mend bridges. Cedar would see how clever and creative his father was. This would restore Yuri's belief in himself and then he would clean up his act and everything would be plain sailing. I was new to this heroin business.

The truth was that I could not afford my philosophy of wait it out and all will be well. I had a mortgage to pay. I had renovation costs to fund. And increasingly, I had a bank account that was shrinking by the day.

There were dark clouds gathering, but still way off in the distance.

The Buddha, whose teachings I was beginning to embrace, exhorted his followers to cultivate a mind that clings to nothing, which is great advice if you find yourself loving a man with a heroin habit.

A drug counsellor in Byron told me I was a 'co-dependent', that I was not acting in Yuri's best interests by being so accommodating, emotionally and financially. But textbooks have no place in matters of the heart, I reasoned. The alternative to what I was doing would be to throw him back on the street.

Would tough love help him slay his demons?

I thought not. And I said as much to the counsellor. A life-long restorer of discarded treasure, I wasn't about to junk a man as worthy of restoration as this man. In fact, I had come to reject the word 'junkie' and all it implied. Maintenance, Yuri called it on the occasions he couldn't dodge the fact he had forsaken his Physeptone medication in favour of heroin. The Physeptone he was prescribed, and for which his GP wrote a prescription each fortnight, was a methadone substitute. If he exceeded his dosage, the alternative was heroin. He needed relief from his pain, he said. His shipwright-damaged joints ached after a day spent climbing up and down ladders. He needed only a 'taste' to feel fit.

This was the usual lament. Eighty dollars, a 'taste' was costing us.

But in my naiveté, I believed I understood the nature of the beast, that I had it by the horns and soon enough I would tame it. And to my still sick brain there was a certain excitement attaching to the life I was living, a life so far removed from my former respectable wifehood and motherhood days, from the strictures of living in the public gaze as a politician's spouse, a businesswoman, from the imposition of dutifully rearing five children to responsible adulthood.

There was something liberating, something rebellious about tolerating a partner's heroin habit. My life had been dramatically disrupted and I was putting it back together again in a way that pleased me. The world could go take a jump. I didn't need to be judged. I prided myself on being mature enough and open-minded enough not to be outraged by the fact my lover shot heroin into his veins.

Brownie points, you might ask?

More likely clinical madness, I would suggest.

~ ~ ~

One day, early in our relationship, I was given a full-on introduction to the life of the heroin user and the company they keep.

Why, I don't know, because we had the mattress in our yet-to-be-renovated shack on which we'd been sleeping rough for months, but one night I slept with Yuri on an old army rug inside a small tent, along with three of his friends, fellow users who had driven up from Melbourne in an old camper van. They had put the tent up in a well-concealed grassy gully behind the Byron Bay football club.

I recall being impressed by their stories. The three had been university students when they morphed into Vietnam birthday lottery draft-dodgers, on the run and resisting conscription on moral grounds. That turbulent era, one that had so often pitted family member against family member, when a son might be thrown out of home because of the length of his hair, had been a time of my own political awakening, a time when I used to call in my parents to babysit the children and go off to moratorium marches in the city.

I wondered, as the four men drifted off into their heroin heaven that night, leaving me stranded on my lonely island of insanity, how each of their lives might have turned out had we never gone to war against the Vietnamese northern peasants and their political leaders. Maybe these men in the tent alongside me would be dentists, accountants, lawyers, motor mechanics or shopkeepers today.

And maybe I would not, at my age, still be playing out my

subversive Seventies fantasies by being in a tent in a god-
forsaken paddock in Byron Bay hiding out with law-breakers.

On another occasion, again in the early days of our
relationship, I accompanied Yuri to Nimbin, a place with all its
left-over Sixties and Seventies symbolism. It was the first time.
Of course, it would not be the last. But first impressions stick,
they linger.

It was a hot Friday afternoon. We had driven up into the
hills after being in Mullumbimby, checking out a closing-down
sale at the Timber Slab Factory.

The smell of marijuana in the air was my first take-away,
then the sight of all the rainbow shop fronts and old timber
cafes and the mass of long-haired hippies wandering the street,
congregating in clusters on the pavement, neighbours drifting
from one gathering of locals to the next with their ragamuffin
kids in tow, the little ones in their rainbow-coloured fairy
costumes running between adult legs.

Peace, Love and Harmony seemed the appropriate order of
the day up in the legendary hilltop village.

The colourful Nimbin scene bedazzled me, and despite
Yuri's impatience to score, we paid a visit to the cannabis
museum, an echo of days gone by, reminding me of how left
out of it I'd felt all those years ago when reading about the
Nimbin Aquarius Festival.

Fast forward for a moment, and sadly, much of the old
Nimbin I marvelled at that day, in August 2014 would be
consumed in a fire. Ironically, I was there to witness the fire,
having gone on my own to a Nimbin retreat where I camped,
and begun this memoir from a tepee by the river in vast and
beautiful fields of green.

So, on this, my first ever visit to the rainbow kingdom's
HQ, Yuri went off and scored his heroin, the transaction taking

place on the street with subtle nods between buyer and seller.

'Now we go up to High Street!' he announced with a mischievous gleam in his eye when he returned with the prize. It was the playfulness he routinely adopted when attempting to put a cute face on his bad ways, not only to make light of his crime, but to bring me into his orbit.

If I were honest, I would have to say it thrilled me to be complicit in the bad behaviour, a fellow traveler on Hell's Highway.

And one man loved the pilgrim soul in you, goes a Yeats' line, one I love for its meaning, but also for its meter. Iambic pentameter has a pleasing rhythm and so did my eventful life with Yuri O'Byrne.

With a heroin-hungry man beside me I drove the Golf past the police station and up a winding side road just outside of the village, a road that ended at the top of a steep hill alongside a giant tank, the town's water supply.

'You weren't kidding. It actually is called High Street,' I said, having noted the street sign.

'Someone's idea of a joke, you reckon?'

'Maybe. But this isn't, Yuri. You get all the fun. It's not fair.'

'Where else would you rather be?' He reached over and roughed up my hair. 'Look at it this way; you're learning something ... a new world. You love it, who are you kidding?' He put his hand between my knees and grinned. 'It's sexy.'

'It'll send us to the poor house. If that's sexy, then yes.' Any resentment I might have felt melted away. Yuri, my soul, my sin.

Sitting beside him, at the top of High Street, I observed the shooting up process with the curiosity and excitement of a First-Year chemistry student entranced as she watches her teacher demonstrate the baking soda and vinegar volcano experiment.

Yuri first wiped his spoon with a swab then dropped sterile water from a tiny glass file into it. He mixed the powder before resting the spoon on the dashboard—the bent spoon and only one of many these days to be found in my cutlery draw—while he strapped his arm with his belt, opening and closing his fist, pumping for a vein. I continued to watch as he sucked up the drug into the syringe and wiped the injecting area of his skin clean with another swab.

By now I knew his mind was somewhere else. The twinkle in his eye was gone, replaced by a deadly earnestness. A man reaching for Valhalla.

'Explain to me what it feels like,' I said.

He took the syringe from between his teeth and looked at me. I was waiting for him to say something profound.

'It's like kissing Elle McPherson,' he said, flashing another of his bad boy smiles before returning to give the preparation all the dedicated attention of a lover, oblivious to everything except the hit. He had left me, gone off in his own obsessive world, his mind focused only on getting on. I saw a look of pure lust as he tilted the syringe upwards and tapped air from it. I flinched when the needle went into the vein and saw a trickle of watery blood swirl back up into the syringe like a soft pink flower slowly opening up. And then he plunged the heroin into his body.

The hammer! Horse. The smack!

It might have been *his* heroin rush, but it made a direct hit on my libido. White horses at full gallop.

I gave him his moment, then took the syringe from his limp hand, bent the stick over and rested it on the floor at my feet. As his head fell back against the seat and his body relaxed, I found my own high. My addiction was him.

Pathetic, you say? Yes, no argument there.

GALLERY

Our Xanadu in Byron Bay

Christine Petersen, Gold Coast model

The detective's card left under my door

The Christine Petersen murder December 1991

General Orlov on the Tsarina's left, inspecting the Guard

General Orlov with sword, presume purloined by the
repo men

The Pittwater renovations, 124 tonne of clay and rocks dug out
and the old house jacked up to make way for ground floor

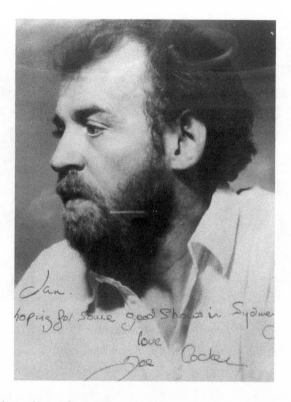

The glory days of my PR consultancy... George and Joe were
special people

My Beauty & the Beast days

Tuska...Anchors Aweigh!

FADE OUT

MAGIC HAPPENS

A soft Sea washed around the House
A Sea of Summer Air
Emily Dickinson

It was almost midday. The summer sun had been building strength all morning and I had just returned from cooling off in the surf.

Yuri was making his way along the ridge of the roof, balancing a long plank of timber on his shoulder.

Watching him up there made me nervous but I knew he had done plenty of this type of work in his time, and he was a sailor after all, used to shimmying a mast, up to the crow's nest in a gale or out on the bowsprit, bringing in the headsail. I had lived my life until now without ever mixing it with a man like Yuri, a powerful man who took physical risks. It excited me and once again I blessed the universe for putting him at the roundabout that day.

He had one long muscled leg either side of the roof's steep pitch, and a carpenter's pencil stuck in his mouth as he ran his tape over the job. His work boots and thick pushed-down socks were part of his uniform, likewise, the much-favoured torn and faded skimpy black t-shirt that stretched tight across his abs and stopped at his midriff. The sleeves had long ago been ripped off. His biceps gleamed with sweat this day. The red bandana held back his black mane of hair.

I saw sunlight catch on the gold earring.

His Zen nature, his romantic dreams, his stories about Californian life in the Sixties, his love of reading that matched mine; all reasons to love the man, but at this moment, watching him up on the roof, I was ready to concede it was his virility, his sheer masculinity that took my breath away.

Since knowing him, I had come to believe the sexiest accessory a man could wear was an old leather carpenter's belt slung low on the hips. It would not be long before the ad industry and reality TV's love affair with tradies caught on.

'Cleo centrefold material!' I called out, and savoured the coy grin he shot back.

'Can you grab my chisel and pass it up ... the one inch?'

I fetched the chisel and handed it to Con the Greek who had scurried half way down the long ladder as soon as the call went out. Con was a tiler, and also working as Yuri's building off-sider. I was the gopher, my job being to fetch and carry, to pass things to the men as required. It was also my job to keep the workbenches clean and to sweep up the fragrant curly wood shavings at day's end. When it was smoko time, I made good with the cheese and chili scones and mugs of tea and for their lunches, served my special man-sized sandwiches and cold beers.

Yuri had brought a couple of his Byron mates onto the job and it had not taken me long to see both men were heroin users. My Byron home; The House That Heroin Built.

Starting work on the job around 7am, it seemed these men flagged around mid-morning. And then at three they went missing. Their business, not mine, I figured. Con was small, dark and unambiguously Hellenic in his choice of food and in his constant veneration of the old country. He was a genius on the blues harp. Instead of my sandwiches, we occasionally trundled around to the pub for lunch where Con would produce his harmonica and entertain the bar. His Zorba got me up dancing, a custom I had recently acquired. The kids I had driven into town that first afternoon had been spot on. You don't wait for someone to ask you up. Not in Byron. The music moves you, you dance!

I jumped out of Con's way as he shimmied down the ladder and ran past me.

'Need a slash, sweetheart!' He grinned, running across to a spot over by the fence and turning his back to me.

A fervent, hyperactive builder's labourer as well as a gifted artisan with tiles, excellent at what he did, according to Yuri. Just a problem if you got in Con's way. Con went at things rather than around them, at a thousand miles an hour, as if the last train were about to leave the station and Con had to be on it. Panic, imperatives and assumed deadlines were how the man got through a working day but, that said, he had managed to turn an ugly little bathroom into something wonderful, laying four walls and a floor of rough-hewn grey slate around Yuri's Japanese red cedar steps that led up to our bathtub. A hole-in-the-floor Asian-style toilet had been suggested but squatting to defecate—according to Yuri it aided bowel movement—was a bog too far. We compromised with a WC concealed within a cedar bench.

We had decided to install a skylight to bring the stars and moon shining down into our exotic little bath house. This was the reason Con, by his own admission terrified of heights, had been up on the roof alongside Yuri this day. I had a genuine soft spot for the funny little man. Janny he called me. Some days he would go missing for hours, but he would go at it like a whirling Dervisher once he was back on the job.

Con's Muma often rang me from Sydney, another worried soul trying to keep tabs on her precious baby. I never failed to

tell Muma how precious Con was to all of us, what a good boy
he was. Why not? What was there that poor Muma could do
for her baby? Nothing. Con was on his own journey.

'Got a minute, Jan?' It was a man's voice.

'Coming.' It was Jay, over by the workbench, the other
carpenter Yuri employed. He was working the drop-saw,
slicing long pieces of pine into smaller cuts. 'Can you start
carrying these over to the boys?'

'Sure thing.'

Jay loaded up my outstretched arms with the timber and
stuck a box of nails on top of the pile. I struggled to the foot of
the ladder. 'Hey, you lot, I'm coming up.'

'Hang on! Coming down.' Yuri met me at the bottom and
relieved me of the load.

'You didn't have to do that. I could have brought them up
to you.'

'It's cool.' He gave me a peck on the cheek and a look that
held a promise before handing up the timbers to Con. I
touched the side where he'd kissed me. A strange man, shy
with his affection, so I took whatever I could get by way of
these spontaneous gestures, aware that gifts bestowed like this
were precious. The way he put his hand on my back to guide
me across a busy road. It wasn't necessary. Some might even
say it was chauvinistic.

But it felt good, dam it. One Sunday afternoon, at the Beach
Hotel, as we drank our beers, ate our meal and listened to the
music, a man he knew plonked himself uninvited at our table
and straight away, leant over and snitched a couple of fries
from my plate.

'Hey, man. Don't do that, okay?' Yuri said. 'You're being
disrespectful to my lady.'

My lady. Blessed are these small gifts.

Heading back to Jay's bench, I stood waiting for another load while he measured and cut. Jay was a different specimen from Con. A laconic one, was Jay. Blonde and bony, a sun-bleached lanky surfer, here since Byron Bay's glory days. Brooding, closed-up almost to the point of catatonia sometimes but Jay, God knows his last name, was an accomplished and thorough carpenter and Yuri, I knew was pleased to have him around. Jay often stood with Yuri, their heads together working out ways to manage tricky design problems. Both builders were used to the ways of Byron. No architects. No draughtsman's plans to work by. Not a council development approval in sight. This was building Byron style. Everything was inside Yuri's head and applied with spontaneity, creativity and precision. Like his lovemaking.

'Pass this up to them too would you, mate?' said Jay, breaking into my lustful thoughts.

I stuck my arms out as he piled two tubes of sealing liquid and the pressure gun on top of my load.

Jay was an interesting man. A heroin user but according to Yuri, more moderate than Con. Jay had a small daughter from a broken relationship. The mother had disappeared when the child was a toddler and Jay had raised her on his own. He had a live-in girlfriend who made a half-hearted effort to help him raise the girl, but I had the feeling it was far from being a perfect arrangement. The woman came around to the yard some days but never left the car, a patched-up 1970's Holden ute.

Whenever she showed up, Jay would hit Yuri up for an advance on his week's wages, a 'subbie'. Eighty dollars bought you a 'taste' on the street. A balloon. A cap. A bundle. I was absorbing the culture by osmosis. The occasional straggler from the previous owner's tenure still dropped by, looking for their sugar man. Silver magic ships. Sweet Mary Jane.

'Take this!' I called out to Yuri, handing up the gun and tubes from the foot of the ladder.

After he relieved me of my load I crossed to the shady end of the veranda and checked the beer cooling in ice in the plastic tub. Con's ouzo and the vodka, the Kahlua and milk for Yuri's White Russians were also there, snuggled in among the party ice.

'You blokes finished with me?' I called out. 'Can I go inside, now?'

Without taking the stubby carpenter's pencil from his mouth, Yuri gave a thumbs-up. It was Friday afternoon, party time. People would soon be turning up, a tally of the people I was beginning to make friends with and who often gravitated to the building site for beer and cheese on Friday afternoons. This one was special; it was Con's birthday.

It was cool inside the teahouse as I set about preparing for the gathering. Kane, an itinerate surfer I had met on the beach earlier in the week, prepared sushi rolls from the back of his van and made home deliveries. Kane and his sushi rolls were on their way, but his sushi would be off limits for the family next door. My vegan neighbours. If they came. But I doubted they would.

It had still been in the honeymoon days of my re-entry into Suffolk Park when I'd made a move to bond with these neighbours, a move that turned out to be absurdly comical.

The young family I had only seen from a distance, lived in the run-down red brick and fibro house next door. The other side of the property was a high vine-covered brush fence hiding the sandy parking area and public walkway down to the beach. A paling fence divided our suburban front yards until the dunes area where there was no dividing fence, only a common

pathway through messy pandanus trees giving access on to the
beach. It was while traversing this communal path that I
bumped into the man, the woman, their young daughter and
two small sons.

'My son and his girlfriend speared a big snapper down at
Cozy Corner this morning,' I announced with a certain
maternal pride and acknowledgement to having acquired some
Brownie points.

Cozy Corner was the locals' name for the protected little
rocky cove at the north end of Tallows Beach, the area beneath
the lighthouse and favourable to diving and snorkeling. 'Come
over later and have a beer. We're going to throw the fish on
the coals after the sun goes down. We'd love you to share it
with us. And bring the kids, of course.'

In the silence that ensued, which I took as hippy shyness, I
pushed on, explaining how Number One son and girlfriend,
visiting for the weekend, had gutted the monster and stuffed it
with lemongrass, ginger, chili and coriander. Believing I had a
salivating audience I went into further details. The mother,
meanwhile, had turned a paler shade of white. Then the father
explained in a gentle voice devoid of any trace of moral
judgement that the family ate nothing derived from living
things. They were vegans.

'Not even honey, milk, cheese?' I asked, fascinated by such
a life of sacrifice. 'What about eggs?'

'Uh-uh. No animal products.'

It's Stardust, right?' I said, looking at the woman.

'Stardust, yes. And this is Rubin.' The woman put a loving
arm around her mate then tapped each child on the head as if
she were their fairy godmother bestowing a lifetime of
promised love and happiness upon them. 'Sapphire, say hello
to Ms. ...?'

'Jan. Just call me 'Jan'. Okay? Just Jan.'

'Hello Jan,' said the girl.

'And these two little monsters are Dashiell and Tarquin,' announced the shy mother. 'Say hello to Jan.'

'Look, I'm sure we can get around this.... and all enjoy some other...some other...,' I was searching frantically for the exit. 'Yeah...some other great things to...barbecue?' I could hear my voice trailing off into the nether regions of lost opportunity. 'I'll find something.'

'It's fine. Really. It's fine,' said Rubin, his palms together in supplication. 'Why don't we do it another time. We'll bring the treats. Leave it to us.'

'You might be surprised how much you'll enjoy our table,' said Stardust, smiling as she pulled her little rainbow chicks under her wing and began heading them home.

'Maybe a beer, then. One day?' I called out, catching the father's enigmatic wink as he followed his brood onto safer ground. We had parted with smiles, but as I prepared for Con's birthday bash I was still contemplating where my neighbourly initiative had taken me. The vegan revelation had me wondering about the correctness even of beer. Beer was made with yeast, which gave it an active life. Mightn't beer also be verboten, might it also be considered a living organism in the Vegan Book of Righteousness?

Although we would remain prandial non-starters, a pleasant get-together over a mineral water and tofu stir fry never to happen, we remained on good terms. But embarrassment of a different kind was lying in wait for me next time I attempted to bond with the family.

Whereas veganism is fairly exclusive, nudity is universal. And yet it has the power to bring on paroxysms of coyness in modest souls.

It was early morning a few days after my return to the Byron from the Sydney dash. Before the vegan revelation. I was pushing my way through the pandanus and ferny undergrowth to the surf as my friendly neighbours were returning from their morning dip.

We commented in passing, on the weather and the state of the surf, a pleasant exchange taking only a few seconds. Thank God. Because I had no idea where I should cast my eyes. The entire family standing before me was buck naked.

Concerned that I may have been embarrassing them, I made my apologies—something to do with having to rush to the hardware store for building supplies—and quickly moved on. I met them again later in the day as I made my way through the shady track down to the sea again. This time I had come prepared. In an attempt to blend in to my hippy New Age neighbourhood I'd daringly left the top of my bikini at home.

While we exchanged hellos and commented on the unusually high tide, and the dad enquired about my proposed renovations I was painfully aware I was exposing my breasts to my dreadlocked friends, who, no doubt in deference to my sensibilities, had come fully dressed!

'Hey, good looking,' said Con as he came running inside the shack through the newly fitted timber doors and made a show of sniffing the air. 'I thought you'd be in here knocking up some spanakopita for the party, hey? Howz about it?' He was about to hug me.

I fended him off. 'Uh-uh, it's sushi.'

Con stepped back, a little-boy pout curling his lips. 'Sushi? Jesus, woman! You'd make a man eat fuckin' seaweed? What kinda party's that!'

It was good humoured. Con gave me the hug anyway and

was about to walk outside, again when I opened the oven door. 'Hey, you!' I called to him. 'This do?'

The smell of my spinach and feta pie drifted towards the door, pulling Con up short. He came running across the room and lifted me by the waist, spinning me around and around. When it stopped, I gave him a serious look. 'Con?'

'What?'

I was about to make the little man's day. I burst out laughing and flicked his bare legs with my wet tea towel. 'It's Muma's recipe!'

'Janny, Janny, Janny! You are a goddess! Woman, I love you! Muma's recipe? Get out! Y'mean Muma actually give it to ya? Shit, hey! She must think you're okay, girl. What you two been yapping about, hey? Me, I reckon. She tell ya what a no-hoper I am?'

'No, Con, she didn't. Funny about that. She said she loved you dearly.'

He slapped a kiss on both my cheeks then darted outside, giving a heel click as he leapt from the veranda.

'Knock off, time fellas!' I called from the doorway.

'Yoo-hoo?' came the call, followed by a laughing woman appearing from around the side of the shack.

Eye-catchingly beautiful in her tall, slim, sway-backed way, and sporting her trade-mark shock of long red untamed curls, the kind of angel frizz I would trade my right arm for any day, it was my friend Deb, recently moved down from the Gold Coast to Byron and unleashing her inner hippy. It was all Indian skirts and gossamer blouses now that she was no longer waiting on celebrity politicians at Spargo's, gorgeous soul that she was. And still is. A mother of adult children these days, the eldest of which, I'm happy to say, was conceived when Deb and her man Leo rented our little Balinese Teahouse one year.

She stepped up onto the veranda and stood there holding a bottle of champagne in a silver ice bucket, and with fingers to her lips gave a piercing whistle.

'It be Deb here, fellas. Ya Champagne Fairy. Come down, it's party time!' She popped the cork, shook the bottle and spun around, squirting Buddha and the tuckeroos with her jet of champagne. 'Time we baptized Xanadu!'

'Xanadu?' enquired the lean young man coming through the pandanus in wet cut-off jeans, a faded towel around his neck and a set of bongos tucked under his arm. It was a random kid I had befriended down on the beach earlier in the day and invited to drop by. I thought we could pull something together with Yuri's guitar, Con's harmonica, the kid's bongos and Deb's singing. *Magic Happens* proclaimed the sticker on the back of the Golf and what we were creating here on our little patch of ground on the shores of the blue Pacific was proof enough to justify the optimism.

I held out my champagne flute for what was left of Deb's offering and watched as Yuri came down the ladder and walked towards us. He acknowledged Deb with a peck on the cheek, and then dropped one on mine.

'I have to go out for a while, guys,' he said. 'Be back soon.'

How often I had heard him make that promise, and how often I had sighed and watched him go, asking myself how such a good man could be so flawed?

I looked at Deb. She looked at me, and we both slowly shook our heads.

BEAUTY & THE BEAST

*From this hour, I ordain myself loos'd of limits
and imaginary lines...*

Walt Whitman, *Song of the Open Road*

Hand in hand with renovating the shack and living the beautiful Byron life alongside my man, I also spent time flying down to Sydney most weeks to record *Beauty & the Beast*.

Over the next decade—for the life of the program until, sadly it folded due to Stan Zemanek's grave illness—my performances would be characterized by my controversial, and uninhibited outpourings. Brian Walsh had been right; I shot from the lip. The Spouse That Roared, one Sunday tabloid had tagged me in headlines years before, during my husband's tenure as Minister.

Opinions were the currency of the program and I believed everyone had a right to mine. I dished them out generously, creating a persona that made television executives nervous. Given that I couldn't take either myself or the show too seriously, I had the advantage of having nothing to gain so nothing to lose and I would just let it rip. Particularly when my moods were in the manic phase, meaning access to my brain's cut-off button was way out of reach.

My years on *Beauty & the Beast* were a hoot. Foxtel would have been surprised to know this motor-mouth might have paid *them* to let her have such unfettered access to the airwaves in order to air her left-wing opinions.

During every episode I held forth on what I perceived as political stupidity, social injustice, lazy thinking, badly behaved bosses, cheating husbands, delinquent children, drug issues, the absurdity of the monarchy, romance, marriage, divorce, indigenous rights, women's rights, the republic, monogamy, grief, consumerism, capitalism, mother-in-law issues, eating disorders, low wages, farm subsidies, the environment, gay rights—all kinds of topics, light and heavy, as per the viewers' letters submitted to us. And always I leant to the left.

When the viewers' letters weren't juicy enough they were created in-house by Trudi-Ann Tierney, one of the show's producers. Trudi was my friend at court. Many times, when I was coming under attack from either the host or one of the Beauties—or all of them at once—I would look past the camera to Trudi and know from her giggles that at least someone in the studio was on my side.

Jamie the Harley-riding Balmain 'boy' who for most of the decade was our leading camera man, was a good sport. Before each show, as the sound technicians were fixing our mics, and the make-up women were busy with last minute hair and gloss adjustments, Jamie would hand around his bag of jelly babies, which we greedily snapped up in handfuls.

As if any of us needed sugar! A panel of women with diverse views up against a moderator determined to lift the angst level of every performance with his sexist, right-wing hectoring.

I wasn't the only bleeding heart taking the side of the underdog. Lisa Wilkinson, a former editor of Cleo Magazine brought her common sense and sound left-wing conscience to the table.

Johanna Griggs was another Beauty who had the right values. And a beguiling full-on smile. The cameras loved her. A huge sports fan with an encyclopedic mind for sports-related data, Jo Griggs was always destined for a television career as a commentator.

And there was the beautiful and refined Maureen Duval, the one-time beauty queen. Maureen was known affectionately among us as 'Mauzzie' and was the archetypal respectable older woman. Older Catholic woman, that is. Mauzzie's quaint opinions never shocked. They sat well with our conservative host. Mauzzie's quirky vagueness often gave us, and the audience, cause for a good laugh. She was the mother of the show and we all loved her.

Belinda Green, former Miss World, and I often clashed. Belinda, a soft-hearted soul, was earnest in giving her opinions on the show and often took exception to mine. But we respected each other. We had worked together in the Eighties. Married to John Singleton at the time, Belinda had been keen to leave the kitchen sink and get a job. Singo phoned me early one morning and asked me to find room for her at JMA. Not asked, but demanded it, actually. And in return, he said, he would put plenty of PR business JMA's way. I employed Belinda, and she was good at her job, but decades later I'm still waiting for the other half of the Singleton deal to drop.

Another of the show's regulars, and another whose opinions sat well with our host, was Ita Buttrose, that familiar Aussie icon, former magazine editor, and a woman who had gone bravely out ahead to help forge the new dawn for feminists. Ita had change, however. The radical journalist editor had settled benignly into middle-age and become more matronly than the Queen.

I often pictured Ita trailing Corgis. Dear Ita was usually

appalled by my behaviour. At least the disapproving glare in those lovely violet eyes, and the tightening of the coral-lipstick mouth would suggest that was the case. Unlike the majority of us, Ita gave little away of her personal life and played coy to Stan's titillating comments. 'Oh, Stanley!' she would sigh. And our host was never rude to Ita. Like Mauzzie, she was considered to be a true lady and beyond his insults.

Often, after one of my go-ins with him, the camera would switch to Ita and catch the shocked look on her lady-like face. The tut-tutting was palpable. I was fond of Ita but I think she would agree; not in a million years would we ever be soul sisters.

And of course, there was the indomitable Prue McSween; potty-mouthed, brash, in-you-face, I'm-here-to-shock-you delightful Prue McSween. Prue was a contrarian in the funniest and most outlandish way. Many were the fierce ideological arguments between Prue and me, often accompanied by flying insults. And yet it was Prue I asked to launch my memoir, *Sheer Madness; sex, lies and politics*, in 2010. We were combatants, but I believe we respected each other as professional women, albeit with diametrically opposed views on political issues. On most issues. On all issues! It was this kind of tension between us that made the set crackle some days and left poor Stan open-jawed and wondering what kind of shrewish company he had fallen amongst.

The times when the show took to the road were some of the best of times. There were the interstate flights, the big limos put on for us, the dinners and parties, and in general, the special celebrity treatment. Not hard to take for a working-class girl from Merrylands.

Beauty and the Beast was the only show at that time to be made by cable television and sold to free-to-air. It attracted the ratings and when the show went on the road, audiences would overflow the casinos and club venues. Afterwards, the fans would line up at tables set up in the foyers where Stan and 'his' Beauties would sit for ages signing autographs. When our mini-bus pulled out, the fans would be there on the pavement, waving. We had made their lives just that little bit more exciting. Not a bad thing.

It seemed, from the daily letters bag that our viewers missed the good old days when neighbours could sort out their problems at the local washing well. Or talk things over with their preacher after Sunday service. Or share gossip over the back fence. Instead, poor souls, they had us. We were the agony aunts paid to listen and offer advice.

But what chutzpa! As if any of us had a monopoly on wisdom? As if we had the right to pontificate?

Most of the Beauties would probably admit to having stuffed up their own life to some extent, and yet we readily argued the rights and wrongs of moral dilemmas, felt confident in dishing out advice to the lost and the love-lorn, and in giving succour to the suffering. Ours was the original reality television show. Apart from the Channel Ten lawyers visiting the set some days and having to wave the Anti-Discrimination Acts in front of Jeannie Little when her mouth ran off about Muslims and 'Aboriginals', we were never censored.

It was a fabulous way to put in a few hours each week and be well paid, but did we really understand how seriously some letter writers took our answers?

A few years ago, a stranger came up to me in the street, a woman in her late forties I guessed. After the usual compliments about *Beauty and the Beast,* how much she'd loved the show, how much she missed that it was no longer on air, she bowled me over with her next comment.

'I did what you said, Jan. I took your advice. I left the bastard! Divorced him.'

That gave me serious pause for thought. Here was a woman who had altered the course of her life simply on a throw-away line of mine, given as entertainment on an agony aunt daytime commercial television show. After I learned from her letter that her husband was a serial abuser and had kept her in poverty while he made whoopee I had called him a maggot and advised her to pack the silverware and anything else that was hers and walk out the door.

For other letter writers with badly behaved spouses I often told them to say "Here's your hat. What's your hurry?" as they kicked the problem spouse out of their lives. No doubt the woman who spoke to me that day had done the right thing by leaving the man. She convinced me that it had turned out for the best for her and her child, but the bottom line was that it had simply been entertainment and not the perceived wisdom of one who had a right to be advising anyone on such monumental life decisions.

The show could get rough. We traded insults and slandered each other with insouciance. But that was the kind of show it was. It was wild and free-ranging and we pulled no punches. I doubt programmers could get away with it today. It seems none are game to try. But verbal dust-ups weren't the only way we got through a show some days.

Dahhling Jeannie Little once tossed her full glass of water over my head, and another time knocked my chair backwards off the platform. I picked myself up, brushed myself down and we all had a good giggle. Stan was known to throw the odd projectile at me. He once hurled a book down the table, aiming straight at my head. Today I would probably be encouraged to sue the network for dangerous work practices.

The contretemps which led to Stan throwing the book, and which can still be seen on Youtube, was over a letter sent in by a young country person complaining about how tough farming life could be for folks such as her parents, who seemed, from her letter, to be wealthy land owners. Stan, in introducing the letter, had taken the girl's part.

When it came my turn to offer an opinion to the letter writer I railed against farm subsidies for rich graziers and stood up for the poorly paid rural worker. In my rant, I criticized the then Prime Minister, John Howard, ridiculing him as "... that pigmy gnome of a prime minister, little Johnny Howard".

Stan became apoplectic. He talked over me, trying in vain to shut me up. I knew I was antagonizing him, mightily.

Unable to stem the flow, in frustration, he picked up a book and threw it at me.

I ducked. It missed!

My immediate reaction was to grab the book and hurl it back at him. But I pulled myself up, and instead, hurled a mouthful of insults.

'Jan! Do you have any respect for anyone?' shouted a red-faced Stan Zemanek.

'Not for a fool like you, I don't!'

Much finger pointing and yelling over the top of each other.

'If you're trying to get me to walk off the show I won't and what I'm going to say is that while ever there's one homeless person—'

'Jan? Jan? I've told you before, I don't care whether you walk off the show or not ... Jan? Listen to me! Jan! I don't care if you walk off the show or not but when I ask you a bloody question you will look at me and—'

'I won't. I won't but what I will say is that while ever there is one homeless person living in Australia we don't give rural subsidies!' I thumped the desk. 'There, I got my point in!'

'Jan...Jan....when I'm asking you a question you will look at me!'

'Why would I look at you?' I pointed to the audience at home. 'I want to look at intelligent people.'

While he yelled at me about my lack of respect for our Liberal Prime Minister, and I yelled back at him, the camera cut away to Ita Buttrose. Poor Ita! The look on her face. She was shell-shocked!

The imbroglio ended with smiles once we settled down, but I was visibly shaken. I believe Stan was, too. But it wasn't over yet, not for Stan. What I learned only recently from his wife—and a friend these days—Marcella, was that her husband had to face her cold shoulder once he got home that night.

'He came through the door and he knew he was in trouble,' Marcella said at a recent lunch where I had arranged to meet her to discuss the manuscript and my memories of her late husband. 'He only had to look at my face when he came through the door to know what I thought about his performance. Oh, yes. The man knew he was in trouble!'

I was chuffed to hear her tell me this. It came as a surprise. During the years of recording the episodes I had little to do with Stan's wife. That has all changed these days and I regret that I've missed out on so much of this admirable and charming woman's friendship. Marcella is salt-of-the-Earth. She works tirelessly for her charity, curebraincancer.org.au and is a wonderful mum and grandmother. We have made up some lost time, and I delight in the behind-the-scenes tit-bits she relates about her husband and his hosting of the show. The big shock came for me when she admitted how often she had barracked for me.

'I don't believe it! I thought you didn't like me.'

'You were my hero, Jan!'

We hugged each other. 'Thanks, my love. But I won't verbal you on that. I won't put that in the book,' I promised.

'Please do,' she said with a gorgeous grin.

And so—immodestly, but gratefully—I have.

It is worth watching, that book-hurling segment of *Beauty & the Beast*. For me, it's always good for a laugh. Stan is probably having a chuckle, too. I always told him I would have the last word!

Often after these recording sessions, as I drove out of the Foxtel car park, I would ponder whether this was why I had slogged it out as a mature age student with five little kids and a busy political spouse in order to gain a university honours degree.

Yet there was never a day, despite the tossed glasses of water, despite the hurled books, the often-inane letter queries, and the terrible behaviour when I cursed that I had to front up and record our shows. I loved the whole experience. And the camaraderie off camera was a blessing.

Carlotta, for instance, was great fun to be around. Carlotta with her lovely husky-throated voice. She, like Stan, also had an infectious laugh and wasn't mean about sharing it. She lit up the set with her responses to Stan, who it wasn't hard to see was fascinated by Carlotta's exotic story; born a male but living her life as a glamorous female.

Carlotta and I hosted the Diva Awards one night in Sydney. I had always taken pride in knowing from the fan mail that I was well thought of in the gay and lesbian community.

The night of the Diva Awards was a hoot. Unscripted, Carlotta and I played off each other to great effect. At least our enthusiastic audience thought so. Big Carlotta and Little Jan. We had them in stitches as Carlotta quipped about my sex on the desk exploits. It was always Carlotta's claim that she came up with the memorable and funny line used in the Yellow Pages ad campaign; "Not happy, Jan!". I don't know whether it is true or not, but I do still own the over-sized t-shirt she had printed with the slogan and presented to me on camera one day.

No one enjoys themselves as much or dresses up more spectacularly than Sydney's gay community on Diva Award nights. Sorry, but it was before we all learned the correct terminology; LGBTQI.

A gay man I bumped in to up at Kings Cross one Sunday morning several years ago, however, wasn't one of the happy celebratory ones. I was sitting in a tiny coffee shop opposite Kinsella's nightclub, waiting for Yuri to come out from seeing his GP when I noticed the person at the next table. A slightly built man in his late twenties, I guessed. His sadness was clinging to him like a shroud as he sat alone silently weeping.

I caught his eye and he came to my table. He recognized me from the show, and knew I faced off Stan and Co on behalf of people like him. "Wooly moofs" was the host's refrain.

Sometimes I was brought to tears when Stan disrespected gay people in this way, and so inarticulate with fury that I would be close to ripping my mic off and making an exit. I know Stan was only performing for the cameras, a kind bloke by nature, but it pressed my buttons; the reason he did it, of course.

I listened while this poor wretched soul at the coffee shop poured his heart out to me on this Sunday morning. It was a story sadly all too common in that age of incurable AIDS. His young partner had just passed away. It was such a small thing I gave him, my shoulder to lean on, but I was humbled by how much he said talking with me, and knowing I empathized, had helped him.

It was moments such as these when I felt that perhaps my 'celebrity' status might serve some useful purpose. The comfort of strangers. We should be ready to lean in and listen when we feel another's pain. It cost so little, and goes such a long way.

A ROSE BY ANY OTHER
NAME

'Celebrity' can be a crazy concept. *Beauty & the Beast*'s regular viewers, having taken us into their homes, felt comfortable and familiar with us, and yet not all that familiar because, to want our signatures on their programs they must have thought there was something special about us, something that set us apart, something that made those signatures meaningful to them.

And yet, of course there wasn't anything special about us. I am still the same person today, for instance, as the so-called celebrity TV personality who sat and autographed programs until her arm ached. But I would be hard pressed not to be shoved out of the way by the same autograph hunter today if I were trying to crowd onto a bus in peak hour.

When you're in vogue, your name can get you the best seat in the house. When they've forgotten you, try getting through the door! It helps not to take one's self seriously. I never did.

I admit, however, to a fondness for the make-up sessions, and the costume fittings before each show. Those luxuries did make me feel just a tad special.

Never one to fuss over dressing—jeans and t-shirts being my default position—nor being a person who visited the gym, the hairdresser, the manicurist or went in for clothes and accessories shopping, I was the rough trade among the Beauties and posed a definite challenge for the make-up women and wardrobe mistresses. I think most of the Beauties supplied their own jewelry and glamorous tops.

I say 'tops' because, sitting as we did behind a long table, there was little need to worry about the bottom half of the body.

Sometimes, having been working on the boat we bought and restored during these years, or on home renovations, I would arrive at the studio and present for make-up with red lead anti-foul on my face and arms, with white paint sticking strands of my hair together, with broken fingernails, and wearing my big Blundstone boots.

The viewers would have been shocked to see what went on beneath those tables.

In fact, one day they got their chance. Stan had feigned disgust at the grey suit and cream silk blouse the wardrobe had done me up in, claiming it was too conservative for the likes of me. He really called me out on it. I stared at him for a moment, copping the insults, and then I raised a leg high up over the desk and gave the cameras full tilt at my paint-stained Blundies and hairy legs in a pair of work shorts.

The vision brought everyone to tears, Stan included. What a delicious laugh that man had!

Two of my favourite make-up technicians—our face fairies as we called them—were Lisa and Georgie. Lisa was the boss-lady in the make-up room and Georgie, exclusive to Stan, worked in the room with the big silver star on the door. Along with the Beauties, we always had fun together when the show went on the road. The champagne we drank late at night at the hotel bar or in our rooms always tasted better on account of us having put it on Foxtel's tab.

One panelist who didn't mind dolling up in glamorous togs of her own was Rose Porteous Hancock, the flamboyant former wife of multi-billionaire mining magnate Lang

Hancock. Rose, a Filipino woman who had definitely, in money terms at least, married up, was not a regular Beauty but a guest panelist.

One day, Rose came into the make-up studio in a dusty pink full-length gown, quick to announce to the interested—and even the disinterested such as me—that the lavish garment was 'Gaultier, darling! Gaultier.' The woman was dripping in jewels. Nothing if not over-the-top stupidity. And irritating to the max. A silly, silly woman, she really got under my skin. And I made no bones about how I felt about the lady. This outsider deserved her comeuppance.

The show was on the road on this particular day when it became my privilege to dish it up to her.

We were performing at the Birdsville Casino in Perth and the pre-publicity was plugging the local gal Rose Hancock as the star. I was already made-up and costumed, in this case, unusual for me, in my own Versace suit—a remnant of my PR days—when one of the producers approached me. She had a deal for me, one that was hard to resist.

'If you can insult Rose to the point she walks off the stage, we'll double your fee,' she said with a wicked grin.

'You're on!' My grin was just as wicked. My contract assured I was paid well in those far-off days of television glory. Double my day's fee was dauntingly attractive.

We all took up our positions on stage, a stage sporting an extravagantly ornate set. From memory, it was a replica of a Roman temple, even to the point of having white satin toga-kitted spunky he-men standing about looking delicious.

Stan, the host, was in his chair, as were we, the Beauties.

Bar one exception.

Rose was going to make a grand late entrance, milk it for maximum applause. Time went on. The prima donna was testing ours and the audience's patience.

Eventually the woman appeared from the wings, primping across stage and stopping near to where I was seated behind the table.

Rose looked out at her audience, delighting in her notoriety as they clapped or cat-called her. It was all the same to Rose. She was the centre of attention and that was enough. That was everything.

Rose had little idea of what was coming.

Dressed in a full-length flowing mink coat—on a hot Perth summer day—the lady announced to the audience in her heavily accented voice that the coat was made up of forty minks.

'Forrrty minks, darrrlings. Forrrty minks have gone into the making of this coat. Forrrty minks!'

'And every one of them with a higher IQ than you,' I said.

The roar went up. The audience was with me. The popinjay had just got her comeuppance!

Mrs. Porteous, aka, Rose Hancock, spun around and glared at the person who had dared to call her bluff. Rose began fuming, brandishing a long shoe-horn at me—why a shoe-horn I have no idea. She waved the thing menacingly in my face as she screeched crazy things, which I won't repeat here but which have been recorded for posterity elsewhere. Did I budge? No way. As the audience laughter and applause kept erupting and the shoe horn continued to work overtime in my face I knew I was on target to earn that double fee.

'Put that thing down!' I said, but Mrs. Hancock preferred to make her grand exit with her shoe horn, gathering up her forty little dead minks, striding dramatically from the stage on her high dudgeon,.

Thank you, Rose! You just made my day, woman.

Thank you, Rose! You just made my day, woman.

One well-known show business journalist now working out of L.A., Michael Idato, claims that my taking the piss out of the vain and haughty Rose Hancock Porteous that day is among his most cherished moments in the industry. He pointed out how significant it was that when the lady thought I was calling her a whore—which I was not—she kept demanding; 'Name the house! Name the house!' Go figure.

Mrs. Porteous, however, was not the only one ever to walk off the show. I did it a couple of times myself during those dozen years. Both times when the show was on the road. In hindsight, I'm sure there was a deal done behind my back, just as it had been done to bait poor Rose.

The argument with Stan was in full swing when suddenly I couldn't take any more of his rudeness towards the underdogs he was railing against. In tears by now trying to address his insensitivity towards those affected by drug abuse, words deserted me.

I was wearing a red dress, as I recall, and red was the colour I was seeing. Absolutely inarticulate with anger and frustration, I stood up and ripped off my mic, slammed it on the table and walked off the set. And I know there must have been pre-arranged baiting, because the camera was geared up to follow me all the way down the long hall and into the green room before I slammed the door shut in the cameraman's face.

When the footage was later used as a promo, it was my chance to hear Stan's voice as it had sarcastically described the walk-off in real-time to the audience. 'There she goes. Look at her. Can't take it. Goodbye. Good riddance!'

The next time I left the stage unexpectedly it would be by order of those upstairs in mahogany row.

The Financial Times had been carrying headlines about the

media mogul Kerry Packer not paying tax. A man who was worth billions was paying less than10% tax on his earnings while your average hard-working battlers were being slogged more than 30% and with no way of avoiding the impost.

I got my chance to address the issue and address it I did, in the fiercest, most partisan way, raging in the strongest terms against the man many Australians revered simply because he was filthy rich and believed Australians who paid their fair share of taxes were mugs. He had given evidence before a senate enquiry much to that effect.

Did it worry me that Kerry Packer owned a third of Foxtel, the company with whom I had my contract?

If it did, it didn't show. By now I was manic, ignoring the horrified looks of my colleagues. I just kept on keeping on about what a low act it was for Packer not to pay his taxes, comparing his privileged situation with that of the average worker who had no recourse to cunning tax avoidance schemes. These poor dopes just had to pay up and shut up and watch while the likes of Mr. Packer and his ilk were paying eff-all in the dollar on their obscene wealth.

This was my rave. And I was still frothing at the mouth when the call came from on high.

'Get her out of the building!' said the voice from upstairs into the director's earpiece. Brian Walsh, no doubt it was, and no doubt the poor man would have been up there pulling his fine and already thinning hair out by its roots.

So, at Walsh's command, get me out they did.

I was booted.

Murray's name was toxic upstairs. Great talent, they agreed, but Hell, she's unmanageable. So disrespectful of our masters. Great for our ratings, that goes without saying, but the woman's a bloody ratbag, unable to be trusted to tow a reasonable line when a reasonable line is what's needed to be towed.

The Powers That Be had spoken and my budding television career had tanked.

Back to Byron Bay to contemplate lotus blossoms.

Or so I believed.

SANDWICH-GATE

To follow knowledge like a sinking star,
Beyond the utmost bound of human thought.
Alfred Lord Tennyson

During my time in the sin bin, Stan Zemanek had a feast day picking over the bones of what he believed was my busted TV career.

In my absence, he implied he was the one who had ordered me out the door, telling the viewers that he was sick of my tantrums. Apparently, it was Stan who dismissed me and Stan who was keeping me from returning. If you believed Stan, that is.

This wasn't the true story, however. Brian Walsh, cognizant of what his masters would think of my outburst against Packer, had been the one who'd fired me. And despite Stan's bellicose posturing about whether or not he would let me back on 'his' show, it was Walsh who ultimately got to say who was and who wasn't on *Beauty and the Beast*.

The ratings always shot up significantly during the Zemanek/Murray imbroglios. It was evident in Stan Zemanek's funeral eulogy that Brian would give one day in the future, that our fights made for good television.

The *Daily Telegraph* gossip columnist Jo Cassamento feasted off the sacking. She was in her glory writing up my shame after the dismissal. Cassamento and I had clashed often when she had made her guest appearances on the show.

There were two Beauties, only two, who called me during my time in the sin bin to ask if I were okay and how was I holding up. One was Gretel Killeen, one of the wittiest television performers I have ever had the pleasure to see perform. Gretel knew how to use that steel-trap brain of hers to toss hand grenades at pomposity. Killeen could smash egos with a raised eyebrow and one witty, succinct remark—and did so with great élan where Stan was concerned.

And always we would emerge from the rubble with a laugh—and me wishing I could have said what Gretel said, and say it the way she said it. She had poor Stanley's number, that woman! She was sensational talent and it was no wonder she was snatched up for *Big Brother* at the height of its popularity.

The other Beauty to enquire after me during my days of shame was one of the sweetest-natured, and one of the most classically beautiful women ever to grace our television sets.

Charlotte Dawson is no longer with us. To quote Sylvia Plath, '... *some darker day than usual had made it seem impossible* ...' Tragically, on a day that must have seemed more than ever unbearable, Charlotte took her life. And left the world poorer for her passing.

I am sad as I write this. There is always the thought that I had too easily allowed her to slip out of my life after *Beauty and the Beast* ended. No excuse that I was geographically far away. I should have been there, let her know that I had faced my own dark demons and understood the pain of malignant sadness. News of her death was devastating.

Vale, Charlotte, our darling sister.

~~~

Apart from the good mates like Gretel and Charlotte, for the rest of the crew at Channel Ten/Foxtel Jan Murray was *persona non-gratis* during her days of disgrace.

Disgraced and disowned. Stuck in the sin bin.

But the fan mail kept pouring in. And it was running at 90% in my favour.

This did not deter Stan, who kept running his own version of the story, giving his own tally of the fan mail opinions as he read out selected letters from viewers complimenting him on how forcefully he had dealt with the recalcitrant Jan Murray.

Yes, he would say, and go on bloviating and complimenting himself on his macho handling of the matter. And you can bet your life, folks, I won't be having that ratbag back on my show, he would conclude, as if it were up to him, and not Walsh, to decide my fate.

Stan was a smart bloke and a darling of the network. The men upstairs would have made sure he was in touch with popular opinion. Together, they would have decided to play it tough, stretch it out, milk the conflict week after week for all it was worth because it made for good daytime television. 'My way or the highway,' Stan used to say. He could go on with his bombast till the cows came home but he was always going to get me back. He just had to do it his way, a way that made sure he didn't lose face. By now the fans had taken sides, picked their team.

And my team won!

I came back. My fans had demand it. Even Brian Walsh came to me on the day I returned and told me his elderly mum and her church ladies weighed in on the issue and demanded her son put me back on the show. Immediately.

The day I appeared, Stan was still trying to put a brave face on things, pretending he was being magnanimous in allowing me back. But for all Stan's bloviating, knowing I had been brought back by popular demand felt gratifying—to have made the big man eat a little humble pie.

Stan's wife, Marcella and I recently had a chuckle about the dismissal incident. She told me that during the stand-off, Stan was confiding to her, nightly, saying that he had to get me back because, together, he and I worked off each other brilliantly. He needed me. He missed me.

God bless the man!

~~~

Despite my popularity with the viewers, I don't believe I was ever in Brian Walsh's good books. Not one of his favourites. And it was mostly on account of "Sandwichgate".

This was an episode that came early in my *Beauty and the Beast* days.

As well as the commissary which was the in-house cafeteria for everyone who worked at Foxtel, there was also a pleasant Green Room for the 'talent'. Green is supposed to be a soothing colour. TV performers are supposed to be highly strung creatures who need calming before they go on air.

In our case, that was rubbish. The Beauties were a hardy bunch of women. The Foxtel Green Room was simply a place where we could grab a bite to eat and a cuppa once we were made up, frocked up and ready for our recording sessions. Brian, to his credit, always laid on a generous repast for us. There were trays of delicious, wholesome sandwiches, fresh fruit and a selection of cheeses.

One day I arrived late. I was booked in for a set of afternoon recordings. They were holding the show up for me, so I was already pretty much in the bad books. But, unlike the rest of the cast and crew, all of whom lived locally, I had to be up early to drive an hour to Ballina airport and then another hour and a half in the air to Sydney, and then thirty minutes in a cab from the airport to the Pyrmont studio.

My plane had been delayed in a holding pattern over

Sydney. I arrived at the studios not only panting, but ravenous. The healthy, nourishing sandwiches I was greedily anticipating were a sad affair by the time I arrived.

No way can I spin it to put myself in a good light. My "Sandwichgate" is my shame.

I was too full of my own self-importance. Word got back to Brian Walsh that I complained about his sandwiches. I was made to feel rude and ungrateful. As I should! I was getting carried away with my own fabulousness and needed to be brought down a peg or two. The incident would live on for many years, with host and Beauties often reminding me of the incident and giving me a hard time for my lack of grace.

Foxtel would eventually move to North Ryde, the hinterland of north west Sydney, but for the first several years of the decade it was based on one of the Pyrmont finger wharves, a wonderful piece of real estate with expansive views of Sydney Harbour.

At lunch time, I would often sit out on the wharf and watch the ships go by. We usually recorded a week's worth of shows in two days of shooting. If Stan and I had been going at each other extra hard during the morning, I would take the opportunity while out in the sunshine, to meditate, sitting cross-legged on my own in a quiet corner.

I often explained my meditation practices on camera as 'pulling a white light down over my body' in order to give myself protection from the slings and arrows that came my way so often from the cast.

This notion of a white light tickled Stan's fancy. It gave him the chance to ridicule me for being a Byron Bay 'hippy'. If I missed the studio call to get back inside after the lunch break—because of my deafness—I would tell Stan as we were being mic-ed up and the make-up techs were doing their last-minute fiddly bits that I had been sitting outside beneath my white light, putting the protection in place against his bad behaviour, assuring him that his insults couldn't penetrate the barrier.

Sometimes when he was giving me grief I would simply mime pulling the white light down over my head and shoulders and wriggling into it, insinuating to the bemused and puzzled moderator that he could carry on all he liked, because once under my white light I was impervious to his rants and taunts. As good as saying "Talk to the hand." It infuriated Zemanek. And it helped position me as the rat-bag of the show, a mantel I wore with pride.

I am still being asked, in connection with my years as a panelist on *Beauty and the Beast,* about these clashes with Stan. Was it a put-up job? Were we simply staging our stormy confrontations for the benefit of the cameras, the pair of us just doing it to give the viewer a thrill and the ratings a boost?

The answer is 'No!'. An unequivocal 'No'. It was not staged. This was reality TV, the original reality television show. We never rehearsed. We were never asked to re-record any segment, no matter how fiery the arguments.

Accepting that the donnybrooks between myself and the host were for real, the fans ask whether Stan and I were friends once the cameras stopped rolling.

And here's the truth; we were never impolite, I can vouch for that, but there was little real camaraderie between us. In the case of my fellow panelists, the arguments and name-calling ceased once the cameras were no longer on us, and between takes we would often have a laugh among ourselves about our performances. Stan was usually busy being spoken to in his earpiece by the director in preparation for the next segment and so was preoccupied.

Often, he and some of the other Beauties such as Prue—who shared an out-of-office social life with Stan and his wife Marcella—would gossip among themselves about their mutual friends and their week's activities. I was an outsider. When Stan and I passed in the studio corridors, we were no more than courteous.

It was the same at the various Channel Ten and Foxtel promotional gigs and end-of-year parties; he was aloof towards me. Occasionally he might grin and have a dig at me and they were good times. As I so often commented on camera, I was the only Beauty never to be invited to the Zemanek Christmas parties.

I wore the snub like a badge of honour. It defined us for the fans, gave the show colour, and that was no bad thing.

SCALES OF JUSTICE

'Tis all a chequer-board of Nights and Days
Where Destiny with Men, for Pieces plays...
Omar Khayyam

Deemed supply was the offence, according to the Sydney solicitor I engaged for Yuri's trial. A person is presumed to be intending to supply the drug if found in possession of a trafficable amount. Under NSW law 2.5 grams was deemed trafficable. Yuri was alleged to have been in possession of 3 grams when busted.

He had confessed to me about the drug offence early in our relationship. Just one more surprise I dealt with along the way to loving him. The bust had come as a result of the motor vehicle accident in Karuah in 1996, the year before we met, the night his angel left his shoulder.

The set of small scales found with the bag of heroin was a serious matter, making it hard to prove the heroin was intended for personal use. I engaged Christopher Murphy Lawyers and we would take several trips down to Sydney over the next couple of years to brief the solicitor assigned to the case.

I knew how Yuri had come to be in possession of the heroin the night he almost wiped himself out down the highway. Con confirmed his story.

~~~

It was April 1996 when the Ballina slipway job came up.

Con knew a guy who knew a couple of brothers up at Surfers
Paradise who needed a competent shipwright, one who
worked with timber boats and in particular, was familiar with
fishing trawlers.

'It's yours for the bloody asking, cobber,' said Con. 'The
guys want these two old decommissioned trawlers converted
to pleasure cruisers, y'know? Fancy cabin refits, teak decks and
fix up any rot? I told 'em, you're the man for the fuckin' job. I
told 'em, mate. And there'll be more jobs coming down the
line. These blokes, they're bloody loaded, I'm tellin ya!'

Manna from Heaven. He would employ the hapless Con as
his off-sider. He was excited about the prospect of lucrative
work in an area of the shipwright's trade that was his particular
passion; the sturdy timber fishing trawler. As he headed up the
hill to his dealer he felt confident he could pull it off, give the
Denmead brothers the kind of results they were looking for.

He had already completed a meticulous set of drawings,
given the men his quote and suggested they check out a job
he'd done on a forty-foot yacht, a Swanson, up at Southport
two years ago. As well as a trawler conversion he'd worked on
down in Ballina last year. With the Denmeads' deposit in his
account, he was awash with cash but had no intentions of
using the start-up capital for anything other than to set up the
job. He could pay the slipway fees in advance, give Con a
decent 'subbie' to kick off with and get down south and source
the necessary materials.

It was the weekend after he'd signed the deal with the Gold
Coast brothers. He and Con were on their trip down to Sydney
in the new red Ford utility leased with Denmead money.

'Why don't you keep a few grand back?' Con suggested.
'Invest a bit of your capital? You'd triple it before you even
started on the fuckin' job. We're gonna need it, mate. To work

the long hours. We're dead-set gonna need some duji on this job, let me tell ya.'

He knew what Con meant. Buy the smack wholesale in Cabramatta; sell it retail in Byron. The dealer Pete Hershey, and plenty more, would take it off his hands.

'Think about it, mate, why don't ya? It makes good sense,' urged Con.

He did think about it. For two minutes. Then told the Greek he intended cleaning his act up now that he had serious work prospects, and what's more, he wouldn't be using any guys on the job who used. He was being given a chance to make it again and he wasn't about to blow it. No deal, no Cabramatta, he told Con.

'Get fucked! You're a fuckin' maintenance junkie like the rest of us,' Con said. 'Guys like us need a little charlie on the job or our fucking bones start aching and our gut curls up. You're taking on some hard, fucking work, cobber. Whadda y'reckon?'

He still believed what he said to Con, that he had quit using.

'Hit me but don't shit me, cobber,' said the Greek, staring at the outside world through the ute's passenger window. 'You don't wanna do it, then lend me the green stuff. I'll pay you back, end of the month ... with interest. Right?'

'Wrong.'

'Who got ya the business? Hey? Who got ya the fuckin' business?'

The Greek got himself out to Cabramatta on the train with a wad of Denmead money.

He asked Con no questions. Didn't want a share in any of it. Not even interest on the loan. He simply wanted the Greek to understand the big 'subbie' he had grudgingly advanced him would come out of his pay packet, straight up. That was the deal. But the actual dirty deal would to be all Con's business.

Driving back up north on the Friday night after two days in Sydney spent sourcing the anti-foul paints, the varnishes, electric tools and other job requirements he found himself with an unwelcome passenger, some loser Con had met out at Cabramatta and inflicted on him. Con had bailed out, staying in Sydney over the weekend, catching up with his old mum, he said.

Catching up with his Kings Cross pals, more likely. And all he knew of the guy Con had foisted on him to share the return trip to Byron was that the dude's surname was Zemiter. Or a name like that. Con hadn't known a whole lot more about him than that when he offered the junkie the ride up to Byron aboard the new Ford ute.

A half hour short of Karuah, the silent, sullen stranger had wanted to bail out, catch up with an old girlfriend.

He pulled off the highway and let the guy out, pleased to be free of his surly presence. He was about to pull back onto the highway when the guy doubled back and banged on the window.

'Here, take this. Can't let her find this shit on me!' Zemiter was holding his set of small brass scales and a plastic bag of heroin in his hand. 'Look after them for me, mate,' he said, tucking the gear tight in under the front passenger seat. 'Catch ya Monday night at the Rails, okay?' He banged the side of the ute and was gone.

'Okay. Yeah, see ya. What the fuck!' He pulled out into the traffic flow, still cursing, little knowing he was hauling a time bomb that would explode before that Saturday night was over.

~~~

'They had to scrape me off the tarmac, the ambos

reckoned,' said Yuri, describing his accident to me. 'I was conscious most of the way up the highway to Taree. They towed the busted ute into town. The boss lady at the smash repair shop's the reason I copped the rap, the tow truck driver's wife. She was the one who found the gear. She was checking the wreck brought in to their smash repair shop when she spotted the bag and scales on the floor. Soon as she found the stuff she rang her copper mates down at the station.'

I could see he was reliving the horror of that night.

'I'm in Taree Base Hospital ... in intensive care ... when these two coppers arrive to interview me. I found out later I would have been in my right to refuse to be interviewed. I was on Planet Morphine. If I could have afforded a lawyer they would never have got near me, for sure. Or if my ex had shown any interest and been in touch with the hospital it might have made them think twice about harassing me like they did.'

Sitting in the solicitor's office, listening to Yuri tell the lawyer his story, I was angered to think he'd endured the whole sorry episode without a soul caring about him enough to protect him.

His ex-wife, a trained nurse, a hospital matron in fact, was missing in action the whole time he'd been hospitalized; not even a phone call when she was told the father of her two children had been badly smashed up down the highway. A bitter woman who forbade their fourteen-year-old son to call the hospital and have them tell his father he was thinking of him. Nothing. The boy had wanted to get on a bus and go down to Taree to be with his dad, but she forbade it. What a woman.

The police, when they came to Yuri's bedside in the intensive care unit early that following morning, claimed they had the evidence needed to arrest him.

'I was just conscious enough to know what they were talking about,' he said. 'The guy's dope and the scales under the front seat. Jesus! I hadn't put it there. I swear. It was the loser Con foisted on me. It was his gear. I never knew the guy's name. Zamita, Zemiter? He's never been seen or heard of since. Never shown his face in Byron or I'd have known about it. Con's my only chance. Doesn't know the guy's name either but he'll swear in court that there was someone else with me on that trip and it was his gear they found.'

'Con will swear in court?' I said, looking from Yuri to the lawyer. 'Get real! Con, a convicted heroin user?'

The solicitor appeared equally aghast.

'Don't you think I know?' said Yuri. 'But he's all I got, man.' He stood up and walked to the window. It was moments before he turned to us and spoke again. 'What's the use? I come with form, anyway,' he said with a shrug. 'Forget about Con. They've got my record. The L.A. bust. It happened twenty years ago but ... who's gonna believe my story, huh? Who?'

I was inclined to agree with him. It looked bad. I was already planning my life to incorporate the trips out to the coast where I'd line up for the regular visits at Long Bay. It was on days like these that I would sometimes look back with a certain fondness on my duller suburban life.

I often wondered what my fellow Beauties would think if they knew what dramas I encountered in my Byron Bay life. I only ever referred to Yuri on the show as my 'Hitchhiker'.

Zemanek repeatedly made cracks about the drug scene in Byron, joking about what he called, 'all that whacky tobacky' we supposedly smoked up in rainbow country. He would have been shocked to his conservative soul had he known how up close and personal I was with the hard stuff.

TWO MEN IN BLACK

Life can only be understood backwards;
but it must be lived forwards.
Soren Kierkegaard

Yuri O'Byrne had been a young Californian teenager during the Summer of Love when all the hippy blissfulness was rolling over the land, and when the great rock concerts were happening in his neighbourhood, Golden Gate Park.

It was marijuana. After all, what kid wouldn't have a puff at those happenings? Even Bill Clinton admitted to smoking the stuff, although the politician stopped short of saying he 'inhaled'.

By the time the teenage O'Byrne was sixteen the troops were coming home from Vietnam with heroin in their kit bags. Records show that by 1968, a third of the US deployed troops had a drug habit.

Haight Ashbury—the home of the Summer of Love, of tuning in, turning on and dropping out—was well on its way to being something different. The drug scene was hardening. Heroine, big time. Haight Ashbury was a dream turning sour under the weight of itself.

China White, the particularly pure form of heroin, was hitting the States. Some vets in the war zone had cottoned on to its popularity and were operating out of the Golden Triangle to make their fortunes, allegedly sending the heroin back in the false bottoms of military coffins.

Young men who had left their hometowns clean, were returning as addicts—or pushers—bringing the white powder back with them. Maybe they had simply been intending to spread the joy. It was early enough for a user to embrace the highs heroin offered, but not yet far enough along the road to realize at what cost. But they were getting there. According to the United States Centre of Disease Control and Prevention in October 1969, "Deaths from heroin overdoses have accelerated, doubling in just two years."

With what we know of the horrors those young men endured in the jungles of Vietnam, Laos and the borders of Cambodia—going from their childhood homes and everything familiar, to killing innocent people for an unknown cause in a hostile environment—who can be censorious about so many of them turning to a drug that gave them some escape from their nightmares?

Not me. They had seen things no nineteen-year-old should ever have to see.

An investigation by the US Congress in 1969 found that around 20% of the young men Congress had sent to the war were presently using heroin on a regular basis. One senator was moved to say that "...a soldier going to Vietnam runs a far greater risk of becoming a heroin addict than becoming a combat casualty." There was evidence to suggest that at least 40,000 veterans returned home as heroin addicts.

The twenty-two-year-old step-brother of young Yuri O'Byrne was one of them.

'We didn't even know where Vietnam was, didn't have a clue where he'd been or why he'd been fighting those people over there,' Yuri said when telling me the story. 'At first, he showed me and my friends how to snort it. 'Riding the tiger, he called it.'

Then for Yuri's sixteenth birthday, the step-brother gave him a belt and the gear and taught him how to shoot up.

The mother he adored was hopeless at the mothering game and unaware of the near and present danger for her only child. Born into Russian wealth and military power but forced to flee Russia during the Communist Revolution, she and her family were among the White Russians who settled first in Shanghai, and later in Hong Kong. The beautiful Katya Sokolov (I've seen the tiny B&W photograph) grew up in Shanghai to become an international model and jet-setting party girl who reveled in the high-flying life of the upper-crust ex-pat China clique.

At nineteen Katya married a Flying Tigers WW11 pilot, much older than his beautiful young Russian wife, but a husband who, most importantly, could provide Katya with a passport out of China.

Captain O'Byrne did not wait around for the baby to be born. He ran off with his Asian mistress and died the following year from a heart attack. Katya would eventually migrate with her parents and her six-year-old son to the United States.

By the time the boy was sixteen Katya, still a hard-living party girl, had married another five times. The step-brother who was packing the heroin was the son of her fourth husband, a gambling man and minor criminal. The fifth one—a P&O sea captain and by all accounts a decent man—Katya married twice; first time for love, second time for his generous P&O pension.

I imagine peer pressure would have been a deadly missile aimed at a teenager like Yuri O'Byrne, flushed with cash but running on empty when it came to parental guidance. It would only be a clairvoyant who could have predicted then, how profoundly his future would be affected by the step-brother's birthday gift.

~~~

Los Angeles 1970

Rising panic had him sweating. He wiped his palms on the backside of his jeans, checked his watch and continued pacing the room. The motel sign out front wasn't helping the situation. Its jittery off-on-off-on-off-on nervous neon was doing his head in.

When he crossed to the window and peered through the dusty slats into the darkness the nineteen-year-old saw only what he'd been seeing for the past two hours; the same four cars in the parking lot. Still only four; his and three others. A Dodge pick-up, an old black Cadillac and a beat-up rust bucket van, psychedelic and stacked with boards, but it didn't mean they weren't parked around the side of the motel.

He returned to the bed and laid across it, his arms behind his head, his eyes fixed on the ceiling and his mind running off with itself.

Minutes passed. Another twenty-two minutes by the watch he kept checking.

Sitting up rigid on the edge of the bed, he reached out and gulped water from a grimy tumbler and tried to ignore the god-awful sensation of a lead weight sitting in his gut. He had already used the john twice in the last ten minutes.

He mentally replayed the phone call and cursed himself again for agreeing to the deal. For being a soft touch. For winding up in this rotten downtown L.A. flea pit, waiting for a junkie to turn up. He had been a kid three years ago, a fucked-in-the-head sixteen-and-a-half-year-old, but big for his age. She pulled sodas at one of the drug stores. Every guy wanted to bed her. He had the bike. L.A. to Chicago. Route 66. The Summer of Love running out of puff, the Haight-Ashbury scene cooling off but San Francisco still the place to be if it was freedom you were looking for.

But he, an L.A. kid, yearned for the open road, and he had the bike. Chicago looked good, Chicago and back again to L.A.. Let's do it. She'd been up for the dare but a drunk pulling out from behind another car somewhere out of Flagstaff put paid to their big adventure. He copped a broken arm. She lost a pile of skin. A few scars. But she still looked good back then. Hot, in fact.

Waiting. Waiting to hand over the gear so he could be quit of her.

She had tracked him down. A pathetic junkie, a sad case. But she'd worked hard on him. Dragged up old times and, against his better judgment, won the day. Now, cursing his stupidity, he was waiting in this dog of a motel room for her to show up.

Hadn't he known the cravings, though? The tigers clawing at the inside of your veins, the violent gut cramps, the god-almighty nausea, the sweats? Yeah, he remembered the bad stuff alright, knew the pain. He had the means to help her. He still knew the beat and had the cash.

So, he had done the deal, scored good Thai white for her. But now he wanted out of this flea hole and quit of the last shreds of obligation. What did he owe her, anyway? Nothing. She had meant zip to him. Just someone to get it on with back then, just one more fellow traveler on the highway to Hell. He counted the minutes and tried blocking out the lousy premonition gnawing at his gut.

He would sure let her know this was a once-only deal.

She had conned him, got him with her pleading. Getting off it, she had whined over the phone. Yeah, aren't they all?

But she wouldn't get him the second time. He would be

long gone after this. Hasta la vista, babe. Out of Santa Monica.
Up to Sausalito, back up with the boats, the harbour and clean
air, away from all the sniveling, ratty-haired pathetic junkies.
His mother's fourth husband, Lars, the only one of Katya's
men who'd ever treated him right, the old boy had a job lined
up for him. The round-the-world sailor and ex-P&O captain
had already taught him something of how to build and repair
the fishing trawlers up there and he wanted to know more,
wanted to know it all.

Another glance at his watch. Another rerun of the phone
call.

Still time to beat it.

He could walk out the door, dump the gear in the nearest
bin and keep walking, forget he ever knew her. Get on with
the rest of his life, which he had now figured out was going to
be a good one. Learn all he could about building boats, elegant
timber ones. And one day sail them across oceans like Lars had
done. There's nothing more noble a man can do than build a
ship and go to sea. Or something like that, he remembered
Lars saying. Robert Louis Stevenson. Neat.

He reached in his back pocket for his wallet and took out
the photograph he had been carrying around since Europe for
no other reason than the old gaff-rigged girl was such a stunner
he hadn't had the heart to trash the photograph. She was
pretty. He wondered; had the Frenchman been leveling with
him about that invitation to sail her? He could work hard, save
up the fare and get back to France and test the offer, couldn't
he? He figured he had made a good impression on M.
Delafeunte. The suit and tie, his polite manners. No trace of
the sorry loser he had been before his mom dragged him away
from L.A. and took him to Europe to get him clean. The junkie
life, a life he had left behind now, a life that disgusted him

these days and the business tonight, a sad remnant.

'Just this once,' she pleaded over the phone. Obviously, she'd got the word from some low-life on the street that he was back in town. 'Just for me, baby. Just for old times. Just once. I'm hurting, man. I'm really hurting. I can work it out after this. Promise. Just this once. For baby. I'll give you a good time. You know I can. C'mon, man, I'm hurting real bad. Y'know?'

He wiped his sweating brow with the sleeve of his shirt and admired the new boots stretched out in front of him. Against the dull shag of the carpet their gleam made a nice contrast in textures. Great boots. Italian leather. He and Katya had walked Rome last month looking for just the ones he had in mind, finally finding them in a shop on the Via Candiotti, a classy establishment, all gilded mirrors and fawning old guys with ruthless comb-overs. Expensive boots, but then his mom had been up for the spend that day.

They had just come from lunch at the St Regis Hotel with her mysterious Frenchman. Katya, having enjoyed the opulence of the grand hotel, and with three hours of M. Delafeunte's fawning and expensive champagne aboard would have bought him a Maserati that afternoon if he'd asked for one. He had settled, however, for his passion; the soft cushiony brown leather boots by Ferragamo.

'A true Russian doll,' the Frenchman whispered in his ear after Katya had risen and walked off to the bathroom, using her shapely figure, the tight skirt and red stilettos to put it out for every male in the restaurant, while leaving her son sitting awkwardly at the table with the stranger, aware of yet another of Katya's incorrigible performances. She had bathed in the Frenchman's flattery that afternoon, flirtatious all through lunch, confident in her mature European beauty.

'*Merveilleux, votre mere.* Such a wonderful girl,' the man said as his eyes followed Katya's disappearing body. He did the French thing; kissing the tips of his fingers and rolling his eyes. '*Magnifique!*'

When M. Delafeunte excused himself and went off to kiss the proffered hands of two painted old dowagers at a nearby table, he had taken the opportunity to study the refined gentleman. Very European, his summing up of the light coloured trousers, the dark navy blazer with its gold buttons, and the maroon cravat. The gold ring and bracelet, something he had never seen on a male before, certainly not back home, gave M. Delafeunte a look of otherness.

He couldn't nail it any better than that. An 'Otherness'. And yet, strangely, he felt drawn to the stranger who was having such a profound effect on his ditzy mother.

Thinking about the way the Frenchman's eyes lit up when he and Katya had first walked into the hotel, and the smouldering looks across the table the pair gave each other throughout lunch, he had guessed that M. Delafeunte must have been part of his mother's wild, party girl life back in Shanghai and Hong Kong. One of her old 'beaux' as she liked to say.

No doubt the young Delafeunte would have cut a neat path through the international jet-setting scene his mother endlessly raved on about, couldn't forget about, certainly couldn't leave behind in her mind. Such a history between the pair would explain why she'd been so excited about the lunch, the reason she had shopped for a special outfit to wear and why she had taken hours back in their hotel room to get herself ready, fussing about her dress and jewellery like a giddy teenager.

'Cosmopolitan' was the word he had finally settled on to sum up M. Delafeunte. Elegant attire, thick greying moustache, olive complexion and hair almost as black as his own, touched up by the bottle, he concluded.

But the dark heavy-lidded eyes. He had noticed those eyes, especially. They had not only lingered long and hard on his mother, M. Delafeunte's eyes had lingered almost as long on him, a thing that had made him uncomfortable, forcing him to either look down at his plate or stare off into the distance to avoid the scrutiny when he caught the old boy looking at him.

'Your mother,' said the Frenchman when he returned from kissing the two women and had settle back at their table. 'Katya ... ah, yes, she tells me that you are a sailor, no?' M. Delafeunte produced his wallet and from it, a photograph which he passed across the table. '*Magnifique!*' Again, a kiss to the tips of his fingers. Women and ships.

A beautiful vessel. He had been impressed. A classic gentleman's yacht of the 1930's, a type he knew had been, and still was, famous around the Mediterranean. He looked from the photograph back up into the hard gaze of the man, feeling tongue-tied, not knowing what he was expected to say other than that the gentleman had himself a fine boat. He was racking his brain in an attempt to identify the design, something beyond a cliché to say in response to this French dude.

'Alfred Milne. The designer,' said M. Delafeunte. 'In your American measurement; Length 105 feet. Waterline 72 feet. Beam 20 feet–'

'And a 12-foot draft?'

M. Delafeunte smiled and nodded his head. 'Maybe one day you will come back. Take the helm, hmm? Sail our Mediterranean waters, no?'

He made to hand back the photograph but M. Delafeunte pushed it towards him again, patting the top of his hand and holding it there a moment longer than felt comfortable.

'Please, you will keep the photograph. *Tres magnifique*, no?'

'She is a very pretty sloop, sir. M. Delafeunte.'

He had slipped the photograph into his wallet, asking himself what good a lousy photograph? 'Thank you, sir.' But when he had looked back up at the Frenchman he saw something he hadn't expected to see. The old guy had teared up, his eyes red and moist. He turned and looked behind him, to where his mom had disappeared. He hoped she wouldn't take forever touching up her face and hair.

At first, it hadn't been clear to him why his mother had dragged him along on her special date that day in Rome but at some stage through the lunch he had figured it out: She wanted to show her son that she hadn't always been involved with bums and losers. Hadn't always hooked up with gamblers and con men, some of the guys he had had to cop as fathers while growing up.

It hadn't been the perfect upbringing, being the neglected son of a much-married lush. Many times, even as a small child, he had been woken in the early hours of the morning to the sounds of his mother's retching, finding her with her head in the john bringing up party stuff. He would wash her face with cold cloths, strip off her soiled dress and put her to bed in her underwear between clean sheets then get himself off to school later in the morning.

But always, he had looked forward to coming home to Katya. Exotic Katya. His adored mother. And he knew that through it all, the many husbands, the lovers, the neglect, he understood that she loved him best, the one he loved beyond words.

He got up and looked through the window again, checked the cars in the lot then came back to the bed. He was about to replace the photograph in his wallet when the tap on the door startled him. He ran to the window and parted the slats.

She was at the door. He checked the parking lot. Four parked cars, still. She must have been dropped off. Too bad. She wasn't going back with him. He would leave her here, leave her to get on in this dump. One more stoned loser.

He dug into his pocket for the gear. No charge. A gift. That much he felt he should do for old times' sake. A gram and a half he hoped would satisfy her habit long enough for him to quit town. As sure as he knew his own name, he knew if he stuck around she would keep getting to him and he dreaded the possibilities, dreaded being sucked in to that hell hole again.

He moved across to the door, his intention being to hand her the junk and walk straight out and not look back. He opened the door. Stood rigid as his eyes scoped the territory behind her.

She took his face in her hands and tried to plant a kiss on his lips. Fierce in his dismissal of her, he pushed her from him and wiped away the kiss. She brushed past him and walked into the room.

It came as a shock. She looked even more of a mess than he had imagined she would after these years on the game. Twenty-one and wild when they hooked up three years ago, now she looked like every other junkie; skanky, defeated, used-up. He had just tasted the sourness of her breath, smelled her body. She was stale. Man, she was stale. Had she got off the stuff, been lucky like him and had an old lady who took you to Europe for a couple of months to get you clean she would have still looked sensational, he figured. But instead, she had stuck with the smack, gone bad.

He took in the whole sorry picture; the pallor of her skin,

yellow, leathered, her hair, once her pride and joy, was lank, its colour anybody's guess. Somewhere between dull and putrid.

She sat fidgety on the edge of the bed, foot tapping, a creature to pity but he felt nothing other than a sense that he had done what she had pleaded with him to do and now he was about to be quit of her. Neither could say anything of any consequence. What did they have to say? He resented what she had asked of him and for her part, she only wanted this one thing from him. No joy, there. He watched as she tugged the belt from her jeans and, with the syringe already between her teeth, stuck her hand out for the dope.

'Enjoy,' he said as he tossed it to her.

They wore black suits, the two men who came bursting into the room yelling and flashing FBI badges, the big one slapping the cuffs on him, shoving him out the door.

He looked over his shoulder just as the door slammed behind him. She would waste no time in getting it on. He copped another shove from one of the narcs and stumbled forward down the motel steps. Move it asshole, shouted the FBI guy, and he saw that the motel sign was still doing its thing, but it would be the least of his worries tonight.

They pushed his head down and shoved him onto the back seat of the vehicle. Just like on TV. And just like on TV, he understood he had been set up. What he had suspected, feared from the get-go, had just happened back in there. She had done a deal to save her own neck. Served him up to them on a platter. The lying cunt.

So much for kindness. Only days short of his twentieth birthday. What would his old lady say? This would fuck things up, fuck things up big time.

He sat staring out the window as the black & white drove out of the parking lot and turned onto the highway, taking him to God knows where and for God knows how long. And now he remembered that in his panic he had left the photograph of the sloop sitting on the bed back at the motel and it struck him he hadn't got around to asking M. Delafeunte that day in Paris the name of his yacht. No matter, he figured, he wouldn't be heading off to the Mediterranean any time soon.

The dice had been tossed.

~~~

Had he never taken the junkie's phone call that night, Yuri probably would have lived the rest of his life as a United States citizen. But he was to become an exile, a man with no country. America's loss would be my gain, I often laughed. Life is weird.

Despite being clean when he faced the L.A. County Court, the twenty-year-old Yuri O'Byrne was ordered to undertake rehab as part of the plea deal. Better than the three years they could have thrown at him.

But his passport was current, and Mom had bought her precious son a plane ticket to Australia—a place neither of them had ever thought about other than believing it to be the furthest place on the planet from California. Katya figured it would be a fine place to hide her boy from the law.

She arranged everything. At her urging, he jumped the bus taking him to the drug rehabilitation unit. She hurried him off to the airport. He was up, up and away.

~~~

By following him out to Australia two weeks later, however, the doting Katya lead the FBI straight to where her son was working as a builder's labourer at a construction site in Coogee. He was locked up in Long Bay's remand centre while the FBI processed extradition orders.

Unlike the L.A. agents, the FBI men sent out to Australia to take him back to the States were decent types, according to

Yuri. The two men acknowledged on the QT that he had been set up by their colleagues that night in L.A.. Both FBI men assured him that if he returned to the States and pleaded entrapment he would doubtless get off, but neither agent put up an argument when the lawyer Katya engaged to defend her son pointed out at the court hearing in Sydney that Mr. O'Byrne already had his get-out-of-jail card and could not be sent back to face trial because Californian Governor Ronald Reagan's extradition orders were invalid.

Reagan had signed all but one of the documents. The final document had received only a stamped gubernatorial signature, a legal technicality but enough for the two FBI men to slap young Yuri O'Byrne on the back, wish him well in his new country and disappear, not taking up the magistrate's invitation to wait around for a valid set of documents to be flown in. The miscreant was allowed to go free.

However, he would never be allowed to set foot in the United States again. If he did, he would be arrested.

At an age when the cause-and-effect mechanism of his brain was still a work in progress, where the frontal lobe responsible for judgment and decision-making was still developing, Yuri O'Byrne made a bad decision. Egged on by a doting mother—who no doubt felt some guilt for all the years of neglect—he jumped the bus and did a runner. It must have seemed like a great idea at the time, but it would mean living out the rest of his life cut off from his home, his country, and the mother he idolized.

Bad things happen to good people.

BANDA ISLES

Wi' lithesome heart I pu'd a rose
Frae off its thorny tree,
And my fause luver staw my rose,
But left the thorn wi' me.
Robbie Burns

It's the dawn of the Seventies. Cue me as a busy suburban mum, her hands full rearing five young children and contemplating a university degree if she can ever cut loose from the shitty nappies and school lunches that are her present lot.

Elsewhere, up in the rolling hills of the Byron hinterland a couple of young hopefuls are just starting out as farmers.

Cue in Yuri and his bride. They had recently purchased from their Channon neighbour a small section of his holding. Flashing two thousand dollars—the total of their savings—the old man had been happy to accept their deposit and finance the balance, interest free. The asking price had only been eight thousand dollars after all, but a fortune to the honeymooners settling down after their big South Sea sailing adventure.

It was an act of faith on the part of the old farmer to take a gamble on a pair of complete novices with only the shirts on their backs as surety for the loan. And in their first year, when they were finding it a stretch to set up the farm as well as meet the monthly repayments, their neighbour still believed in them. According to Yuri, they were so broke at times that they resorted to all kinds of means to get by, one of which was to place blankets under the olive trees on their property and shake out the ticks, gather them in jars and sell them to the pharmacies and vets down in Mullumbimby and Byron.

It was not long before the young farmers purchased more of the old man's land. And more, again.

They were good for the place, working hard to clear the run-down banana plantation and get it going again. Although they fell behind in their repayment plan, they improved things, rejuvenated the plantation after its years of neglect, got rid of the noxious weeds and set up a production line, Yuri digging out the suckers from the base of the banana stools and his young wife, with her machete, working with the bulbs, hacking four or five sections from a large bulb then trimming the roots of each section before putting them in the bags for him to gather.

Fifty to a bag. Going at it from sun-up to sun-down, and often by the light of hurricane lamps, the two of them out in the shed with the bulbs seven days of the week, filling each day's orders until there was only three and a half thousand dollars left owing on the property, and they were ready to buy the even bigger property up at Wilsons Creek.

Their business was tough but rewarding, and harvesting the suckers was an important part of their expanding business. There were farmers, not only all over the north coast, but even across to Western Australia, where growers were ready to take whatever cuttings Yuri could provide.

It was the same story with their fruit. They had orders to fill. Big orders. The vegetable co-op down in Mullumbimby was taking all the bananas they could deliver. Their bananas, unlike any of the others in the district were organic and the market for organic was just taking off. Again, even over in

West Australia they found a market for their organic specialty.

By the time both children were at school, however, the wife was resenting being stuck in the back woods. She was over the hardships of rural life. She had harvested banana crops even while heavily pregnant, working alongside her young husband as helpmate to create a viable enterprise.

She was a nymph who ran naked down to the rainbow creek on their hinterland property with her husband and babies to swim beneath their own special waterfall. And she was the wild young thing who danced all night under a harvest moon in the local community hall and wandered home under that full moon to a tiny cabin up in the hills behind Byron, no power, no running water but a husband-lover with a slow hand who took all the time in the world to pleasure her.

But she had grown tired of the husband and of the life. To turn a derelict plantation into a thriving organic one had been their dream, but by the time it was a reality the wife was wanting to come down from the hills.

It was at this time that Yuri considered buying the Alcorn Street property, the one I would purchase one crazy day in the future.

Instead, he bought thirty-five acres of prime headland around at Broken Head, installed his wife and two young children in a makeshift cabin on the property, and started planning something much grander. He also invested in a mobile timber mill and employed upwards of half a dozen big strong men like himself to work it with him. They were exhausting days, but ones filled with promise.

The house on the headland sounded sensational in the telling. His own design, he envisaged it being part-buried into the the hill, with huge wrap-around windows open to the Pacific, because by now it was the wide blue ocean that was calling him. Time had moved on. He was over the tough work of taming the headland and starting construction, all in the limited time he had after the long drives each day up into the Whian-Whian State forest and the arduous work entailed in running his mill, using his timber cutter's licence to drag the huge fallen trees out of the forest.

His dream by now, the thing he wanted above all else, was to buy a sailing boat and take his family to sea. It was the life he wanted for his children.

Meantime, the O'Byrnes were doing it the hard way, living in the small make-shift hut on the Broken Head headland while he started constructing the foundations for the main house, and running the mill.

The doctor was the first of the boyfriends. There was a lawyer who, against the ethics of his profession, represented her in the divorce process.

'I called in on her one night,' he said. '...at the house that she and the kids had moved into, and the guy was there, his feet up on the coffee table, the one I'd made.'

'She kept asking for more and more,' he said. 'She wanted our Broken Head property sold. It broke my heart, but I sold it. She wanted the cash. I gave it to her. She wanted the big four-wheel drive. I gave it to her. And all the time, the lawyer boyfriend was urging her on, telling her to threaten me that she'd take the kids to Melbourne where her parents lived unless I gave in to her. She used my love for our kids to blackmail me out of everything. It was me who'd done most of the parenting. I used to carry them in a sling on my chest when they were little while I'd be working in the paddocks. I fed them, bathed them, played with them and was the one who read to them at bedtime. It was me who picked them up from school most afternoons, along with a bunch of the other kids whose hippy parents up in those hills were often too stoned to remember that school was out.'

As a postscript to this story, the thirty-five acres of prime land he was forced to sell in the divorce settlement would eventually be broken up into large lots and devoured, with their multi-million-dollar price tags, by the rich and famous, some of whom were Hollywood blow-ins.

These days, you can't step outside your front door around at that headland without bumping into a celebrity musician or actor.

I was sitting in a Byron cafe one day with Yuri when a woman called Margaret from First National Real Estate, who had sold his property for him at the time, came over and whispered in his ear the kind of sensational prices she was getting for 'his place' these days.

~~~

It was a typically beautiful Byron Bay Saturday morning, sunshine and rainbows caressing Mother Earth; at least it was caressing our part of it. And this was a special day for Yuri. It was his daughter Chloe's wedding day.

A few days prior, his son, Cedar had dropped by to let his father know that his sister was going to marry the young man who had fathered her baby. And then he had come back again the following day with a message from his mother saying that Yuri was not to attend the wedding.

Not under any circumstances.

His precious daughter's wedding, and he was not only left off the invitation list, but was being ordered by his former wife not to come anywhere near the event.

One of our earliest conversations when Yuri and I first met was about how he had assisted at the birth of his two children. It had been strange for me to hear a man talk so tenderly about

what I'd thought of as secret women's business, describing
unselfconsciously his emotional response to the miracle of
birth. The order not to be with his only daughter on her
wedding day hurt me, and I can only guess at how much it
must have devastated Yuri, a man not given to showing his
emotions but more than capable of registering emotional pain.

'I'll stay out of sight, down the back of the church,' he said
to his son who was obviously embarrassed having to pass on
such a callous message to his father.

Unlike his sister, the youth had resisted his mother's bad-
mouthing of their father in recent times. He was an intelligent
young man, a handsome, lanky, blonde laid-back surfer
kid—the archetypal Byron Bay youngster who would go on
one day to be a talented musician, the base player in his local
Byron Bay band.

Yuri was sure he could squeeze in an un-noticed appearance
at the wedding. And he let it be known he would not
embarrass his daughter by being anything but respectful.

On this Saturday morning, he had already taken his early
dip in the surf, showered, shaved, tied his dark hair back in a
pony-tail, and enjoyed a breakfast of muesli, fruit and yoghurt.
He had purchased a suit and tie for the occasion—ironically,
for this, *and* for his up-coming court appearance. While down
in Sydney, I had scored a pair of good black Bally shoes from
my ex to compliment the wedding weeds.

Come the morning of the nuptials, the father of the bride
was almost unrecognizable. Despite the shoes pinching him,
the tie choking him and the suit jacket tight across his biceps,
he was one happy dad.

Happy, if a little concerned. He laid the responsibility for
their young daughter getting pregnant at his ex-wife's feet, and
being only human, I guess there was a sense of schadenfreude

on his part, given the history of the marriage break-up and the unfair custody arrangements the court, at the wife's request, had imposed.

When the issue was dealt with in the Family Court, the wife had failed to notify her ex of the date of the hearing so that he could fly down from the Whitsundays where he was working. She misled the court, saying that Yuri was in Thailand, implying he was there to purchase heroin.

It was a total lie.

As a family man, working his farms and his mobile timber mill, he had stayed 'healthy'—a term he used to describe his heroin-free condition—for the fifteen years of the marriage. It had only been with the marriage breakup, and the separation from his children that saw him relapse.

The fall off the wagon occurred when he was up on the Whitsundays working as chief carpenter for Keith Williams who owned Hamilton Island. In his spare time, he was refurbishing the local doctor's timber cruiser. The cunning—and I would say 'despicable'—doctor read the signs, would have seen those purple train tracks inside Yuri's elbow, and instead of paying in cash for the work, he offered his shipwright powerful opiates as remuneration.

He did this, according to Yuri, by leaving his medical case enticingly open on the boat's deck one day, in full view. Being by now, an empty man who pined for his kids, it was too easy for the one-time addict to succumb to the doctor's challenge. Easy to forget the pain.

It was downhill from there. He became what he called, "a fully-functioning maintenance junkie". He was a man who held down a solid job but who, if his Physeptone medication wasn't at hand, needed heroin, not to get high but to get relief from his knee and his back pains in order to keep working.

And now, on this lovely Saturday Byron Bay morning, having taken his Physeptone medication, he was all kitted up and ready to go off to church, to sit down the back unobtrusively and witness the marriage of his daughter.

I made herbal tea for him, hoping to calm his anxiety, and he was still sipping it when we saw the two men in dinner jackets walking down the front yard and coming towards the teahouse.

Yuri knew at once who they were. They were his former brothers-in-law.

'I know why they've come,' he said, already loosening his tie and throwing off his jacket.

And he was right. The pair had come to make certain he stayed away.

I have a loving family. We care for each other. I cannot for the life of me understand people as vicious as the ex-wife and her people. Or as weak-willed as their daughter who let the hurt happen. It must be Hell to live with such black hearts.

I took Yuri in my arms to comfort him, but my overtures were rejected. I understood he had gone to a dark place, a place where he needed to be alone with sweeter memories than this day would ever provide.

~~~

The moment he came through the door I could see it. He was stoned. He and Con had said they had to see a man about timber. It was after midnight. They had been gone three hours.

'Been having a good time, have we?' I said. I was furious. 'A lot of timber talk, hey?'

He tossed his canvas bag on the couch. 'How y'doin'?' He was carrying a long rolled up document under his arm and he hit me playfully on the rump with the scroll. 'Wait till you see this.' He was as high as the moon over Cape Byron lighthouse.

'Our boat, the plans for our boat, me salty ol' mate.' He grinned. 'This guy up at Federal give me the plans.'

It was the heroin talking, again. I wondered what tonight had cost me. I walked out onto the veranda to cool my anger. 'There's no way we'll be starting from scratch to build a yacht. No way,' I called after him.

'Wait till you see this,' he said. 'Come here. Give us a minute. Come on, pal.'

He stood at the table, spreading out the boat drawings. The man collected these charts like others collected memorial spoons. Every week, a new idea, another design, plans for a timber yacht he knew would be just right for us. He understood the intricacies of naval charts, I'll give him that. And celestial navigation and logarithms, as well. He was an intelligent man whom heroin transported to fantasyland. An intriguing enigma.

'Sail pathless and wild seas, remember? Pathless and wild seas, you and me! You'll write your articles, I'll work on boats. We'll make enough to get by. She's a British pilot cutter. Only sixty-four of these ... in timber ... ever built.'

He tapped the plans he had laid out.

'Man, the rest of our lives just cruising the world. Starting with the Banda Isles. What a way to go, hey? The Bandas? Guitar, me. You can learn the air pipes. You're poetic, anyway. You can write lyrics. Nothing but sea, sky and music. It's gonna be the best life. Like the Pardys. The things we're gonna do and see, I promise you!'

It came gushing out of him like water out of a busted mains pipe, his devotion to his yacht plans, and the life he envisaged for the pair of us. Lynne and Larry Pardy, a middle-aged Canadian couple, wrote prolifically about their life as a long-time cruising couple. We had their videos that demonstrated what a glorious life the pair experienced cruising the world on their beautiful old classic timber yacht, *Taliesin*.

It seemed an idyllic life. If Lynne and Larry could do it, so could Jan and Yuri. Right?

The Banda Isles held a special fascination for Yuri. Once we'd purchased our boat, fitted her out and were under sail it was where he wanted to take me first. And particularly a small island called Sumba. The rug he had brought with him when we began living together, and which he kept in his sea chest, was from Sumba. He had even called the family's dog Sumba, a dog long dead who still wandered beside him in his dreams, apparently.

I was fascinated when he told me the story of his honeymoon adventure on Sumba. As ever, when he set forth to tell me bits and pieces of his life story—with the Californian accent that so charmed me—he could colour in the settings and fill them with interesting characters. In this story of Sumba in 1972 he had me dreaming about the exciting horizon just beyond our present days.

On his honeymoon, crewing aboard a fifty-foot cruiser heading for Indonesia, the disabled yacht ran out of supplies. They were down to apportioning sultanas between five crew members by the time land hove into view. The adventurous honeymooners bailed out on the remote island where the local postman befriended them.

One day he spirited the pair off to the interior. From the top of a hill, in secrecy, they witnessed a weird ceremony going on below. It was the burial of the tribal chief, the Rajah, complete with wailing virgins and offerings to the gods, including the horrible slaughter of the chief's white stallion, which was to be interred with him.

The honeymooners were intruders, foreigners who shouldn't have witnessed the primitive all-day ritual. No wonder Sumba left a deep impression on him.

'Okay. Let's see what you've got in those plans, sailor boy' I said, carrying my tea cup over to the table and dropping a kiss on his neck.

It was useless to stay mad at the man. The money was running out, but life was good.

A MILLION BUTTERFLIES

The host with someone indistinct
Converses at the door apart...
T S Eliot

Candlelight illuminated the room. A warm glow blessed everything, especially the golden bamboo walls. Sitar music played softly in the background, and the air smelled sweet with patchouli. This was our lovely *Teahouse of the Splendid Moon* around midnight.

Earlier in the evening I had cleared the mess on the veranda, including our noodle bowls, an empty bottle of Petaluma, a couple of burned-down incense sticks, and the tail end of the joint Yuri had rolled earlier in the evening. Afterwards, we lay on our backs on the veranda boards, watching the moon glide overhead, undisturbed when one of our pet pythons slithered past. Or maybe it hadn't. Maybe we imagined that part of the beautiful evening.

We were possibly still a little high when the intrusion came, but maybe not. Certainly, we were happy. Who wouldn't be?

Yuri, in his traditional sarong and bare chest, sat at the table—and as was his way when he was happy—was pouring over his future yacht plans. I had just finished scribbling some notes for a scene for the script Phil Avalon still wanted. I was at the fridge—also in my sarong because it was a steamy hot night—dropping ice cubes into our White Russians.

It was about then when I heard the tinkling noise of the

wind chimes outside.

And then the tinkling stopped abruptly.

Too abruptly.

Instinctively, I felt something was amiss out there in the dark. It hadn't been the gentle rustling noise you would expect when wind stirs the bells. They had tinkled as though knocked, and then they had suddenly stopped tinkling. Someone had accidentally bumped into them, and was holding them, not wanting us to know they were out there.

I put down the glasses and crept across to one of the windows that looked out onto the veranda.

At first, I could see nothing but blackness. The moon had gone under clouds and the night was dark. And then I saw the silhouette of two male figures, their backs to me as they scurried down the veranda steps.

I flicked the switch for the outside veranda light. 'Sorry. Can I help you?'

The two figures on the step, now fully illuminated, propped and looked around at me. Both appeared as comical players in a B-grade movie. Both were big men, both wore bright floral Hawaiian shirts and khaki shorts and sandals. One man had a camera draped around his neck. These weren't drug customers of the previous owner looking to score, as I'd half expected. This pair looked like tourist straight out of Central Casting.

'Yes?' I said.

'Ah ... we're looking for Bernie. We've just driven up from Sydney,' said one of the men.

'This is Bernie's place, right?' said the other.

I turned to Yuri. He was still seated, his back to us, and hadn't lifted his eyes from his charts. I turned back to the strangers and shrugged. 'Sorry. Can't help you. No one by that name lives here.' I was about to slide the door shut and lock it when Yuri piped up.

'Go down the end of Alcorn,' he called out to them. 'You'll see a lane on your left.' His head was still bent over his work as he ran his slide rule across the parchment. 'Can't miss it.'

He turned and faced the intruders, a congenial smile lighting his face. 'There's a yellow house on the corner. Go down that lane and at the end there's a tin shed on your right. You have to go in behind the shed and walk about another fifty yards up through shrubbery to a row of houses. Look out for the Rottweiler. You'll see Bernie's when you get there. It's the one with the green door. Say hello to ol' Bernie for me, will you?'

The 'tourist' wearing the camera bristled and started towards Yuri but the other pulled him back by his shirt, and together they left the veranda and started around the side of the teahouse.

I hurried to the other side of the room and stood looking out the kitchen window to make certain the strangers were leaving the yard. When I saw them under the street light, and saw them get into a car parked there, I turned to Yuri. 'Bernie's place? A green door? What the Hell was all that about?'

'Undercover cops.'

'Undercover cops?' I was stunned. 'Why? What the hell were they doing here?'

'What do you reckon? They were sneaking up on us. Hoping to catch us out. I'm on charges, reporting every Tuesday around at the cop shop. What do you reckon? They'd hoped to bust me.'

I was rocked. This was getting serious.

Yuri went back to his charts. 'Come to think of it, I might be wrong. It's probably about you and your mate ... all that "whacky tobacky" nonsense he goes on about. They'd be onto you, don't worry. The ex-wife of a politician and a lefty TV celebrity who mouths off? You'd be a notch in their belt.'

On *Beauty and the Beast* I'd often aired my views on what I believed was wrong with the federal government's zero tolerance policy. Heroin is a medical issue, not a criminal one—was—and is, my contention. And on cannabis, I accused all our politicians of gross hypocrisy for not decriminalizing it while continuing to reap massive excises on the other vices; tobacco, gambling and alcohol. All addictive and dangerous and more insidious than smoking a bit of naturally grown marihuana. 'If God grows it, we can smoke it,' was my mantra.

Apparently, I was also in the crosshairs of the law. We were a subversive couple, me and my wayward hitchhiker. Little wonder the law was checking up on us.

The night had just put its laughter away.

~~~

Phil Avalon was waiting for me to deliver the *Claudia Christiana* screenplay. I still had plenty of work to do on it. But I had set it aside to work on a first draft of the novel I'd decided to write, using material gathered since meeting Yuri. I believed his life experiences were rich pickings for a novelist and had been keeping notes in my journal, appreciating there were characters, settings and stories I could work up.

There was Katya's glamorous life in Shanghai; Yuri's wild teenage years in California; his Russian grandfather who had been a high-ranking Cossack general in the Tsar's army, aide-de-camp to the Tsarina, a man who in old-age worked as a janitor in San Francisco stoking the furnaces; Yuri's life as a sailor; as a banana farmer; as a timber mill owner in the Byron Bay district; and of course, the heroin story.

It would be more than a decade, however, before I had a novel published and it would have nothing to do with Yuri

O'Byrne.

It would be the story I adapted from my 1991 screenplay, the project that never quite made it, despite the grind, the expense and the heartache.

Goodbye Lullaby is the novelised version of that screenplay, a story set in the Vietnam era exploring the infamous Birthday Lottery, and the forced adoptions of the Fifties, as well as the cruelty of the so-called Aboriginal Protection Board during those years.

I had worried about these issues for a long time and had written my screenplay years before forced adoptions or the stolen generation issues became part of our national conversation. I dreamed back when I was trying to get my film funded that it would help to highlight the disgrace of our past.

Unfortunately for my dreams of being a prophet, I was never able to stitch together the five-million-dollar budget for the project, and it would be many years into the future before our leaders stood up in Parliament and apologized for the way the state had intervened between mothers and their children; namely, as in my story, the forced adoptions of the past and the Stolen Generation. And, also in my story, a third way; conscription.

This morning, we were working out of the big garage at the front of the property, Yuri at his work bench, me over in the corner pounding away on my old Olivetti. We were finally making use of the extra space the ugly triple garage offered; Yuri as a workshop where he created miniature figurine carvings—netsuke, a Japanese art, and for myself, I fancied the space as an office. Around at the local industrial centre we had scrounged a decent oak dining table and a small set of filing draws, enough that I could call a corner of the garage my writing nook.

'What are you doing?' Yuri asked.

'I don't know. When I do, I tell you.' I waved a dismissive hand over my shoulder as I bashed away at the keys.

Too curt, but the sudden awareness of another's presence had jolted me back into the here-and-now and when that happens, when I've been lost in my own world of images and words, it can be troublesome spiralling back up into real time; at least, in a gracious manner.

Yuri pivoted on his stool and held his work up to show me.

It was lovely. I gave it a cursory thumbs-up. My soulmate was planning to produce a collection of jewelry pieces and netsuke from his collection of whales' teeth, stones and shells, the plan being that as we cruised the Pacific, he could earn money when we pulled into ports by spreading a black velvet cloth on the deck and displaying his artistic pieces for sale.

He was also a scrimshaw artist—that traditional skill of sailors—and had some elegant pieces in his collection. My contribution to sustaining us during our cruising life would be my writing for boating magazines, articles about sailing and our experiences in ports.

From this distance today, when I'm no longer plagued by a bi-polar mental illness that tends to distort reality, our business plan looks naïve in the extreme, to the point of embarrassment, but it—and our tiki bar set among swaying palms on distant white sands—was at the heart of our relationship, our *Ultima Thule*, our north star, and it shone bright for many years.

Yuri passed across two Maori tiki tokens he had carved from his jade collection and threaded onto leather strings early in the day. 'Like them?'

'I love them. They're great. They'll sell.'

I laid the pendants across the small coffee table he had

crafted from tamarind wood, a brilliant yellow timber, creating it from his own design to reflect the Asian look of the teahouse. I blew him a kiss and went back to my writing.

'A Russian?' he asked.

'Love one.'

I turned from the Olivetti and watched him leave the shed, observing that odd gait of his that I had first noticed the morning down in Yamba when we said goodbye to each other, believing it was all over, believing that his habit had destroyed our chance of happiness. I ripped my pages from the typewriter and stuck them in the filing cabinet. The surf was calling down beyond the dunes. And a cool White Russian.

Along the way, as I headed down to the teahouse, I yanked out some of the rapacious vines strangling the native trees. It was a pastime that gave me great pleasure. You pull and pull. It's energizing work. The vines are never-ending, they just keep on coming away in your hands, so much verbiage entwined around the poor struggling ti-trees, banksias and tuckeroos.

In Byron's lush climate, these villains practically grow while you watch. Yuri was pulling at them one day and was bitten by a funnel web spider, which sprang at his wrist. I wasn't home. He called a cab but when the driver found out his anxious passenger had jumped in the cab without his wallet, he dropped him off at the corner. Yuri walked back home, poured a White Russian and lived to tell the tale. No wonder we liked the cocktail.

On this morning, as I busied myself freeing up the native plants from others that would strive to strangle them, I uncovered an amazing creature: An albino snake, possibly a baby one, a sickly pale pinkish, almost transparent, white thing.

Yuk. Ugly to the extreme.

I was about to yell for Yuri to come and look at it when it slithered out of sight. I can still see the weird reptile in my mind's eye today, and a search of Google shows that the creatures are rare and valuable. But I can't help thinking that the over-population and commercial expansion of Byron Bay these days has cleared the district of its exotic flora and fauna. Even the rapacious vines. Nothing that untoward would be permitted to exist in the now-sanitized rainbow district.

Despite albino pythons and funnel web spiders, I worked daily at the vicious vines, aware I would probably never get the better of them. But as I pulled at the greenery this day, I reflected on my life in the Bay and knew it was a good one. I was the luckiest woman alive. What could be better than this? I had my gypsy man, I had our *Teahouse of the Splendid Moon*, I had a couple of interesting writing challenges, and at least every second week I would get a phone call from Annie O'Brien, the producer of *Beauty and the Beast*, inviting me to be on the panel that week.

Eventually, as my fan base grew, I would become a regular, recording three or four shows a week most weeks, but while consolidating my life in Byron, I was happy to have what was on offer.

I loved my rainbow life. The locals were friendly, Mother Nature blessed the landscape, and whenever the whim took me, I could go sit on the sandy dunes out front and either hail a new sunrise over the Pacific or dive into said Pacific on the tide.

We could hike Mount Warning or go for a drive over the stunning Burringbar Ranges. On summer nights, we often packed a picnic and drove to nearby Brunswick Heads and sometimes beyond, to South Golden Beach where we slept under the stars—until the mosquitos and sandflies sent us scurrying for cover.

Mullumbimby's Friday fresh food markets were a delight. As was the hippy-trippy arts and crafts one up in the Channon.

Going south there was Bangalow and the pub on the rise where we could grab a delicious meal of grilled fish and salad and wash it down with a beer while we sat out on the deck overlooking the rainforest gully. Or there was the option to take a drive out to the place Paul Hogan had made famous, Possum Creek.

We could drive to Mullumbimby and watch the late afternoon sun set behind Mount Chincogan. Or explore the hinterland villages of Wilsons Creek, Rosebank, Dunoon, Clunes, the Pocket, Main Arm, Federal, and always Yuri would have a story to relate about these places and the characters he'd known who had once inhabited them in the Seventies and Eighties when he and his family lived in the hinterland. Whenever I listen to Neil Young's *Harvest Moon*, I'm reminded of the stories, and I get a yearning to be there in those communities of the alternative folk of yesteryear.

It is a magic part of the world, the rainbow country; the Whian-Whian state forest, Tuntable Creek, the Channon, Terania Creek, Nightcap Mountain, Nimbin, Kyogle, Huonbrook, Binna Burra, and of course, the majestic beauty of the Minyon Falls. All ours.

One time, we took a few days away from Byron and our labours to drive down the coast to a hidden beauty Yuri knew about, an isolated place that out of pure superstition I won't even name here, only to hint that it is close to another idyllic location famous for its oysters, the food of Aphrodite.

I want it always to be the remote, white sandy beach hideaway, deep in the Yuraygir National Park that will always linger in my memory as our special place.

We erected our two-person tent on the river sands and, from there, set out each morning—after a dip in the placid waters and a breakfast fry-up cooked on our camp fire—to try and spot Yellow-tailed Black Cockatoos or the rarer Glossy Black Cockatoo. We found that the area teemed with wildlife, being able to thrive in the isolation of that magic place. Shhhhh! Forget I mentioned it.

It is a fact, I left little of the district unexplored. I was up for the full thrill, having relocated my life to this part of the universe, and having a native of the area to guide me was a bonus. On a more pragmatic level, I loved the place because in the Nineties Byron's traffic was still manageable. I could pull up out front of my bank or park on Main Beach or Wategos without putting money in a meter. Go for a dip in the surf. Rest a while on a beach towel. Take a hike along the beach. All without the worry of being booked.

It seemed there was always music in Byron Bay—especially there was music on a Friday and Saturday night at the Rails Friendly Bar and at the Top Pub. It was all new to me. Music came out of stereo players.

I remember one Sunday afternoon at the little bush pub at Billinugel—one of our favourite weekend haunts—when, as usual, there was an open mic. Musicians of all stripes were getting up on stage and jamming with the local band, wailing their mournful blues tunes, giving us their Janis Joplin impersonations, generally showing off and accepting their dues from us merry pranksters. Then, up stood one extremely elderly, thin, crooked little character in flannies and daggy shorts and shuffled onto the dais.

Just as I was starting to feel embarrassed for the poor man, believing he was about to make a fool of himself, I looked at

Yuri, who gave me a wink. He knew more than I did about this loveable local identity.

The old boy's timing was superb. His audience waited as he lit up a cigarette, sucked in a mighty draw and then gulped a swig of whisky from the glass he had carried to the stage. All this done, he began in a husky but tuneful voice to sing the old refrain, "*Cigareets and woosky and wild, wild women, they'll drive you crazy, they'll drive you insane...*".

He was a hoot! After bringing the house down with his lusty contribution the old codger took a nonchalant bow and returned to once again hold up the bar inside.

The life of the Bay was agreeable. I assured my adult children that their mother had found her groove. Occasionally, we paid them visit in Sydney. Yuri met John one day. They shook hands, and I later teased him that he had addressed my ex-husband as 'Sir'.

He reminded me he had been raised an American, and that was how a congressman would be addressed. I suggested he call me 'Ma'am' and he laughed and chased me down to the surf.

The only hitch in the magic Byron Bay life we led was the gorilla that sat four-square in the corner.

~~~

It is a terrifying experience to be pricked with the needle of a used syringe.

It happened to me one day as I dived in under the veranda for a piece of timber and emerged with a stick injury.

A panic attack does not herald its coming. It hits you from behind like a fast-moving locomotive. One moment you are enjoying a fruitful day, relaxed and at one with the world and preparing to make a small vegetable garden at the side of your house. And then, in an instant, your well-ordered world is spinning crazily out of control. You can't reign in the pieces of your brain. Bits go flying off everywhere. Panic. The adrenalin rush that has your hands sweating, your lips numb, your legs collapsing from under you, and your heart jumping the corral.

It took all the steady deep breathing I could muster to calm my body and brain, enough that I could think rationally about what to do next.

I knew, despite his protestations, that Yuri was still using occasionally, but his blood was clean, and I knew he was scrupulous about safety. He would never have tossed a used syringe under the house. And yet I'd just had one jab my middle finger. I had landed in the nightmare, slap bang in the middle of all the uncertainties and dangers that are part of the heroin culture.

I hung on while a clinician from the HIV clinic down in Sydney came on the line to fill me in on the risk to my life.

'Yes. I guess it would be an old syringe,' I said in answer to his question. 'It's dirty and dusty. It was a fair way in under the house.'

'Twenty-four hours,' the man informed me 'Twenty-four hours is as long as the virus can live outside the human body. After that, a needle is no longer contaminated.'

Relief!

'Thank God! Thank you,' I said as I lowered the phone down and let out a heavy sigh.

A million butterflies had just been released from my tummy into the atmosphere, soaring up high into the cloudless sky. I floated with them. Not a care. A magnificent sensation.

But ephemeral. Fading on the wind.

I put down the phone and laid on my bed and thought about my lucky escape. Yes, I had missed the bullet this time. But for how long?

How had I arrived at this place in my life where I needed the HIV / AIDS hot line on speed dial?

MONKEY BRAIN

The man of wisdom is never of two minds;
the man of benevolence never worries;
the man of courage is never afraid.

Confucius

Grandfather Orlov lifted the small boy up to the railings of the big white P&O liner and told him to wave goodbye to Hong Kong.

The Orlovs were sailing for America, never to return. The six-year-old was leaving behind his beloved amah, the girl who had looked after him since birth, his jet-setting mother never around long enough for him to learn her English. Only his grandparents' Russian and his amah's Cantonese.

I believe Yuri acquired his Zen ways from his amah.

It was also his amah who taught him to guard his emotions, be brave, be kind and be silent. It was she who taught him to count on the abacus, who taught him to use his chopsticks, who proudly hauled her small charge with her every morning through the noisy street markets of Hong Kong, through the old wet markets of Kowloon with its flowers and produce. His amah it was who screeched over the heads of stall holders and fought for the best bits of seafood for his dinner, weighed live hens in her hand so she could serve him the plumpest meat, bartered at the top of her voice over a piece of pork belly.

He remembers the live ducks for sale on the street. And as

they hurried frantically from one place to the next on these daily exertions, it was his amah who showed him off to her friends, women who fussed over the little boy with small gifts and noisy affection.

I never tired of hearing him relate his memories of those vibrant markets, the typical Asian smells, the bustling ambience, all of it tied in with the memory of his young amah, a memory that would never leave him.

Compared to my suburban upbringing in the boring stultified Fifties, his oriental life intrigued me. I've seen a tiny black and white photo of Yuri's sixth birthday party. Lots of well-dressed little ones sitting along a large table, all the children with their personal amah standing behind each chair ready to fuss over her charge. A different world. If his glamorous mother had been present at the party that day Yuri did not recall. Possibly not, he thinks.

He told me how he had looked for his amah among the crowds gathered on the docks that day, searching the shoreline as the big white ship, draped in colourful streamers, pulled away from the shore.

But the person dearer to the six-year-old than his own mother had slipped silently out of his life the night before.

Aware she would be too upset to come down to the ship to see him off the following day, she had taken him aside at bedtime and told him always to remember the things she had taught him. And always to be brave like his grandfather. In saying which, the amah would not have been aware of an episode in the General's past that was not covered in glory; the time he sat by and watched a terrified baby animal suffer horrendously. And then partook of a feast that featured the creature's living brain matter as the highlight of the night.

Had I not seen the photographs, I might have doubted

Yuri's illustrious Russian heritage; the grandfather, an important general in the Tsar's army and close to the Tsarina. But I've seen the pictures; the large oil painting showing General Orlov in full military regalia astride his decorated horse as he accompanies the Tsarina—also on horseback—on an inspection of the Guard in the grounds of a grand palace. All feathers and gold epaulets, all pomp and ceremony, they are images from history. Yuri carries them close to his heart, a reminder, he claims, that although his family might consider him a bum, they cannot deny his forebears had class.

The photographs had been well hidden in a tight cranny below the deck of his boat when he lived aboard her. They had survived the Yamba repo men's best efforts to plunder his personal belongings while repossessing the boat after his 1996 road accident.

Until his death, the old General would play an important part in his grandson's life. Yuri told me about the ceremonial sword his grandfather bequeathed him and how, despite fleeing the States, despite sailing half way around the world, despite raising his young family on farms—all up, having lived the gypsy life—he had always managed to ensure the Orlov sword was in safe keeping.

Sadly, despite having hidden it deep in the bowels of his boat while living aboard, the precious heirloom did not survive the onslaught of Yamba's repo men. But he still had his grandfather's stories told him in childhood and no repo man could rob him of those; one, in particular, the grizzly story of the baby animal sacrificed for supper.

'The live monkey brains came after the soup and the moon dumplings,' was how Grandfather Orlov's story would begin. Yuri said he would shiver and slide up closer to the old man, wanting but not wanting to hear the awful tale. Hot monkey brains were a special treat offered by the Chinese hosts in honour of their exalted guests, according to Orlov's memories of the China he had known after the Revolution; White Russian fighting men exiled to Shanghai because their Tsar had lost to the Bolsheviks, the Red Russians.

As the story goes; they brought the baby monkey into the banqueting hall, manacled and oozing shit between its legs. Somewhere in its state of terror, the tiny animal would have hoped for a reprieve. But no man would show it mercy that night. 'Mercy was not on the menu,' his grandfather would say. 'Instead, we in the grand Chinese banqueting hall raised our glasses and toasted the petrified creature. Our hosts considered the tiny animal's fear to be an essential ingredient of the feast. Its dread was intended to whet our appetites.'

A Cossack, the General was no stranger to terror and death. He would have seen men die in agony on blood-drenched battlefields. He would have proudly done his Tsar's bidding, killed on the battle field, ordered traitors shot.

At this point in the grizzly story the grandfather would confess that in the lavish Chinese banqueting hall—all sumptuous silks, oriental rugs, lacquered screens—he had felt his entrails rebel against the ceremony being laid out before him and his men; the ritualized death of an innocent creature.

But those Chinese nobles, hosts to the elite of the Tsar's army that night, would have dared any man in the great hall to look away.

Each White Russian soldier would have had to watch as the metal band was positioned on the skull of the frightened animal, would have had to endure its primal screams as the band was being tightened by painful degrees, endure the blood-curdling minutes it took for the soft warm brain to be squeezed up into the top half of the monkey's skull until the fissures in its cranium were able to take the pressure no longer and the still-living creature's head exploded and the warm matter of its being poured into the ceremonial bowl.

For the sake of patriotic pride, the Tsar's men would have endured the whole barbaric ceremony. To do otherwise would have brought shame to their rank and to their lost homeland.

As Yuri grew up he understood that his grandfather told his tale as a *mea culpa*, and also as a parable intended to teach his grandson a moral lesson.

In his Californian dotage, as he went about his janitor days, the old man must still have heard the pitiful, high-pitched squeals of the terrified infant monkey, and never forgiven himself for having taken the coward's way out by not defending the defenseless.

It would be a lesson I believe still resonated the day Yuri made a choice to risk personal danger rather than cut and run.

DAY OF SHAME

*I believe compassion to be one of the few
things we can practice that will bring immediate
and long-term happiness to our lives.*
                                                        Dalai Lama

In writing of the Keats Street incident now, I have to hope
that the statute of limitations saves me.

As a mother and grandmother, and someone with a high
national profile at that time, had I been caught in a drug bust,
not only might I have landed in jail, but the notoriety would
have destroyed what chance I had to recover sound mental
health. I was still experiencing Bi-polar One episodes that had
flayed me in 1995, still having good days and bad days, manic
highs and depressive lows, rational moments and pretty
irrational ones.

It would be years before I plateaued, more like my old self
again, the one who did not act capriciously and did not take
risks, a woman who knew it was necessary to respect the law.

At the time of my Byron story however, I wasn't too
concerned with the niceties of the law.

Similar to the time I visited the Gold Coast hinterland to
get a feel for Christine Petersen's murder—putting myself in
harms' way in the service of primary research—so it was on
the day I sat in on a drug delivery in Byron.

It shames me to recall it today, but it was a pivotal
moment, the moment I believe things began to change for the

better around the teahouse.

Many times, when we drove down to Sydney, Yuri would make a b-line for the Cross. Always with the excuse he had to see a man about timber or machinery. But my credit card statements told the truth. I knew what he was up to. Three hundred dollars from my account would be taken out at a Kings Cross ATM. And for countless hours some days I would wait around for him outside a house in Kellett Street in the Cross, knowing he'd gone in there to score. On a couple of occasions, I sat at the wheel of my car in a mangy Kings Cross lane keeping watch while he sat beside me shooting up.

Yes, I was a fool. An idiot. No argument. My actions on the day of the Keats Street incident were not those of a sane person, either. I had a mental illness. Yuri had a heroin habit. We were both damaged souls. I doubt, however, if that story would have played well in court.

The Gold Coast couple, Cheryl and Gavin, told me during the afternoon of our Mermaid Beach meeting that the drugs so prevalent in Byron Bay came down from the Gold Coast.

As a writer who intended setting her story in that part of the world, I was curious to know how the trade operated. Many times, in Byron I had waited out in Tennyson Lane behind an old wooden house while Yuri went inside to score.

I knew who was dealing. I often thought of going to the police. But I'm more inclined now to think the local cops already knew. They would have had to be blind not to, given that the worn-out path to this man's door on any Byron Bay day would have been a dead give-away.

The Keats Street house, circa 1960s suburban ugliness, had none of the usual Byron ambience. No Bangalow palms, no rainforests down side paths, no ti-tree fencing, no carved Balinese entrance doors, no temple bells to welcome the visitor, no chimes or Buddhas, no greying weatherboards; just bland-as-they-come pale brick veneer ugliness.

Desolation on a grand scale. I tripped on a child's plastic dinky left laying on its side on the front path. The once-flourishing rockery made me feel sad for the good souls who must have designed their garden years ago with hope in their hearts. The rockery on this occasion boasted only a few never-give-up-the-fight cactus plants amongst long grass and tangled weeds. Sadder still was the sight of the rubber tires forming a guard-of-honour up the pathway to the front door. Someone, sometime, had lovingly white-washed them for use as garden beds. Once, they might have bursts with colourful blossoms. Now they bloomed with petrified dog turds.

'This is crazy,' said Yuri, shaking his head as we approached the front door. 'You shouldn't be here.'

'I need to know how it works, okay? I've got a right to be here.' My voice was as cold as my heart. By now, there had been too many lies. Too many disappointments.

Of late, there had been no pretence about sticking to his Physeptone tablets, the surrogate methadone treatment overseen by his GP. It was costing me. He would disappear from the job and be gone for hours through the middle of the day. One recent Saturday night he returned home late with a bleeding nose. Scoring in public toilets would do that, I had said to him. I was losing faith in my plans. On the bad days, even losing heart, overwhelmed by the whole business of being the financial backer for his deepening heroin addiction.

This visit to Keats Street was to be the last hurrah, the last time I produced the cash. I had concluded that it was madness, and Yuri agreed. He was ready, he said, to clean up his act. Just this last score to help ease him out. I was to take control of it and dish the powder out in ever decreasing amounts. His commitment, his promise, offered up voluntarily. And accepted naively.

We walked together up the path and a skinny male opened the door to us. He immediately fell back onto the couch. Bare feet, dirty off-white singlet, torn khaki shorts. His hair was long, straggly and partly hidden under a grey beanie. He lolled in front of a screen running a football match, ignoring the whimpering of the small child stuck in a play pen in the corner of the living room. Two long candles of yellow snot ran down the baby's upper lip into her mouth. I took a tissue from my bag and wiped her nose.

'Can I get her a dry nappy?' I asked the man who had yet to look up from the television set. 'Does she have a bottle?'

'He's on the nod,' said Yuri and kicked the man. 'The lights are out, aren't they, buddy?'

I grabbed a warm washer from the bathroom and ran it across the child's grubby face and hands then went to the kitchen and organized a Vegemite sandwich and a mug of milk. It seemed to sooth the poor little girl.

Three women roamed backwards and forwards through the house. Nobody acknowledged me. They talked to Yuri, but only in monosyllabic grunts from what I could make out. A man wandered out into the living room and for a moment, looked as if he had a purpose but then he disappeared again.

'You shouldn't be here,' said Yuri as I took a stool in the kitchen. He was right, of course. I should be a long way from this place and its business. It was dangerous. A different world. The darker side of Byron Bay. The world of heroin users and their suppliers.

'It's me who's feeding your arm, sailor boy. I've got every right to be here.' The household was irritable and so was I.

The minutes ticked over. The household's lethargy was

only punctuated when one of their number would split the venetian blind to check the street and the room would hold its collective breath.

Once or twice a rush of jittery expectation rippled through the sorry precinct, but the house fell back into its sullen torpor once the sighting proved a false alarm, or the knock on the door produced nothing more comforting than another customer slipping furtively inside.

A delivery from the Gold Coast was on its way, but I could see it was taking way too long for this strung out mob. The inhabitants drifting in and out of the various rooms were all of a kind; lank hair, dead eyes and ratty clothes. It was hard to tell how many people were actually in the house. I would say, not including myself or Yuri, that there would have been half a dozen strung-out customers wandering aimlessly around the place.

Every so often someone would sit down beside the couch stoner. The football match had ended but no one turned off the television or seemed interested in discussing the game. There was little if any joy anywhere in the dimness of the mean house. It all seemed so incongruous. Outside, it was a beautiful golden sands blue water day where the clean and healthy were enjoying the blessings of Byron Bay.

Time passed with no sign of their sugar man. I vacillated between being bored and being edgy, which was much the way everyone else was in the room, except that my condition wasn't chemically-induced.

'A dime for your thoughts,' said Yuri as he handed me a chocolate bar. 'You were a million miles away.'

'Closer than that.' I checked my watch and accepted the chocolate. 'Thanks. When's this business going to be over?'

'Soon.'

We were sharing the kitchen with two customers standing over by the sink. I was catching drifts of their conversation—for the note book—the language of the heroin aficionado.

Good gear from Thailand coming in. Street stuff being cut with sugar. Thai white. Dolexene. Sleepers. Picks. Spikes. Caps. Balloons. Gear. Physos, Meth. A mate who was getting out next week. A guy who got caught with three grams last month.

A self-contained culture.

Junkies didn't have friends, they just had other junkies, people the same as them, with nowhere to go because no one but them spoke heroin. I was about to call it quits, leave Yuri to do his deal. I knew he felt uncomfortable about me seeing this pathetic side of his life.

'It's here!' yelped one of the agitated females who had been keeping watch at the blinds.

Suddenly there was a pulse in the room! As if a bolt of lightning had zapped the place. As if a switch had been flicked and the robotic inhabitants suddenly came alive.

The living room filled up with people who had previously disappeared up the hall into other rooms. This was the moment the ménage had been sweating on and I noticed that even the dolt on the lounge looked up from the TV screen. A female, the one in charge—and who would soon be at the centre of a frightening drama—came down the hall into the living room and, after checking through the blinds, opened the door just wide enough to allow two diminutive Asian men to slip inside.

Without a word, the men were led through into the kitchen. Nobody eyeballed anybody or uttered a word, just a silent, but tangible nervousness, a sense that danger had arrived, but so too had the good stuff. Scales and other paraphernalia were produced and the weighing and measuring on the kitchen bench began, one courier bagging the heroin and the other bagging the cash. I attended to the small girl in the playpen who had been woken up by all the hyper-activity and had begun to cry again.

The mission completed, the inscrutable pair left the premises followed spasmodically by most of their clientele who seemed to melt into the afternoon, leaving behind only their sad histories and a sense of defeat. The child's mother, ignoring the little girl's screams for attention, took off down the hall with her booty.

'From the Gold Coast, that pair,' said Yuri, explaining the Asian men. 'The business operates out of Surfers Paradise. The casinos.'

I had just watched him hand over two thousand dollars of my dwindling cash in exchange for the heroin. The milk of Paradise. Coleridge's laudanum, I wondered had it come at such a price?

I had seen more than I needed to see. It was ugly. It was tragic. It was scary. And, as well, the money thing rankled with me, especially when I thought about it going into the pockets of such low life as those two Asian mules and their Gold Coast bosses. 'Let's go, come on,' I growled.

Yuri was checking his canvas bag. 'You go on. It's okay,' he said as he headed for the bathroom. 'I can make it home. '

'I'm waiting here.'

'It's okay. I can get home. You go.'

I went up to him and thumped his chest. 'I said I will wait. Got that?'

'What's your problem?'

'Where to start? With this!' I waved a hand around the house. 'That poor baby over there? How about her, for starters? I saw that the child had fallen back to asleep. I took a jacket from the arm of the lounge and placed it over the toddler's tiny body.

'And the drop-kick there on the lounge?' I said as I sat down at what, in any other home, would have been the dining table, but here, was a bench strewn with household junk. 'And that stupid bitch up the hall?' I looked across to the sleeping child again. 'No doubt Mummy's busy. Mummy's shooting up. Right? Who looks after this little pet when she wakes up, huh? Him?' With disgust, I nodded my head at the junkie on the lounge I thought might be the child's father.

'You wanted to know how it worked.'

'And now I do. Okay? Now I do!' I had just witnessed a federal crime, making me an accessory to the fact. I had known this, going into it. But now the reality, the stupidity, the lameness of my behaviour these past months disgusted me. 'We need to talk,' I said. He turned from me and was about to walk back in to the bathroom when we both heard the thud.

'Christ!'

The woman, the mother, had fallen in the hallway. Yuri ran to her and kneeling beside her, started slapping her face. We had to get away. We couldn't get caught here! Long Bay for a long time for Yuri O'Byrne. And everlasting disgrace for me.

'Help her, man!' Yuri yelled to the dolt on the lounge. 'She's dropped, man! It was bad shit they sold us! Bad shit. She's O.D.'d! Do something, for Chrissakes!'

He kept slapping the woman's face and shaking her. 'Fuck you, man! She's your fucking woman!' He ran over and kicked the junkie's shin, dragged him to his feet and shook him.

It was useless. He threw him back against the couch, looked at the woman who was in serious trouble. My head was spinning. Fuck! How had we got ourselves into this?

The woman's body was convulsing, her face turning blue and her eyes rolling back in her head. She would die if she didn't get a shot of Narcan, that much I knew about this heroin world. I'd been a nurse long, long ago, as well, and I'd seen the O.D. patients brought in to Emergency at Parramatta District Hospital. But I had been only a junior nurse. Only an observer, the one who cleaned up their dribble, piss and shit afterwards—or dispatched them to the morgue. And now, right here, with her child nearby and the dolt on the lounge not lifting a finger, I knew this woman was going to die.

I grabbed my mobile and was about to hit Triple O.

'No!' he yelled, snatching it from my hand and flipping it closed. 'Not on yours!'

In a blind panic, I ran around the messy chaotic place looking for the home telephone. This was a nightmare. And the yelling had woken the toddler. The poor frightened little mite started screaming, standing up in her pen, her arms reaching out frantically through the bars to her mother spread out on the floor, her body twitching and Yuri hitting her face with repeated blows.

The baby, with a child's intuition knew that something bad was happening, that she was losing the most precious thing in her world. She was hysterical, desperately reaching out between the bars of her playpen for her mother.

I found the phone and dialed Triple O. 'Keats Street. A woman's over-dosed. Heroin. House on the right. Half way up the hill. Blonde brick. Front door's open. Please hurry!' I knelt down and reached in to the mother's mouth to clear her airways. It was all I knew to do.

Yuri shoved me aside. 'Go! Get out of here!' He slapped the woman again, a savage palm across the side of her face that sent her head sideways, then dragged her up on her feet and lugged her around the room, trying to get her to walk.

'Come on, bitch!' He looked at me, desperation cramping his face. 'I'm losing her!' He looked over his shoulder, to the guy on the lounge. 'What's her fucking name, pal? Her name, man. What is it?' he yelled.

There was no response. Yuri let the woman fall back. 'Fuck it, we have to beat it! Come on!'

This was crazy! I looked to the door. He was right, we had to run! Get away! The ambos, the police would be here any second. This stranger, this stupid irresponsible junkie woman wasn't our concern.

The child's screams reached a crescendo, until, in an instant they stopped, and seconds later, the most pitiful sobs I had ever heard wracked the tiny body. She was petrified.

Yuri's eyes turned to the door. I saw him look again to the mother. I guessed what was going through his head; he would be thinking about the court case pending and knowing that if he were caught now, in this house, it would ruin any chance he had to plead his case when he faced the judge.

Yuri looked across at the terrified child, the pathetic little creature who, for an instant, took her eyes off her mother to beseech the only adult in the room who could save her.

When Yuri turned back to me I saw something in his eyes that told me he wouldn't run. Couldn't run. It was his moment of truth. It wasn't the little girl screaming for help but a tiny monkey, screeching in terror and a room full of cowards ignoring its plight.

'Fuck you, bitch!' He grabbed the mother under the arms and dragged her across the carpet towards the bathroom. 'Go!' he yelled at me.

Ignoring him, I picked up the baby and followed him into the bathroom.

He heaved the woman up and over into the tub and turned the cold tap on full force, holding her head under the water. 'She's going, man. She's dropped! Help us, for Chrissakes!' he yelled over his shoulder. 'Come on, lady! For fuck's sake wake up! Wake up!' Another slap, a punch to the woman's gut. She half-opened her eyes. They rolled back in her head and then she threw up. He turned her over to stop her choking on her vomit.

'Clear out! Clear the fuck out! Get away! Now! Give me her, quick!' He reached out for the little girl. 'Here! Your daughter, lady!' he said, turning the woman on her back again and thrusting the child at her chest. 'Touch her! Hold her!' he said, wrapping the woman's limp arms around the toddler. 'She wants her Mommy, so wake up, you stupid, fucking, dumb bitch! Wake the fuck up and stay awake for your daughter, bitch!'

I knew Yuri as a man who never cursed, but I also knew from my nursing days that these gross insults helped stir something in the person's fading brain that caused them to fight back.

The child climbed over her mother, trying to find her place. Yuri, perched on the side of the bath was trying to stop the woman from choking, trying to get her to recognize her child. I was panicking and keeping an ear out for the sirens.

'Go! Beat it!' He looked at the woman and back up at me. 'Start the engine! Go! Go!'

I tried to estimate how much longer we had, how long it would take for the paramedics and the police to get here. Not long. It was only minutes in a speeding vehicle from the Police and Ambulance Station on Shirley Road to Keats Street. I left the house, ran down the path to the car, jumped in, and got the ignition running.

And then I heard them, the sirens screaming down Bangalow Road. They would turn into Keats Street any minute. And no sign yet of Yuri.

CEMETARY ROAD

Will his name be Love
And all his talk be crazy?
Or will his name be Death
And his message easy?

Louis MacNeice

I had the engine running and the car in gear. As the ambulance turned into Keats Street I saw Yuri coming through the front gate of the house next door as he walked towards the Golf—not running because that would raise suspicions—but not dawdling.

'Quick. Let's go!' He slammed the door and shot a glance across at me. He knew how I felt about what had just happened. 'Step on it!' he said with rude impatience that I knew masked his fear and shame. He bent over and tucked his canvas bag under the seat beneath him.

'Christ! Get rid of that!' I took off at respectable speed down Keats, remembering Karuah.

He flung his bag onto the back seat.

Not what I'd meant.

'I could hear the sirens. Figured it'd be okay to leave her. She knew her daughter. She kissed her. That couch smackie came in the bathroom ... didn't do much, the drop-kick. I wanted to punch the prick's lights out but there was no one home to hurt.'

I had never seen him angry before. All trace of his calm Zen nature had vanished. Before we got to the end of Keats Street, an ambulance turned in and raced past us. I put my indicator light on to turn left towards Suffolk Park and home. He flicked it the other way and spun the wheel to the right. I was confused. 'But we live down that—'

'Just head up to the roundabout and keep going. Please?'

'Into town?'

'Just go. Please. Go!'

Before I turned I checked the rear vision mirror. The paramedics were running up the path of the drug house. He sat, statue-like beside me as I drove towards the roundabout. He seemed not to move a muscle, not even when a police car took the roundabout at speed and came racing towards us, its lights flashing and sirens blaring.

The police car passed us, and in the mirror, I saw it turn left into Keats. Only then did I let out my breath.

'Okay,' he said. 'We can go around the circle now and head back down Bangalow.'

The roundabout. The place where it had all begun one afternoon as the sun set over Byron Bay. 'Home?' I said. 'Good.'

'Uh-uh. Throw a right when you get to Cemetery Road.'

I was in no state to argue. I drove in silence until we came to the road that runs off Bangalow Road.

'Go in, all the way to the end.'

While I bumped the car along the rainforest track, over potholes and rocky stretches, through heavy groves of Melaleuca trees and swampy undergrowth, the man beside me stayed silent, staring out the window, no doubt contemplating the near miss he'd had back at the Keats Street house. If he had been a moment longer getting away and the police had arrived, our chances of convincing a judge of his good character would have been nil.

I imagined him being hauled in by those same two detectives so pathetically camouflaged in their Hawaiian shirts and ridiculous shorts who'd dropped by our home pretending to look for their mate Bernie. Those two had felt the sting of Yuri's wit that night, and I doubt they would have shown him much mercy had they caught him in the act of scoring heroin.

'I did the right thing by the kid,' he said, finally turning to look my way. 'That was something, I guess.' He shrugged. 'Not much, but something.'

My tolerance had been shredded by now. I was a partner in crime. The ex-Cabinet Minister's wife a getaway driver in a drug deal. Me, Bonny. Him, Clyde. I wasn't about to pat him on the back for his nobility any time soon. And yet, I couldn't help thinking about the monkey story, and feeling that he must have seen something of the terrified animal in that baby girl and felt the need to defend the defenseless, to save her by saving her mother.

'This'll do. Pull up here,' he said.

I had been bumping the Golf along the ups and downs. Now I looked around. 'In a cemetery?' I said.

'Good a place as any.'

He was hanging out, I could see the signs. When he was strung out, he claimed it was like tigers inside his veins, like their claws scratching him from the inside trying to get out. The cravings. The gnawing at his gut, his nerves strung so tight as if they'd snap, the sweats making him want to puke. He needed to get on. I understood, but I couldn't let him do it.

This day, if it meant anything, had to be a turning point. I had just seen up close what heroin could do to someone. Those people back in the house weren't kind, artistic, creative, active people like Yuri, not clean and well-dressed, not people who made plans and who wove dreams for me. They weren't a fully functioning human being like Yuri O'Byrne, those people back there.

'Give me five?' he said, reaching over for his bag.

He left the car before I could stop him.

'They're all dead out there, cobber,' I called after him.

He kept walking.

'Stick that stuff in your vein, you're just as dead. You're not getting any younger, remember. I hear the older you get, the greater the risk. Every shot's a gamble ... until the one comes up that's got your name on it.'

'Something like that,' he said over his shoulder as he walked off towards a cluster of ancient tombstones laying lopsided among the swampy Melaleuca gums.

I watched as he sat down on one of the raised burial spots. Just a few stones and the remnants of a rusted iron fence, but the last resting place of some pioneering resident of Byron Bay, and for all I knew, a favourite hang-out for the strung-out.

'Wait!' I yelled as I jumped out and ran up to him.

'It's okay,' he said. 'Get back in the car.'

'Stop it, you idiot!' I grabbed his wrist and tried to wrench the bag of heroin from him. 'Give it to me!'

He unpeeled my hand from his wrist with ease. 'Don't worry. It's all good.'

'What are you thinking? You saw a woman almost drop dead just now. From that junk!'

'She was greedy. Just greedy. There's nothing wrong with it. Promise. She just shot up too much of it in one go.' He shrugged. 'Desperate junkies,' he added.

'And you? You're not greedy? You're not desperate? Not a junkie? For fuck's sake, Yuri! Look at yourself!'

We glared at each other. When I sat down beside him and put my arm around his shoulder, my other hand on his thigh, he took my hands away from his body and laid them back in my lap. He turned his head from me. I couldn't be expected to feel what he was feeling, I knew that, but being the rational one at the moment, the onus was on me to stop him risking his life.

'Please, you can't do this. Look at me. Please? Turn around and look at me. I'm the one person in your world who gives a fuck about you, don't you see? We live a good life, Yuri. I can help you get through this. We can fix it. I don't want you to die on me. Please don't go through with this? At least not here in this place? No one's around to help me if what happened to her back there happens to you.'

I was in a state, in a nightmare. I had to get him out of this place. Home. We had to get home where things were normal. Where I managed.

He bent over, resting his elbows on his knees, his head buried in his hands. The world was black for him. I felt his pain. There was nothing in his world at this moment but the cravings, the savage hunger. Heroin had cost him his country, cost him his mother, cost him his boat, cost him his precious children. Now, if it was really bad heroin, as it seemed to be, it was about to cost him his life, and what could I do about it? I was a poor runner-up to the drug.

He looked up at me, stared into my eyes for moments. His voice was not much more than a whisper. 'It robs you of your soul, y'now?' he said, shaking his head. 'Man, it robs you of your fucking soul!'

I tried to comfort him, but he stood and walked further into the cemetery.

I followed, and when I reached him I hugged him and

rested my cheek against his chest. 'I love you so much,' I whispered. 'Be strong for me? Please?'

It was a small word, said softly. 'Please?' But I think he knew it held our whole world inside it, everything we could be, every good thing that lay in front of us, all inside that word 'please'. I dragged him back towards the fallen tombstones stacked on top of each other among the bracken ferns. 'Let's sit down. Over here.'.

'I've stolen from you. I've lied and I've—'

'I know.'

'Then why—'

'We're going to get your soul back from the devil.'

'Let me go. I'm not worth it.'

I tried to prize the bag from him. 'Let's tip it out. It's just put us two thousand dollars further away from our boat but tip it out. It'll kill you. I just saw how bad a thing it was.'

'She was greedy.'

'She was dying.'

I tried again but no way was he giving up his 'precious'. 'You saved the child's mother. You felt for the little girl. You're a good person, a good person, Yuri. Tip it out.'

The heroin was in his hand. He was staring down at it. 'Everything's fucked. They're coming for me. I'm going to jail.'

'No, you're not. The lawyers don't think so.'

'The layers are full of shit. They don't know diddly.'

'You can't tip it out, can you? That's the truth. You can't tip that poison out.' I knew that by now he was resenting me, resenting my presence. He just wanted me to go away, and for him to hit up.

He took his time to answer. 'No. I can't.'

I stared hard into his eyes, those dark Doctor Zhivago soulful eyes that had won me when I'd first looked into them.

'Yuri. You're strong. You're courageous. You're the man who's battled raging oceans in tiny boats and you're telling me you can't deal with this? Of course, you can!'

'I need it bad. I'll start ... tomorrow ... knocking it off. Like we said, I'll get back on the tabs and then ease the lot back. Promise. That's what this was for, wasn't it?' He held up the bag.

'Yes, but that was before I saw what—'

'Promise. You can make me do it. Tomorrow.'

'You've done it before. For everyone else. Do it for me? For us? We can't go on the way we've been going. We can't. I can't, I know that. I can't keep going.' I started to get up. 'And I won't!'

He grabbed my arm and looked up at me. 'My gut's in a knot. I just wanna forget. They're gonna throw me in Long Bay. Long Bay, for Chrissakes, Jan. I'm looking at two to three years. I'm too old. It's gonna kill me!'

'No. This stuff is going to kill you, old sport!'

'It's going to stop, I promise. I promise! Hand on heart.'

I stood up and walked away. 'You're pathetic, that's what you are.'

'I'm trying,' he called after me. 'Just not today,' he said.

I returned and faced him. 'It's my fault.'

'What are you talking about? Your fault?'

'I'm a joke. That's what I'm talking about. I'm a sick joke. And you're a pathetic ... I was about to say 'junkie', but I shouldn't. No one's junk. You are someone I should have helped instead of letting you ... because I thought I was doing ... No. That's a lie. It was because I didn't want to look like a boring old woman. I wanted to look ... I didn't want to lose—'

'Man, that's bullshit. You're not—'

'A boring old woman? No. I thought I was so cool. But

what's cool about shooting heroin into your veins, huh? It's
not cool at all, is it? It really isn't. It is very fucking lame, in
fact. That poor little baby back there in that hideous house?
Not cool. Con's Muma eating her heart out, wondering if her
beautiful boy's dead or alive? Not cool. Your own mother, the
same. The Brisbane mate you told me about ... hanging
himself. HepC and liver cancer, poor bugger. Not in the least
bit cool! He had kids, didn't he? Like you. You have a son and a
daughter. And a grandchild. Don't you? Well, don't you?' I
shook my head. 'Not cool.'

'Jan, I—'

'You, stealing from me, lying to me?' I snatched the packet
from him while he was distracted. 'Not fucking cool! I threw
the bag into the long grass.

'Jesus, man! Why did you do that?'

'You don't know why?'

He grabbed me by the wrist, glaring at me. I had never seen
violence in his eyes before but for an instant it was
unmistakably there. He wanted to kill me. Then the moment
passed. He let go of my wrist and turned from me. I headed
back to the car and stood leaning against the driver's door, my
arms folded, my eyes fixed on him as I watched him kicking
the grass, looking for the heroin.

'You do it, and it's over,' I called out. 'I mean it.' I walked
back to where I knew I had thrown the stuff. Eventually, I saw
the bag, picked it up, opened it and then, turning to face him, I
held his gaze while I scattered two thousand dollars' worth of
heroin around the grounds of the ancient cemetery. Good luck
to the ghosts. Yesterday's stoners would be partying tonight.

I wasn't to know he had other ways to get high, but when I
saw him reach in his shirt pocket for his Physeptone tabs and
tip the lot of them out onto his palm, I knew what was going

to happen. And realized I was helpless to stop him.

At least it wasn't dirty heroin, I reasoned, watching him as he crushed the tabs and mixed them in a spoon with his sterile water. When the tabs were dissolved, he pulled the plunger back and filled the syringe with the milky brew. No filter. He strapped his arm, squeezed his fist and found a vein.

'Tomorrow. Promise,' he said as he took the loaded spike from between his teeth and tried for the kingdom.

~ ~ ~

A few tense moments passed before I realized he was in trouble. I could see he knew it, too. He was burning up, and soon his body was giving off furnace heat. I had to get him into the car and go for help, and fast.

I ran back to the Golf, blood pushing its way so fiercely into my head it felt it would come out my ears. I was going from one nightmare to another on this terrible, terrible day! I jumped in the car and bumped over the rocky ground towards him, dodging fallen headstones and culverts as I brought it to a halt alongside where he sat, now stripped to the waist and pouring water from his bottle over his head.

'Get in!' I screamed at him. He shook his head. 'Get in!' I yelled again.

'More water. You got water? Give me ... your bottle.'

I grabbed his shirt and dived into the pockets, searching for the tiny Nokia he always carried. I found it.

He snatched it from me. 'Are you mad!'

In a blind panic, I looked about the empty cemetery. 'Oh my god! Don't die on me! Don't fucking die, do you hear? Don't die!' I tried pushing him into the car. 'We're going to the hospital! Get up, come on, get in!' I was trying to drag him up on his feet. It was useless. The man was built like a military bunker and twice as hard to move. 'Fuck, I hate you, hate you, hate you! Do you hear me? Do you?'

'It's gonna be okay, I promise. Just sit here with me. Please? Just sit.'

His eyes were massively bloodshot. His chest heaved in an erratic rhythm that terrified me. He was having a fierce toxic reaction.

'It's okay. I've done this before. Take a break. It's okay. It's all fine. I'm cooling down. See? It's all good.'

It was true. I could see that his skin was slowly regaining something approximating its natural colour, still red but no longer quite the same fiery, pulsating blotchy red it had been a few moments ago when the junk first hit his system. I touched his forehead with the back of my hand and felt his pulse. This was horrific. Mainlining on something he was meant to swallow. I just knew I had to get him into the car and to Emergency. I softened my voice. 'Alright, home it is. Now get in. Please?' I held open the passenger door.

As we drove out of Cemetery Road onto the t-intersection at Bangalow Road, I put on my right turn indicator but had every intention of turning left, racing back toward Byron Bay village and the hospital on Ewingsdale Road.

Again, he was a step ahead of me. He reached out and spun the wheel. 'Home. Let's go.'

As I reluctantly drove south I recalled his fantasy about dying at sea. He had told me of his wicked plan a long time ago. His idea was to drill holes in his dinghy's floor and bung them with candles then sail his little funeral boat out to sea where he'd throw away his oars, light his wax candle bungs, shoot up the best grade heroin and by the time his candles melted and the boat was sinking, he would be in Valhalla. Told to me once as a joke, but today, it wasn't funny.

I thought once again about the roundabout behind me.

Had I never pulled over for this man beside me, had I kept going that afternoon, I wouldn't be caught up in this horror show now. He would be someone else's problem.

I looked across at Yuri. His soul was mortgaged to the devil and I had just vowed, back there in the cemetery, to get it back for him. But these years had been dramatic, like my mental condition our lives were full of ups and downs, great highs some days, but great disappointments on others. I was feeling drained of the energy to keep fighting the scourge of heroin, keep pretending it would be alright someday soon. But I had committed to him just now, looked him in the eye and promised to help him reclaim his lost soul from the devil.

Was I up to it? Did I have the strength and the resources to help him overcome his addiction?

Did I even have the will to try, I asked myself as we turned in to the yard and I watched him walk towards the teahouse and disappear around the corner.

A LETTER FROM HOME

The time has come,
For us to polish you...
Let us cremate your impurities.

Rumi

Six thousand dollars on the table and the patient walks away drug free, rather than being a person who can't think past his next fix.

The rapid detox treatment administered under anaesthetic washes the blood, I was told by the Israeli doctor at the clinic in Bondi Junction where I took Yuri for a consultation. He would emerge from the procedure, so we were assured, with his blood as clean and pure as a newborn baby's blood, the heroin memory erased altogether.

Such a promise!

It sounded too good to be true. How could I not find the money, six thousand dollars, for this much-touted silver bullet? I was earning a good income from Foxtel, and so I made the commitment. The procedure would be carried out at a private hospital in leafy Castlecrag on Sydney's North Shore. Over a weekend; in on Friday night and out Sunday morning. A couple of post-operative consultations at the clinic, a group therapy evening, plus a course of prescribed Naltrexone medication. Happy days.

This was not yet a time when it was commonplace to jump on the web and research a subject. It is only now, as I come to

write about it that I find there was so much controversy
floating around at the time about the effectiveness, or
otherwise, of the Israeli program, the rapid detox program
using what was touted as the wonder cure, Naltrexone.

Professionals such as Dr. Alex Wodak, head of drug and
alcohol rehabilitation at Sydney's St Vincent's Hospital was,
from the beginning, a Naltrexone skeptic, cynical about the
marketing hype and the money being made by providers who
had jumped on the band wagon.

In a *Sydney Morning Herald* article by journalist Ben Hills,
Saturday 14 March 1998, Dr Wodak is quoted as saying "It
began (here) as a marketing exercise in the pages of the
Women's Weekly, not as a scientific paper in the Medical
Journal of Australia." Hills, in a blog entitled *The Dollars of
Detox: A dodgy treatment for heroin addicts that makes its promoters
rich*, wrote of a seminar held at Westmead Hospital. "Doctors
... could hardly believe the response—it was more the sort of
crowd you would expect at a pop concert than a medical
briefing.

More than 1,000 people crammed into four lecture-theatres
to watch the presentation on closed-circuit TV, another 250
were turned away at the door, and several thousand more
telephoned to express interest."

According to the Bondi Junction clinic, addiction was a
neurological issue and the Naltrexone worked by blocking the
opioid-induced euphoria and so decreased the craving for
heroin. Their accelerated cleansing process was a
comprehensive one. So, said their literature. The treatment
would rid Yuri of all drug cravings, now and forever after.
Amen. Naltrexone was the opposite of methadone, it was a
"methadone antagonist". Methadone was simply a synthetic
substitute for heroin—something evil created by Hitler for his

troops, I was told on the QT.

The receptionist at the clinic, the doctor's wife, offered me a contra deal if I would sing their praises on *Beauty & the Beast*. I thanked her kindly but emphatically declined. In a decade on the program, I would never compromise mine or the company's principles by accepting cash for comment.

Andre Waismann, father of the whole Naltrexone idea, in his blog of October 2008 entitled *Extreme Rehab: Inside the World's Most Radical Drug Clinic* explained things this way: "Our bodies produce natural opiates called endorphins. But when you start using heroin, your endorphin levels go down because your brain doesn't need to produce it any more. The system collapses. Your dependency on heroin increases until the day you no longer produce endorphins and you become totally dependent on heroin. The more you put in your brain, the more receptors your brain produces and the more receptors you have, the more heroin you need. Eventually you reach the point where the amount of heroin that you need to feel high is the amount that kills you."

Not aware of the counter arguments at the time, I paid the money and Yuri was booked in to undertake the procedure.

My only concern was the instruction the Israeli doctor issued. Before the treatment could be undertaken, the patient had to have been off methadone—his Physeptone tablets—for at least two weeks.

The Naltrexone procedure to be successful, required that the body be free of all trace of methadone. Naltrexone only countered heroin. The addict therefore needed to substitute his Physeptone with heroin in the lead-up to the procedure.

It being too dangerous for Yuri, being on remand and awaiting trial, I was the one who had to score two weeks' worth of heroin for him. On doctor's orders.

I did. And I've since tried to forget about it.

I was terrified the day I ducked into a back lane in Cabramatta and handed over a wad of cash in exchange for the—medically prescribed—heroin.

Often, in front of the television cameras, when a letter about hard drugs came up, I would think about the Cabramatta incident. If only they knew. All I would say was that I believed communities and governments should have the courage and the will to acknowledge the serious health issues of hard drugs and act upon it. One of my chief gripes against PM John Howard was his zero tolerance policies on drugs.

My wish is that it would have been easier, that there would have been more information available to me back then, when I was trying to cure a heroin user, that there would have been proper government-run, medically-overseen facilities made available for treating addicts, that there would not have been the medical sharks out there ready to exploit the issue in the time I was trying to rehabilitate a sick man.

But that is wishful thinking. The more things change the more they stay the same, unfortunately. Families continue to be torn at the heart if they are having to deal with the drug addiction of a loved one. Today there's worse than heroin doing the devil's work.

~~~

The Naltrexone miracle held out the promise of a new start. Things looked good. Yuri was free of his addiction. I had stolen back his soul from the devil. His only highs these days were from talking over the cruising plans we were making.

And then he relapsed, disappointing us both, but proving the naysayers correct. It was snake oil medicine, not medicine at all but a get-rich-quick scheme, one that played on the desperation of addicts and their loved ones.

I am eternally grateful that I was not sucked in to the cash-for-comment deal the Bondi Junction clinic had offered me. At least it was my problem, my money I had gambled. And the experience reinforced a principle I had lived by since I had gained my so-called celebrity status as a result of my 1987 *Sixty Minutes* story about love on the ministerial desk.

As I relate in my previous memoir, following that media madness I was bombarded with rich offers to endorse office furniture, ash-trays and underwear. Bendon pulled out all stops to convince me to promote their new sexy underwear line because of the knickers in the ash tray business. When I declined, Bendon went looking for someone else—and found Elle McPherson!

In passing up those golden opportunities to put my name to products, I differed from those celebrities who have sung the endorsement on everything from toilet paper to home building products, and dog food in-between.

I've only ever given one 'celebrity' endorsement and that was for an Australian start-up medical product, Veda-scope, an instrument I fervently believed was the clever alternative to that dreaded cold steel horror forced upon women, the duck-billed speculum, the implement used since the dark ages for Pap testing.

Veda-scope's inventor, Clemens van Der Weegen, approached me in 2002 with his alternative vaginal probe. On several of my *Beauty & the Beast* appearances I had taken the opportunity to encourage every sexually active female, young and old, to have regular Pap tests. I was speaking from personal experience, having been a victim of cervical cancer at age twenty-eight, resulting in a hysterectomy in the second trimester of my pregnancy while carrying our sixth, and much-wanted, child.

With that in my background, and the audience credibility I enjoyed, the publicly-listed company backing Veda-scope, sshmedical, believed I could propel their share price. And I did. Into the stratosphere. As I came from a public relations background, I had also taken charge of the media promotions and special events that in the PR business are called 'famils'. I used my little black book of contacts to bring together high-profile women in politics, business and medicine.

Within nine days of my endorsement and media coverage, including my voiced radio ads, headlines in the financial press announced that sshmedical's share price had jumped by an amazing 88%.

I will add a footnote here: The Vedas-cope instrument had problems which needed to be ironed out and thus, its penetration into the market would be limited until such times as Clemens van Der Weegen tweaked his new alternative to the horrible cold metallic duck-billed speculum. I believe the prototype has since undergone several incarnations and the Veda-scope Mk11 or Mk 111 of today is expected to be welcomed by the medical profession and by the women and girls whom, I trust, are rocking up in great numbers to their GPs at least every two years for their Pap tests.

Meanwhile, the heroin issue; it must seem to those who have never been close to the problem of drug addiction that Yuri, having relapsed after the Naltrexone treatment, was something of a loser, a hopeless case—and that I was pathetic not to walk away.

Okay, I understand. Members of my family were certainly concerned for me. But it comes back to that Gerald Manly Hopkins thing, doesn't it? Inscape. The man I knew, despite his addiction, was an intrinsically good human being. He was kind, he was intelligent, he was creative, he was employed, and to me, he was unique. He was not a lay-about. He was a fully functioning carpenter and shipwright who happened to be cursed with a heroin habit acquired in his youth, a time when his country's governments were complicit in the scourge.

He was worth the effort. Worth the price. Worth the punishment. And, believe me, anyone who is supporting a loved-one with an addiction of any kind—drugs, alcohol, gambling—knows just how punishing, in both emotional and financial terms, it can be. But Yuri and I had big plans for a future together and he meant so much to me. There was never really a time when I seriously considered walking away.

And I had another reason for standing by him and trying to rehabilitate him. As a mother myself, I empathized with Katya O'Byrne, an elderly woman in poor health who longed to be reunited with her only son. In the letters and our occasional phone hook-ups she had begged me, and I had given her my promise, to always look after her son.

But we had tried the Israeli Program, the so-called magic cure and found it wanting. So, he was back where he had started; at the mercy of his cravings. It would take the disturbing phone call we received one night to finally shock him into action.

~~~

It was a warm Spring night. The call came as we were enjoying dinner outside on the veranda—candles and mosquito coils and cheeky brush turkeys hoping to cadge bread from our table.

Yuri had made one of his delicious Beef Thai salads and coconut rice dishes. Sometime during the night, he disappeared and when he returned to the veranda there were no prizes for guessing what he had been up to. He was on the nod. And I was angry. There is no joy in sharing intimacies with a person who is on Planet Heroin. I stood up and began clearing the table, shutting down the night and its possibilities for further pleasures.

As I came and went, clearing the dishes, my mood eventually lightened. I gave a sigh and joined him when he beckoned me to sit beside him on the big Bali couch with its colourful and comfortable cushions.

As usual, we started rabbiting on about our idyllic plans to sail the South Pacific and live a nomadic life. He was a dreamer, but I was a willing party. It would take the sad news we were about to receive to bring it home to him just how little time he had to get better, to clean up his act and be quit of his addiction if it were to happen.

So, once our romantic escapist talk began to wane and the dreamy atmosphere of the fragrant evening made us drowsy, I broached the subject of his promise, post-Naltrexone, to go cold turkey on the heroin.

'As soon as I've got the roof on the bedroom. Then I'm all set. Promise. I can do it, I know I can.'

He was referring to the roof for our new sleeping quarters. We had decided, one lovely night of wide shimmering oceans and a high moon rising, that we needed a bedroom separate from the living area. One up there on the roof, that would have an ocean view.

Why not? he had asked. I had quickly fallen in with the plan. We could lay back in bed up there and float among the galaxies. Even in our sleep, we would hear the ocean. And by day, we could watch the ships sail by from our conning tower bedroom.

Along with Jay and Con he had already taken off part of the existing roof of the teahouse at the north end and had almost finished constructing an upstairs bedroom, a diminutive yurt-shaped Balinese-style room accessed via outdoor stairs made from recycled Australian cedar. At the top was a small landing and a carved golden teak door at the entrance. As with most of downstairs, the walls would be lined with the same woven bamboo. The conical ceiling would be raw timber beams over woven matting. Retiring for the night would be even more of an adventure. Our special country.

'You'll just have to leave the tarp on the roof till you're ready to go back to work,' I had suggested. 'Con's going off to Thailand, anyway, for a couple of weeks. And Jay's on another job.'

'Yeah, but—'

When the phone rang, I darted inside thinking it might be one of my children. They were still keeping a watchful eye on their mother, albeit by long distance. I took the call. And then I had to wait a few moments before I felt able to go back outside and break the news.

'Yuri?' I said, rejoining him on the veranda, my voice a whisper.

'What's up? What's wrong?'

'That was Jay.'

'Jay? What's he on about this time of night?'

'It's Con.

'Con? What about Con?'

I came across and put a hand on his shoulder. 'They found Con ... last night ... in a Kings Cross alley. Con's dead.'

It was the saddest of wake-up calls, but it was a wake-up call, to be sure. And it was the reason we would soon be walking together on Tallows Beach at sunset with Yuri tormented by his cravings and me recalling the words of T.S. Eliot who said, April is the cruelest month.

~~~

We were coming towards the close of April—albeit a warm southern hemisphere one—as we walked along Tallows Beach. Yuri was sick, in the truest sense of the word. Over thirty-six hours without heroin and I was starting to question myself whether I had the right to expect someone I loved to go through this kind of Hell.

If I gave him the Golf's keys and my EFTPOS card, his agony would be over, his cravings gone, along with the crippling aches and pains and the nausea and the sweats. Just my keys and my card and he would be released. But Hell is where the Devil is supposed to dwell. It was the Devil heroin that we had in our sights. Game on, he'd said a couple of days ago. Let's do it. And somewhere in the universe I believe poor Con smiled and wished him all the best.

I jumped as a wave crashed high on the shore. Yuri had dropped back and was sitting on the dry sand, holding his head.

'It's like the worst dose of influenza and then some,' he said. 'A hundred times worse than the 'flu. You can sit the 'flu out. You know you're gonna get better as soon as the virus runs its course, but man, this ...' He ran to the shoreline and vomited into the sea.

'And this'll get better, too,' I said as I sat down alongside him and held his hand. 'It will. Soon. You know that.'

He turned to me with his usual cheeky grin. 'I know what'd make it better.'

'Don't you go there!'

I jumped to my feet, dragging him up with me. 'Come on, let's keep walking. We're going all the way down to Broken Head and then back. You can lay down, sleep, do whatever when we get home. I'll squeeze a jug of juice for you, you can take a long warm bath, watch some TV until you fall asleep.' The way he looked at me, I knew he knew I was making it up as I went along, this hour-to-hour nightmare he had to endure while I could only watch.

For the want of something to distract him, I suggested it was time he wrote to his mother. 'I wrote the last two for you, remember?'

'Yeah, yeah. I will.'

'Her letters are sweet, Yuri. She misses you. She loves you dearly. She worries about her little boy.'

'It's old age talking, that's what it is. Let me tell you about Katya's mother love, pal.' He kicked a conch shell along the beach then turned to me. 'Even if she had ever noticed her little boy, she couldn't have held a conversation with him. The fabulous Katya didn't speak Cantonese, the language of her little boy, never took the trouble to learn.'

'And you had no English at all?'

'Uh-uh. Cantonese from my amah and a bit of my grandparent's Russian, that's all. That was me as a kid. Not until I was six and we got to the States and I started to pick up her lingo. Too busy being fabulous for everyone else, our Katya. The Shanghai and Hong Kong ex-pat scene was where her head ... and body ... were when I was a kid. I'd been an awkward mistake. Palmed off the minute I was born.'

'She worries about her beautiful boy, Yuri. You hurt her, the way you won't write.'

'You're doing it for me.'

'It must have been hard for you.'

'Wasn't great.'

'Sailing single-handed out on the ocean. I reckon you got your dare-devil ways from your father, the fighter pilot. And some of your looks, too. But mostly I think you look like Katya. A bit of both. I can see it in the photograph.'

I knew how much he cherished the one snapshot he had of

his parents. A black and white of the young, beautiful Katya sitting on the edge of a bed holding a cigarette. Her dark curly hair untamed. Unusual for those days of bangs and rolls and hair lacquer. The face of the man sitting close to her was not in as strong a light, not as distinctive as Katya's features but it was clear he was tall, well-built, had a strong jaw and dark hair. I knew that Yuri had been carrying that tiny ragged-edged photograph of his parents close to his heart ever since his mother had thrust it at him when he fled the States for Australia.

'It's weird, y'know,' he had said when he first let me see the photograph. 'I couldn't have known him, could I, being so young and all? But it always feels that way. Like his face is familiar. Like I knew him in another life.'

'Of course, you'd feel that way, dopey. It's your own face looking back at you.' Studying the tiny photograph of his youthful parents he had said it was odd that they looked to be so in love in the candid shot, and that it didn't fit with the story, a shotgun wedding and a Chinese mistress.

We had been walking for over an hour and were coming close to the end of the long beach. Yuri groaned and rubbed his limbs.

'I know now's not the time to give you one of my poetry lessons but—'

'Go on,' he said, straightening up.

'Huxley wrote that the martyrs go hand in hand into the arena but they are crucified alone.

'Man, that kinda nails it then, doesn't it?'

'Do you want to keep walking?'

'I do.' He reached for me. 'Hand in hand.'

'Cheesy!' I laughed and dragged him forward at a trot.

~~~

Sleep wasn't happening for him and he knew from experience it could get worse before it got better. An hour here and there was all, and the sleepers we'd laid in for this ordeal seemed useless. He laid about, got up and tried to walk, tried to watch TV. Lame daytime television, crazy females arguing with a man called Stan Zemanek. Not me. I had begged off for the week in order to see this thing through.

He took a shower and staid under too long. I came in and turned it off. And again, the same thing an hour later. More hours where he stayed curled up, moaning, cursing the wracking pains in his joints. The shakes that came on without warning. Starbursts of pain behind his eyes, is how he described the headaches when he could be bothered talking. Saying he'd done this before, but he'd been young back then.

This was a thousand times worse, spewing his guts, a crazy newsreel running inside his head he couldn't shut down and still the blinding ache behind his eyes. Scratching at the itch that couldn't be reached.

Now more than ever seems it rich to die. To cease upon the midnight with no pain. Keats had yearned to exit the world on a nightingale's song. I rubbed and pummelled Yuri's tortured body, even though I could tell he didn't want me touching him. Every part of him, too strangled and knotted and sweating to take someone's touch.

Nothing but the cravings. Heroin. Hammer. H. Horse. Smack. He craved the rush. The relief.

What had I done with his Physos? Why had I tipped out his stash? He knew I'd hidden the keys. Hidden our phones, too. He resented me. Why couldn't we call it a day and just admit it. He was a junkie. Pete Hershey. He needed Hershey, his dealer around in Tennyson Lane. Not me. He didn't need me. I fixed him a dish of ice-cream. He left it to melt. He dragged himself across the room and slumped on the lounge. I had been copping his tantrums and tears for days. He got angry with me. But, somewhere in his sore head, I believe he was grateful I was sticking by him.

'Guess what? I've got something to show you,' I said, pulling out from my beach bag the magazine I had purchased in the village the day before and was keeping as a reward. I had just come up from the beach, and was stripped down to my bikini, bare-footed and my hair dripping water over him as a tease as I flipped the pages. 'Your new *Wooden Boat*,' I said. 'Take a look.' He cherished these magazines, had all the volumes going back many years, and poured over them endlessly. 'Go on, have a look.'

He brushed me away. He had zero interest in the magazine.

I kept on. 'It's a thirty-foot timber cutter,' I said. 'It's up at Tin Can Bay. We can go up there on the weekend and check it out. And there's one at Southport we could also have a look at on the way through.'

But he was far beyond being impressed by anything that spoke of the future. He was in the here and now and wanting the heroin he knew he couldn't have. He reached over and grabbed the bucket just in time, dry retching into it. Nothing in there to bring up. He wiped yellow bile from his mouth, turned from me and curled himself into a foetal ball.

~ ~ ~

'Tell me what's the matter,' I said. 'Look at me, Yuri. What is it?' It was late in the evening. I had found him sitting in the dry bath tub.

His eyes were hemorrhaging misery. 'They all knew,' he said. 'No one ever told me.'

I saw he was nursing a letter close to his chest. He waved it at me.

'No one told me.'

I took the letter from him and saw it was from his mother. 'When did this arrive?'

'Doesn't matter.'

The letter told us that the elderly Katya had serious emphysema. Rather dramatically, she had written that she could 'go', any day. So, she said, it was time to tell her Yuri the truth. The man in the tiny black and white photograph seen sitting beside her on the bed in Hong Kong wasn't Frank O'Byrne, her husband, and the man Yuri believed to be his father. The man in the picture he so treasured had been her lover for many, many years—her French lover—and yes, Yuri's biological father!

'You will remember him, son. In Paris,' wrote Katya. 'He was the one who took us to lunch that day in the beautiful hotel. He offered to take you sailing.'

'Sailing!' said Yuri and punched the wall. 'If I ever came back! I'd been around for eighteen years when he met me. Eighteen years, his son, and he offers to take me sailing ... if I happened to drop by someday.'

'She robbed you.' I handed the letter back to him. 'Your mother robbed you.'

He shook his head. 'Him. He didn't want me. He didn't want his own son. Didn't want to ...' He couldn't finish his sentence. I massaged his neck and shoulders. 'I'm so sorry. I'm so sorry.'

'He had his own family. Read it! "His own sons".'

He slunk down in the tub and looked up at the skylight he had put there so we might see the stars. 'What was I? Wasn't I his son, too?' He sat up and glared at me. 'No. I'll tell you what I was; I was a nobody, the kid always trailing behind the ones with real fathers. Real fathers who carried their sons' camping gear up the mountain, showed them how to build a campfire, how to fire off a rifle, dodge the grizzlies. I lagged behind, lugged my own tent, struggled with my own fire. Just grateful they let me tag along. I was a piece of shit, Jan. Some Frenchman's little bastard. He never wanted to acknowledge me because he had his own sons!'

I brewed herbal tea for him and when he finished it and seemed calmer, he climbed into bed, assuring me he felt tired and sick enough to sleep the sleep of the dead.

I ran myself a hot bath and slipped in to the fragrant water. He had designed the bath in the Asian style, a tub with two steps up a platform to enter it. All made from warm red cedar on a grey slate floor. A wooden bucket with a pitcher stood alongside the tub, which we kept filled with ti-tree water for hair rinsing and in which I floated fresh frangipani blossom most mornings. This evening the blossoms were the pink variety, yellow at the centre, changing to varying shades of pink on the tips of the petals.

By the time my bathwater was cooling and I was about to step out, I heard a vehicle pull up out front.

I went to the tiny bathroom window and opened the wooden slats. I waited, but no visitor came walking through the pretty Balinese arch Yuri had built to highlight our rainforest passageway. I donned my kimono and as I walked out onto the veranda, about to go around to the front of the teahouse and investigate, I caught Yuri coming down the steps from our bedroom.

'I thought you were sleeping!' I said, surprising him.

He ignored me and kept going around the side of the teahouse. I grabbed the long torch from the window ledge and raced after him. As I broke in to the front yard I was just in time to see a vehicle's lights shut down. It was there, but in darkness.

'Yuri!' I ran and overtook him, coming up to the van, to the man behind the wheel. 'Get off this property before I call the police!' I yelled at the stranger, knowing without being told that Yuri must have found his phone and that this creep was his dealer.

Yuri approached the van. I grabbed his shirt and tried to hold him back. He was too strong, too determined. He brushed me away and kept going.

'Yuri!'

'Quit it, Jan. Go back in the house.'

I watched as he went around to the passenger side. He shot a look at me over the roof of the van before he got in. The look said it all; he felt hopeless.

'Is this really what you want?' I said through the driver's window. 'Well, is it?' I yelled. 'For Chrissakes, answer me! You've come this far. Don't blow it! Don't give in. You can finish what you started, I know you can. You're strong!' I stepped back and shone the torchlight across the front of the vehicle. 'I've got your number, buster,' I said to the dealer as I came around and put my head in his window again. 'You're gone, old sport! Gone, big time. You hear me? Fuck-nuts?'

The man mumbled something. The woman passenger slid over, making room for Yuri then turned and grinned at me, a stoned, vacant grin. She whispered something to Yuri then gave me the bird.

'You dirty junkies! I'm on the phone. You're gone. All of you!' I shone the torch directly in the smirking woman's eyes. 'Think I'm kidding, do you? Try me, bitch! The cops will wipe that grin off your poxy face!' I turned the torch's light onto Yuri. 'Are these your people? Are they really? Think what you're doing. You're better than this scum. Way better!'

His head was turned away from me.

'You idiot!' I yelled at him in frustration. 'Yes, you, Yuri O'Byrne. I'm talking to you!' I bashed the roof of the van with my torch and felt the gratification of metal hitting metal and leaving its mark. I stood back from the van and waited. He made no effort to get out, instead he gave the dealer a sign to get going. I kicked the van.

'Fuck you! Your things will be up on the road!' I gave the van another heart-felt whack with the torch and started walking back down the yard. The torch was busted. The light had gone out. There was darkness. That wasn't my Yuri back there in that ugly rust heap, squeezed in there with those two deadbeats. But I wasn't about to cry. If I did, that filthy maggot at the wheel and his grinning harpy would think they'd won.

Tomorrow, I would have to go look for him. I would find him somewhere in Byron, maybe sitting on one of the outdoor tables at the Rails nursing a VB and nodding off. Maybe up the lane at Pete Hershey's place. Or he might be in the bushes behind the hospital or hanging around the Commonwealth Bank on Jonson Street trying to score. Or on the nod in the park under the big tree where the addicts congregated. Black, white, young, old, back-packers, tourist and home-grown. All kinds, all stoned. Talking the same language. Talking smack. Talking heroin.

Whatever. Wherever. I would find him and bring him home.

~~~

'His Honour was impressed with the plaintiff's efforts to rehabilitate himself,' the Sydney lawyer said to me as we stood on the steps of the Downing Centre building on Castlereigh Street after he had just successfully represented Yuri against a prosecutor Hell-bent on putting him away.

'Those pictures of your building renovations and the fact he underwent that Naltrexone program last year ticked the right boxes,' said the lawyer.

The Court did not need to know about the failure of the Naltrexone treatment, only that the plaintiff had undertaken it in good faith. His Honour might well be telling people, even to this day, how miraculous the Israeli program is. It doesn't matter.

The fact was that Yuri had returned home the day after having gone off with the dealer, shame-faced and repentant, and more than ever determined to knuckle down to the hard slog of ridding his system of its heroin cravings.

By the time of the court case he had been 'clean' for several months, able to present to the Court successfully rehabilitated. According to the advice I was given, his blood would never be totally free of its heroin memory, but with the will and the courage to succeed, which he now had in spades, the heroin cravings could be kept at bay. Like alcoholics, however, it would always be a one-day-at-a time effort. Yuri would not go back to feeling the need to fill a void in his life with drugs if given an incentive to enjoy life. I understood it was about motivation.

And it was for that reason we would eventually become the proud owners of a beautiful classic timber yacht, a British pilot cutter, big and beamy, but neglected and in need of serious refurbishing.

We two pilgrim souls had hungry hearts and our hearts were set on becoming an intrepid cruising couple, a la the Pardys. Fortunately for us, the stars were beginning to align. Meanwhile, we were standing out on the steps of the Downing Centre this day congratulating ourselves.

'One hundred and twenty hours of community service,' the lawyer said as we talked over the morning's event. 'A triumph of good judgment, I'd say, considering His Honour could have thrown the maximum penalty at him—given the amount the police found in the vehicle and the business about the mysterious passenger leaving the bag and the scales in the utility? That one was never going to fly.'

'Particularly as we'd lost our key witness,' I added, thinking of Con.

'A key witness found dead last year in a back alley up at the Cross? Really? You think?'

I could do nothing but shrug and agree with the man's skepticism. It was true. Poor Con was gone but even had he been in court to testify for the plaintiff this morning, it would have been just more grist for the prosecution's mill.

'It didn't hurt him having a person of your stature standing beside him, going guarantor for him. And the Honourable John Brown's character reference. You know, don't you, he was looking at two years in Long Bay?'

I looked at Yuri, standing off from us a little way. He seemed even more Zen at that moment than usual, somewhere inside his own head. He had just dodged a great big bullet and had much to consider.

'We know,' I said. 'And I agree it couldn't have gone better in there just now. Thank you.'

'You'll get the bill,' he laughed.

I didn't laugh. I knew the bill would be savage. But I did offer to take him to lunch. Of course, being of the law, his time was too valuable, and given that lunch with us was probably not billable hours now, he declined with thanks, and that was okay because Yuri and I had plans for the afternoon.

We were off to look at boats. We were people who spent

endless hours walking up and down marinas along the east coast, him explaining to me what was good or bad about a particular boat design, and me suggesting we go indoors for a G&T.

We had a couple of likely sailing boats to look at while down in Sydney this week. *Tuska* was the name we had already chosen for the one we would eventually buy. Yuri said the word in Swahili translates as "the brave warrior who goes out ahead of the tribe". I made no objection to naming our future boat *Tuska*. I would be happy to play First Mate. Had the court case gone the other way, I would have been driving back up to Byron alone and with no intention of checking out likely cruising vessels.

I felt the hard yards were now behind us. Yuri had delivered me the graceful Balinese teahouse he had promised, and he was 'clean'. I felt confident of him staying that way.

All that was left was to go to work on the dream; the cruising yacht, the tiki bar and the wide blue sea. I had already made approaches to Capitol Finance to see if I would be able to finance the purchase of a boat.

Of course, they said yes. And at 17% interest, why wouldn't they? Dreams don't come cheap.

FORECLOSURE

Parting is all we know of heaven,
And all we need of hell.
                                                    Emily Dickinson

As wonderful as our Byron Bay home was, and as much as we loved living there, I felt it necessary after Yuri's court case to remove him from his old haunts, get him away from the kind of people who would tempt him back into their dark vortex, the drug dealers and their sad clients.

If his rehabilitation was to be sustained he had to look forward, not backwards. And there were more opportunities for his obligatory community service work down in Sydney.

I rented an apartment in Balmain.

My friend Debbie—she, late of Spargo's—and her husband, Leo, occupied the teahouse, loving it and caring for it, and even crowning its glory by conceiving their first child under its magic roof.

Yuri found useful voluntary work in Sydney, putting in many days in an old seamen's home where, in addition to emptying spittoons and ashtrays, he shared his scrimshaw skills with a few of the elderly inhabitants. The majority of his time was served, however, by putting his shipwright and carpenter's skills to work on the restoration of the *James Craig*, a grand old 19thcentury square rigger, a heritage ship moored at Rozelle.

Later, when she started taking paying passengers, the ship

would be moored alongside our Foxtel studios on the finger wharf at Pyrmont. This was great. Some days when I was recording, I could take my lunch out on the wharf and share it with him.

A couple of times he brought me onto the *James Craig* and sneaked me below deck to show me, proudly, the work he was doing on restoring the sleeping births. Another day, a lovely sunny Sydney day as he was coming to the end of his community service period with the ship, he was given the honour of helming her, under full sail, as she made her way out onto Sydney Harbour.

And before he left, he was given a small off-cut of the historic timber which he used as a base for a barometer, presenting the nautical piece to me as a gift. I still have it and still tap it every so often when I walk past, but I have no idea how to tell from a barometer's dial whether it is going to rain or not, and how soon. Never the less, it's a pretty piece and a fitting memento of a special time in my life, being that it is an instrument for reading atmospheric pressure and making predictions.

It was while we were living in the Balmain apartment that the New York twin towers and the Pentagon were hit, and the brave souls in the plane heading into Washington agreed to sacrifice their lives for what they thought to be a greater good. Yuri had gone to bed. I was still up, watching a TV drama. When I came back from making myself a cup of tea and saw the first tower had been hit I thought it was a promo for the show. I watched, horrified, as this proved to be a wrong assumption and the nightmare unfolded.

~~~

Eventually, with Yuri's obligations to the state all-but satisfied, and feeling confident he could withstand the temptations of the Byron scene, we were ready to return home. He was yearning to be back near his children, even though his daughter was still wanting nothing to do with her father, nor allowing him to see his baby grandson. Yet he wasn't giving up hope. Cedar's birthday was coming up, and acknowledging he was now a member of a band that was playing gigs around the Byron traps, we bought him some serious music equipment and Yuri was looking forward to celebrating his son's birthday with him.

If I have never done another good deed in my life, I will always know I played a part in bringing father and son back together. For a time, at least. It had been in my thinking from the get-go when I counted on the teenager being so proud of his father's efforts in converting the run-down shack into the splendid teahouse that he would be able to withstand his mother's onslaughts on his father's character. And as the youth matured it seemed he had.

With fond farewells for my own family, we packed the Golf and departed Sydney. With sweet anticipation, we were heading back up the Pacific Highway to our Xanadu.

I had no idea, however, of the news that awaited me.

~~~

I went to the letterbox one rainy morning a couple of months after our return and learned to my horror that the bank was calling in my loan.

The NAB, left to itself, might not have foreclosed on me so peremptorily but it was in league with an American home lending firm at the time—one which would shortly go belly up. Call it schadenfreude, but I was delighted when I read the following year about that motherfucker's collapse.

I was never going to stand a chance. The US bank was merciless. It was foreclosing on me, end of story. And what made it seem more unfair was that the guillotine was about to fall despite the fact the NAB and I were still in negotiations over an amount of $5,000 of mine which the Byron branch had misplaced, funds that would ultimately turn up a year or so later, discovered to have been dropped into the account of a Mr. Roberts!

While I had been disputing the run-away funds—the result of their weird and wonderful bush accounting practices—my financial situation had deteriorated. My Foxtel fees had not been sufficient to cover our Balmain rent as well as service my mortgage, pay the rent on a work shed for Yuri, pay off the boat loan and the lease on a Toyota truck I had purchased for Yuri's new handyman business.

In addition, my sister and I had been providing round-the-clock nurses to care for our invalid mother after our father's passing.

When purchasing the Byron property, I had reckoned on my monthly maintenance payments meeting my mortgage obligations, but some time ago those payments had ceased. It was always going to happen that I would wind up this broke. Not only had I been extravagant with the renovations; not only had I been foolishly irresponsible in maintaining a man's heroin habit for so long, but the divorce settlement had been wobbly from the outset.

The Family Court had ordered John to make monthly maintenance payments to me until the year 2005, at which time the order was to be reviewed and adjusted in the light of our circumstances.

But now I was out on my own financially. John had a legal right to stop the payments. The divorce settlement had a clause stating that the payments would stop if I were to cohabit with a man for a period of three months.

I had not factored this in the morning I signed up for twenty years of home mortgage repayments and then picked up the man of my dreams at a roundabout later that afternoon. It shows you should always read the fine print.

John—no doubt rightly angered that his Family Court payments were helping fund a heroin habit—had eventually put a stop to the madness. Now, with no regular income, and a whole lot of outgoings, the bank was forcing me into a fire sale. Their actions seemed unfair. They held the deeds to the property, and at my expense not theirs, I had significantly enhanced the value of it.

They could reasonably have waited until the missing $5,000 dispute was settled and I could find alternate funds. But the NAB's American partner was going down the tubes, its marriage of convenience with the NAB having gone sour, and they were determined they were foreclosing on me.

Put it on the market now or we will do it for you and you suffer the consequences, I was told.

Goodbye little *Teahouse of the Splendid Moon*. Goodbye glorious blue Pacific Ocean out there beyond the dunes. Goodbye Byron Bay. It looked as if my sortie into the world of property ownership would be short-lived.

I tore up the letter and tossed the pieces to the wind. Fuck 'em! I walked through the rain, stripping as I went down to the beach and for a time, lost myself in the chill of the glorious wine-dark sea.

~~~

Those who put a romantic spin on poverty are fools and dissemblers.

Being in debt, owing money when you don't know where your next dollar is coming from is Hell. Even today, as I drive by the NAB in Jonson Street Byron Bay I still get a sinking feeling in my gut recalling how I used to fear punching my numbers into that ATM and waiting for the machine to tell me whether or not I had sufficient funds.

In the weeks to come, as Yuri worked off the tail-end of his community service, we eked out an existence—some days on not much more than Weetabix and water—while I tried to scrape the funds together from my Foxtel pay-packet to get my repayment schedule back on track. I invoiced Foxtel at the end of each month, but the funds could take time finding their way into my account.

Meanwhile the Shylocks kept demanding their pound of flesh. It was during a period when I had been sin binned by Foxtel and no fees coming in, that in order to buy groceries and pay the household bills I was forced into lining up at the Byron Bay Centerlink office for what was referred to in those days as the Deserted Wives Pension.

It was a humbling experience to stand in line with my hand out for the hand-out. I could not afford to think about the days of glory when, as the Minister's Good Lady I had been duchessed by wives of diplomats in foreign lands, been escorted through Paris, London, New York and Rome in limousine convoys bearing the Australian flag and outriders on motorcycles clearing a path.

Such times as I had taken tea with the Queen at Stoke Lodge in London; flown to New York in the Concorde at Mk 11; sat alongside Pele at an international soccer match; met Mohamed Ali in the garden of his Chicago home.

And at a party given during the 1984 Los Angeles Olympics, had sat between Dustin Hoffman and Jane Fonda; and at another party during those L.A. Games, had told a rude and arrogant Duke of Edinburgh to get fucked after losing my temper, believing he had insulted me with one of his snobbish remarks.

When in the course of my PR business I had worked with legends like Frank Sinatra, Joe Cocker and George Harrison.

Aaahh, the Eighties!

As I shuffled a little further up the Centerlink line that day, I recalled what Katherine Hepburn's character, Eleanor of Aquitaine, in *The Lion in Winter*, asks the universe when she feels she has reached her nadir; "From where we started did we ever get this low?"

This certainly felt like a low point in my life.

Sadly, there was nothing more I could do. I was forced to sell our sweet little Balinese Teahouse, sell it for a miserable sum of $326,000. Less than I had paid for it a few years ago.

To fast forward the reel for a moment: The Gold Coast couple who purchased the property would eventually build a low-cost Asian-style longhouse at the front of the yard incorporating the big ugly garage, the one that in a former life had been a hydroponics greenhouse. When they put the place on the market in the mid-2000s it would have a price tag of $2.8million! I have the clipping from the real estate section of the *Byron Echo*, a full-colour half–page advertisement for the property.

And on my most recent visit to Suffolk Park—the suburb my colleague Wayne Young had disparaged as "Sufferers Park"—I noted that the beach front properties along Alcorn Street are being referred to now as prime real estate, the Dress Circle of Byron, with prices hitting the three-million-dollar mark.

John Singleton and Jerry Harvey moved into Suffolk Park with their luxury resort, attracting a high-paying clientele. There is also a gated community at one end of Alcorn street and a fancy subdivision estate at the other. So unlike the Byron of old.

It is probably little wonder that I feel my Byron Bay—the one that had once enchanted me—has lost its charm, and the neighbourhood gone to pot. The Buddha exhorts his followers to cultivate a mind that clings to nothing. I try, but it ain't easy.

Subsequent owners ravaged our beautiful *Teahouse of the Splendid Moon,* conceived with such imagination one magic summer-blossomed night at a table in a small Tibetan cafe that no longer exists, and whose purchase I celebrated in lusty fashion with a gypsy man on a candle-encircled rug down by the water's edge.

The old order changes, making way for new and God for-fills Himself in many ways. One of those ways was for the new owners to spread a tonne of white hardware pebbles under the tuckeroos and scatter their kitsch tubular plastic outdoor furniture under the palms where my Buddha and Ganesh and wind chimes had once kept watch over us.

As if that weren't enough, they deconstructed our lovely, if minuscule, Asian-style kitchen, trashing the beautiful antique Coromandel screens and the lovingly polished rosewood bench slab, replacing everything with an ugly, pragmatic store-bought red plastic kitchen.

And sacrilege of all sacrileges; our perfect little eyrie, our bedroom up among the stars, was pulled down so as the occupiers of the main house could have an uninterrupted view of the ocean.

Tough luck for them however, as they did not count on the rapacious nature of Byron's bushes.

These days, there is no way to see the ocean from the big house, thanks to the fact Yuri and I cleared away the strangling bitu bush from the tuckeroos. And because they tore it down, there is no way to see the ocean from the little yurt that once sat above our *Teahouse of the Splendid Moon*, a teahouse the owners these days promote to the tourist trade as *Bamboo Cottage*.

In 2012 I heard from the local real estate agent that *Bamboo Cottage* was rented for as much as $1,500 per week in the holiday season and enjoyed a 90% occupancy rate all year round.

God knows what it is bringing in now. While Debbie and Leo lived there they would drop $100 in the fruit bowl—on a good week.

The weird thing about buying a house is that a contract is exchanged, and your house shuts you out and promiscuously opens itself up to its new owners. In the case of my iconic little shack, that was always going to seem a betrayal. Walls that had once been privy to our intimacies, to our whispered secrets and our dreams, by dint of new ownership become privy to new intimacies, other people's whispered secrets and dreams. Strangers lay where Yuri and I had lain and made love, talking well into the night as we planned our pilgrimage to far off places.

And where we had laid out on our starry veranda, chasing away the pesky brush turkeys while we looked up at the skies and he described the constellations for me, others now lie, doing what? No longer mine to know, of course. No longer my business. I became a stranger to my precious teahouse.

The Buddha teaches us to cultivate a mind that clings to nothing. All suffering comes from desire. Let it go, okay?

We packed up our belongings and watched them go into the removalist's van to be taken around the corner to a storage place in the Byron Bay industrial estate until we made other living arrangements.

When I find myself in Suffolk Park these days, I take the

walk, not through the pandanus and ferns track that was our special path through to the dunes and down onto the beach, but the public route, the one I took the morning long ago when I stumbled on the jogger in yellow budgie smugglers running along the beach, and then came upon a young real estate agent in shiny shoes, hesitant about showing a middle-aged woman a property, as yet unlisted, and in a dilapidated and sorry condition.

On these occasions, I stop half way down the steps to the beach and peak over the ti-tree fence, and I see what once was mine, where once so much happened that would change my life. I cannot help it; I go into a melancholy fug, crazy Celt that I am.

If only walls could speak—that's the common sentiment. But what if our *Teahouse of the Splendid Moon's* lovely golden bamboo walls could speak but have chosen to stay schtum?

I do hope it's the case. I really do.

TUSKA

You must tear down parts of an old building to restore it,
and so it is with a sensual life.

Rumi

It was August 2000 when Yuri and I were invited to a party at
the Gazebo Hotel in Kings Cross. Invited in my capacity as a
Foxtel Channel Ten personality. It was a lavish Olympic
Games event put on by the Murdoch family, part owners of
Foxtel. Rupert was in town for the Games. Cathy Freeman
triumphantly brought home the 400 meters final that night,
giving the world a thrilling moment of heart-stopping joy.

We arrived at the venue in time to go into the bar for a pre-
arrival drink and were able to see on the giant overhead
television screen Cathy winning the race. A memorable
moment, even for someone like me who is not the sporting
type, despite having been married to the Hawke government's
Minister for Sport in a previous life.

Yuri looked dashing in his hired dinner suit. I think I had
polished up well, myself, considering that at this stage we were
stone motherless broke and living aboard—and working on
restoring—our classic old timber yacht in Balmain. By now,
Tuska was not merely a dream but a reality.

The cocktail dress I wore that night came courtesy of my
son-in-law, Michael Bracewell who owned the successful
eponymous fashion house. It is not easy to dress in evening
gear in a cramped yacht cabin, with only a communal

bathroom on the marina for showering, make-up and hair styling. Being only able to afford a swing mooring out in the bay at this stage, we had to row in *George*, our tiny dinghy, to get to the shore and walk to my car, parked further along the street.

Not exactly door-to-door limousine treatment. But we presented well; a couple of toffs, in fact, and the night would reward us with the odd compliment. Being a pair of feral Yachties these days, we appreciated whatever flattery came our way.

When we walked into the crowded and noisy Gazebo ballroom, I looked around for my fellow Beauties, expecting to be placed at their table. Through the crowd, I spotted Prue McSween, Ita Buttrose and Jeannie Little sitting at a table half-way down the room. I took Yuri's hand and started to head in that direction.

It was then I felt someone tap me on the shoulder and looked around to see a woman shaking her head. Uh-uh, she said, and took me by the arm.

Okay, I thought. We are the rough trade. Lucky even to have been invited, knowing what Brian Walsh felt about his troublesome, unpredictable and often erratic Beauty, Jan Murray. I wasn't teacher's pet, not by a long stretch. Fair enough, I figured we were about to be frog-marched to a table even further away from the action.

I shot Yuri an apologetic look and had already decided we would cut and run early. Stuff 'em. They can shove their high-falutin' fancy-pants Olympic Games hootenanny up where the sun don't shine.

Imagine how surprised I was to find that we were being ushered through the crowded room, eyes following us, up towards the dais at which sat Lachlan and Sarah Murdoch.

We were warmly greeted by husband and wife and introduced to the rest of the table.

Apparently, as I later learned from Lachlan, he had especially requested my presence.

Well, I'll be buggered! Imagine it; me, the bad girl of the show, the pariah when it came to scoring invitations to the Zemanek Christmas bashes, and here we were, me and my mate, being invited to sit with the nearest thing Australia has to royalty. At the top table, no less.

I can't remember—and best I don't—just how many glasses of Krug I downed that night. All I know is that when Yuri and I finally rolled out of the Gazebo, the bubbles in my head meeting the cold night air of Kings Cross, I passed out.

I came to, laying prone on a park bench just a short way up from the hotel. In the shadow of the police station. I was drunk, for sure. But the heavy doses of SSRIs I was taking for my Bi Polar condition did not help, either. The medication and the Krug was a volatile combo that would have been best avoided had I been of sound mind.

It was late, the early hours of the morning in fact, but the place was pumping. Thanks, mainly, to Cathy Freeman's victory it was a wild, celebratory night. Sydney took to the streets determined to carouse. A party mood more exhilarating than any New Years' Eve bash had overtaken the place. Total strangers—boozed up or not—seemed to stop and embrace each other. Everlasting friendships were cemented in the glorious excitement of the night. Drunks fell down. Cops smiled at everyone. Car horns blared. Whistles blew. Balloons and streamers floated among green and yellow fighting kangaroo flags adorning terrace houses.

Our Cathy had shown the world what we Aussies could do. Rejoice and be happy Nation!

Me? I was leaning over in the bushes throwing up.

I felt a hand tap me. Another one. This time, however, I recognized its owner. Donna Bracewell, my son-in-law's sister was out and partying. Donna was no less drunk than me, but Donna was able to stand straight. Maybe she'd had more practice. Who knows? We hugged, she met Yuri, we raved about Cathy's victory and then she caught up with her crowd.

There are many things in life I don't understand.

For instance; why don't seagulls sit in trees? They don't. I know, because I've been observing them for years, watching them fly high, past perfectly reliable tree branches until they can land on water, on sand, on boats or on jetties. What do they have against trees? You will never see a seagull in a tree. And yellow writing pads? Who decided, and when, that first drafts and rough notes would be written on yellow pads and not green or pale blue or any other colour? Another mystery that plays with my mind is why do historians always speak of past events in the present tense? They could be relating some event that took place in 1770 but they tell it in the present tense as if the characters were in the room beside them. Why?

And how about this for the million-dollar question? How low was I prepared to go in my relationship—albeit vicariously—with heroin? I think the night of the Murdoch's Olympic Games party when I ended up drunk, to the point of blacking out, in a Kings Cross brothel is possibly the answer to that one.

More later.

~~~

Each time Yuri fell off the wagon it took a serious toll on my finances and on my will. Only an understanding of the issue, an empathy with his needs, my affection for him, and a good dose of stubbornness kept me working towards the prize.

It also took courage and determination on Yuri's part, of course. The encouraging thing was that the episodes became further and further apart. It seemed easier than in previous times for him to clean up his act, and to keep from sliding back into the old ways.

We both understood, however, that the Devil never takes a holiday.

Eventually, after my mother's passing, I was able to use my share of our parents' modest legacy to put down a deposit on another house; this time a small waterfront fisherman's cottage on an island in the Pittwater close to Sydney.

Again, I would be buying the property with my heart rather than my head. The modest little three-bedroom fibro house, sadly dilapidated, had been sliding down the side of the hill for years, evidenced by the wide cracks in its brick foundations. Another orphan. Another dwelling no one wanted. The owner was a district court judge, and apparently the gentleman had suffered a family tragedy and the grieving man had lost all interest in spending his weekends with his sons in a fisherman's cottage on an island in the Pittwater.

The waterfront house I was being shown reminded me of 'Ettalong', a rough old holiday house on the Central Coast of NSW that my mother's relatives used to own and in which I had enjoyed many holidays during my childhood. Robert Drew, the Australian author has written admiringly about the quintessential Aussie beach house of the Fifties. And here I had found one waiting for me.

As soon as the agent walked me through the door of the property I was sold. Memories came flooding back of the holiday house of my childhood and all those glorious summer days. Sticky salty crystals clinging to the hairs on my small sunburnt limbs. Days when the rubber of my black blow-up tube was so hot it burned my tummy when I raced with it into the surf and rode waves that dumped me. Memories of zinc cream, thick, white and sticky on my sunburnt lips and shoulders. The gritty sand in my bum, piles of it settled in the crutch of my red and white bubble suit swimmers that had been a gift for my seventh birthday.

While the agent left me to roam the modest property I became a kid again, imaging I was running inside 'Ettalong', feet covered in sand, stretching up on tip toes to reach what I needed on the big scrubbed pine table in the centre of the kitchen, making a Vegemite sandwich on doorstop slices of white bread hacked from a fresh loaf my Aunty Amy had baked that morning before any of us were even awake—heaps of cold butter piled on, lathers of the dark yeasty spread on top. My dopey father laughing about it, sitting on the veranda steps in his shorts and bare chest patiently untangling my fishing line, putting on another sinker and hook for me that was going to hurt me later when it caught my finger and made my finger bleed.

And my baby sister, Carolyn, and cousins galore, all of us running wild in the house, jumping on beds, hiding from each other, yelping when we were caught. Playing Snakes & Ladders out on the big closed-in veranda as summer rain pelted down on the iron roof and we threw the dice, squabbled, laughed, made our moves and planned our next foray down to the beach as soon as there was a break in the weather.

Yes, that little waterfront cottage on the Pittwater I was being shown had, for the moment, shot me right back in time to those magic places. I felt it all around me.

Easy to see the property purchase was sentimental one. But not quite as capricious as the Byron Bay one because I had been checking out the small island's best aspects for some time.

I stood with Yuri one afternoon after a bush walk on top of West Head with its wide vistas of the magnificent Pittwater, and spotted the island sitting there in its sublime setting.

It was then that I understood I could honour my Mum and Dad's modest legacy.

I would create a place where the huge Murray-Brown clan could come together in a uniquely Australian way; swimming, fishing, sailing, beach barbecuing, snakes-and-laddering, and generally cousin-to-cousin, sibling-to-sibling, friend-to-friend enjoying a pure holiday experience.

And as a bonus, being an island, I figured it would insulate Yuri from any bad company that might threaten his health. It would be a long trek to Kings Cross from this off-shore location if the cravings got to him. It was still a one-day-at-a-time effort, as the medicos had predicted, and there had been lapses, of course there had, times when his Physeptone medication wasn't enough to ease the pain of his accident-affected ribs and back or his shipwright's knees, or the heartache of rejection that came with being the father of children who continued to reject him.

I had been naive in thinking heroin would be exclusive to Kings Cross. There was always someone in his orbit ready to take him to, it is that the insidious drug is everywhere. It's just that most of us live lives oblivious to the devil in our midst.

The price on the island house was right; an absolute waterfront, an hour from Sydney's CBD, a deep, forested hillside piece of land running down to its own private beach—all for just a couple of hundred thousand more than Alcorn Street had cost me.

Overlooking the building's shortcomings, dreaming of how we could make it to our liking, I put down my deposit and took possession of the cottage, along with everything inside it, including not only a vintage windsurfer board, but bed linen, furniture, dog-stained rugs, cutlery, crockery, and a full tool shed, all of which the judge had inventoried, and most of which I immediately donated to charity.

Moving on and off an island, I would soon discover, is no easy matter. Many sellers simply walk out on the mother-load of things they have accumulated over the years, finding it easier and cheaper than having to contend with the tides and the weather in barging their belongings off the island.

I had fallen for the house's exposed timber ceiling beams, its many-louvered windows, the veranda, the tiny bedrooms each with their bespoke bunks, the old-fashioned pull cords for light switches, the 1950s kitchen cupboards.

I loved the dark old cobwebbed shed under the house with its collection of vintage shovels, spades, various shaped glass containers from an earlier age, and a bench of long-forgotten workman's tools, tools my darling Dad would have loved to get amongst had he still been alive. All together I loved the cottage's rough and ready ambience and, of course, its proximity to the magnificent Pittwater on its doorstep.

Given the dilapidated nature of the house, I knew it would take most of my earnings and a powerful amount of Yuri's imagination and back-breaking labours to breathe life back into the place. Building on the side of a steep hill, on an island was never going to be easy but Yuri seemed unfazed by the prospect and time would prove what a sensational job he did in creating *Glencairn*, our perfect beach house.

We missed Byron Bay but soon settled in to life in Sydney, albeit, not the mainland, but an island.

~~~

Yuri had been working hard, not only on the house

renovations—a mighty task that would further damage his shipwright's knees and the back he had injured in his 1996 road accident—but at the same time, on restoring *Tuska*.

I had also been working hard on both jobs, learning shipwright skills on the go. The boat needed a lot of work to bring her up to speed. I spent weeks burning off old paint with a heat gun and learning how to caulk a teak deck in the old-fashioned way by using a great big heavy iron caulking ladle full of a hot tar-like substance to pour between the planks—after having spent painful days digging out the old rubbery gunk from between the boards to make way for the new.

We were down to our last dollar most weeks. I was up to my neck in house renovation expenses, boat restoration expenses, house mortgage repayments and boat financing repayments, plus the Toyota truck, and a small barge boat with a 60hp engine, both required for our building work. Someone gave us a huge pinwheel of Turkish delight they had been given as a Christmas gift. Someone else gave us a bunch of MacDonald's burger vouchers. We lived off such offerings, grateful for all donations.

There were days when, on the way up to the island from Balmain to work on the house, we would call in to Woollies at Frenchs Forest and pick up some fresh fruit and vegetables, not from the shelves, not groceries you put in your trolley that you pay for at the counter.

No, we didn't go inside Woolies to pick up our provisions, instead we joined the ranks of the Saturday afternoon skip jumpers around the back of the building. Amazing how many perfectly good punnets of strawberries get tossed out, how many edible bags of onions and potatoes go in the refuse bins.

When I look back, at the extraordinary financial liabilities I took on with nothing more than my Foxtel income, I appreciate the concerns of my family. I spent years being incapable of acting rationally, living proof that the bi-polar person is often financially promiscuous in the manic phase.

~~~

I knew Yuri had been clean for a decent stretch. But I guess on that crazy Olympic Games night of nights he was going with the flow, the Krug not having sent him high enough to satisfy, but just high enough to make him irresponsible.

And so, I found myself in the dawn of a Kings Cross morning walking towards a knocking shop down the end of a god-forsaken lane. Maxim's, I think was the name of the joint. Or Maxine's.

What I mostly remember is being led by Yuri up a set of horrible stinky steps in the dark, to a hideous little cell-like room with a bed and a concrete floor. I remember the smell; vomit and things unmentionable.

The night had certainly thrown up its share of weird experiences. I remember thinking, somewhere in my challenged brain, that I should be recording it all in my writer's journal.

I didn't. Instead, I passed out on the bed while my handsome brave shot up.

~~~

To make the beach house large enough to serve as a suitable holiday house for my family of five adult children, the partners and, at that time, ten grandchildren—the house had to be jacked up for us to be able to build our living space on the lower level.

That was fun, jacking a whole house up while Yuri and I, and one other—a local man named Tim—worked beneath it, digging out one hundred and fourteen tonne of rocks and clay, all of which had to be sent down a make-shift shoot to sea level and dumped into one tonne bags to be barged off the island.

Given the cottage stood on a slippage site, we had to sink a dozen massive peers into the ground to claw the building into the hill. The concrete pour took from six o'clock in the morning, when the first barge loaded with a cement truck hove into view across the bay, until eight o'clock that night when the last of the two barges that had been working the pour all day, finally sailed off into the night.

Only then did a gentle rain come down. We celebrated with an all-nighter down on our beach.

Sometimes, at a particularly wearying days end, Yuri and I would look at each other and feel we had taken on too much. Many around us thought likewise. But we kept going.

Once the house was jacked up, we were separated from the house's plumbing. Thankfully, the old place had an outdoor WC, but our shower was two buckets of cold water we poured over each other after lathering up. Sometimes a shower could take a long, lovely time.

All this, and I was still fronting up to Foxtel to record B&B. No wonder I gave make-up and wardrobe headaches some days, arriving with paint in my hair and chipped nails.

Meanwhile, days spent scouring demolition sites for recycled flooring boards and old doors and windows was part of the happy experience of bringing the old place back to life while maintaining its integrity as a typical 1950's Australian holiday house. One window we unearthed in our search was a huge oval-shaped affair which we rescued from a Sydney hotel demolition site. It took up the whole wall of one of the bedrooms and commanded a stunning view down the Pittwater to Newport. Today I marvel at how Yuri and his men managed to get it up the hill and installed.

We more than doubled the size of the home, beautifying it with the use of contrasting textures—timber, sandstone and louvered glass. Yuri made the folding doors that opened out onto the large deck from Alaskan cedar, a lovely soft golden timber.

The sandstone work which we did ourselves was among the hardest and heaviest work I've ever undertaken. The shape of my hands changed forever under the daily assault of breaking up great rocks, rolling them up or down the hill and then chipping away at them with heavy tools and putting them in place to form the walls of the ground floor.

Lugging forty kilo bags of cement on my shoulder, up from the jetty, and helping to mix and pour the concrete behind the arranged sandstone did wonders for my physique. The Council's certifying engineer who regularly checked on our work was in awe of Yuri's sandstone walls, saying they would resist a tsunami. They were certainly a thing of beauty when the morning sun, reflecting off the bay, caught their sandy creams and golds. *The splendour falls on castle walls.*

So that I would never feel too far from Byron Bay, when we completed the renovations on the main house, Yuri built a Balinese-style writer's studio for me, up at the back of the property, among the forest of giant spotted gums.

Like the main house, it too had uninterrupted views over the sparkling Pittwater. This one we christened *The Teahouse of the August Moon,* having finished it and christened it with love one wintery August night.

The teahouse became Yuri's showpiece, his legacy.

It is a true work of art, built totally without nails or screws, using the traditional carpenter's joinery technique of mortise & tenon. We shipped the woven bamboo for the walls down from Byron, and with soft red cedar, he made louvered windows for ventilation beneath the large fixed glass picture-windows. A woven rush ceiling was held in place with carved timber beams. The double doors were teak, a treasure I had been storing for many years, having purchased the beautifully carved piece in the Eighties in Semenak in Bali from an octogenarian in whose home I had been staying. He told me he had carved them as his sampler for his mentor when he was a fifteen-year-old.

We hung two red Chinese lanterns below the wide eves and laid a randomly shaped rockery path up to the teahouse from the main building, setting large fern fronds and sea shells into the wet cement to leave an impression.

The Balinese teahouse, just big enough for a four-poster carved antique Balinese bed, a lounge and a bookcase, was admired as an exotic hideaway nestled on a hillside in a landscape of Hawkesbury sandstone escarpments and giant eucalypts. To remind us of other days, and to shed his blessing on the place, we sat our Byron Buddha at the top of the steps.

Once we considered the job done, and fully fitted and furnished, thanks mainly to the local Vinnie's stores, we planned to leave it to the family and be off. The Pittwater was sensational, but it wasn't big enough to contain our dreams. We were ready to sail pathless and wild seas. Away from all formulas, towards our magic tiki bar and white coral sands.

Building our little wooden dinghy to compliment *Tuska* was a learning experience for me. Yuri insisted that everything was done in the way of traditional boat-building.

We hired a storage workshed in Balmain and Yuri set about framing up the hull, with me helping him steam the timber planks over an old copper so that he could bend them to his design.

He taught me how to carvel-plank the small boat, using the

roving method, a traditional form of boat building used to attach the outer planking to the hull's frame. It was a fascinating process, building a boat with the roving method, time-consuming but rewarding.

The shipwrights of yesterday believed in the magic qualities of a piece of timber that could allow mankind to challenge wild oceans, and they gave building those vessels their patience and devotion. What I loved was that the roving method required perfect team work.

They were happy days, working alongside my mate, being impressed with his shipwright's knowledge and abilities, and to feel I was not only useful, but learning an important aspect of traditional boat building.

We christened our sweet little dinghy *George*, in honour of my dad. The shape of *George's* hull followed the same lines as *Tuska's* hull, and, like the yacht, it was painted white with a dark green line along the bulwark.

It was a mini-me, replicating the mother ship. When *George* was eventually launched and being towed behind *Tuska*, it was a comical sight.

Tuska was a Lyle Hess design based on the British pilot cutters of old, and a replica of *Taliesin*, the Lyle Hess yacht owned by Lin and Larry Pardy.

The *Classic Wooden Boat* magazine once featured the design on its front cover, nominating it as the boat most likely to go out—into the roughest seas—and come home. With her nine tonne of keel and her finely shaped hull, she was a champion of the wild waves. The British pilot cutters were the boats once used by Lloyds of London. These sturdy vessels waited in harbour until the bell was rung over on the French coast, and then, braving all weather and no excuses, they would cross the Channel for their cargo and bring it safely back to England.

Eventually we secured a mooring out front of the beach house for *Tuska* and after a laborious day of carting timbers, mixing concrete and putting tonnes of iron in place to support the upper story, it was pleasing to load up the boat with wine, beer, cheese and whatever else, and sail her up the Pittwater towards Lion Island, to moor her in one of the secluded bays for the weekend and observe the sea turtles, the sea birds and the dolphins that played around the boat, and generally bliss out on *Tuska's* warm and inviting teak deck.

ANGELS OF FATE

O'er the glad waters of the dark blue sea,
Our thoughts as boundless, and our soul's as free.

Lord Byron

I have a few memories of sailing *Tuska* that still give me goose bumps, novice sailor that I was when I embarked on the nautical life.

One day, after finishing up some particularly dirty and heavy building work on the island house, we decided to take the boat out for the rest of the afternoon and sail her up the Pittwater, to Patonga, a small holiday village with a great fish 'n chip shop and pub on the beach.

As ever, when *Tuska* was under full sail, with her headsail and main bellied out, sailors on other vessels would signal their admiration by tooting horns and waving as they sailed by. Even sailors on the big, flash fiberglass moulded racing yachts that famously plied the Pittwater would acknowledge the old lady.

With her 6ft bow sprit and bumpkin supporting a full display of sails, *Tuska* was a beautiful sight to see, one that reminded those who love timber boats of other days when quality trumped quantity, when a 30ft timber vessel with an 11ft beam was big enough, when a sailor could take on the wildest of oceans without the flash navigational instruments and all the other whiz-bang appurtenances which the luxury gin-palaces boast.

Tuska had few marine instruments. Yuri navigated by the stars, using his compass, slide rule and charts. For a depth-sounder and speed gauge we used what the ancient Greeks and Romans used; an old-fashioned method of dropping a heavy lead plummet over the bow, the rope of which has knots tied in it at regular intervals. By letting the hollow tube hit the sea bottom and then retrieving it, we could gauge from the number of wet knots the depth below our keel, and by emptying out what had surfaced with the cylinder we could tell whether we were over rocks, mud or sand.

It was my job to sink the primitive depth sounder and there would be times when we sailed the Whitsundays that my heart was in my mouth, hoping I was getting my readings right. If not, we were going to be in a world of pain. As Captain Cook discovered.

On the sunny afternoon of gentle breezes when we set out for Patonga, all sails to the wind, with me taking the helm while Yuri ducked below deck, I became aware the weather had suddenly changed. I heard a roaring noise and turned to look behind me, down the long stretch of water, back towards Bayview.

'Oh, my god, Yuri! Quick!' I could hardly see the mainland. The sun had been obliterated by a dark and swirling grey mass of cloud. Trees were bent over in the gale and leaves were eddying off the ground and flying through the air. And all of it coming our way, fast.

'Reef in the main!' Yuri called to me as he came topside and ran forward to bring in the headsail. As the waters of the bay turned from calm to violently choppy, he slid out onto the bow sprit and hauled in the headsail.

I, not nearly so bravely, tried to do my bit to reef the main sail.

A squall is a sudden, violent gust of wind, and that was what had just hit us. With so much sail up and me not able to reef the main in as quickly as I should have, the boat part capsized, traveling on its hull with most of its deck submerged.

My memory is of clinging on to the ship's railing with one hand, and trying to reef in a wet, heavy sail with the other, while flying under water.

When she started to right herself, the force of the gale tore a cleat from the deck. It flew past my face, missing my eye by a prayer.

Eventually we managed, thanks to a seasoned sailor's calm hands and the boat's reliability, to survive the squall and emerge from the wind tunnel in one piece. Yuri had ultimate faith in his boat and unlike me, hadn't panicked. Faith in his boat, he would later say, and laugh, but not so much faith in his First Mate.

It was extreme sport, a frightening experience for me, but proved to be a good test run for what we experienced in the days ahead, when we sailed the Whitsundays.

Before we set off for our Queensland sailing adventure, however, we took the boat down to Batemans Bay on the south coast of NSW. We had Tim, our builder's labourer, with us.

It was 6am when we brought *Tuska* down the Clyde, from where we had laid at anchor overnight, and sailed her into the bay. We planned to meet up with my sister Carolyn and her husband Alan for breakfast on the beach. Once through the deeper waters we were going to cruise into the shallow reaches and drop anchor then row ashore in *George*.

That was the plan, at least. We were not to know there would be a maniac out on the waters that morning.

Batemans Bay can be problematic. But not on this early

morning as the rising sun kissed the blue water and made it sparkle and dance for our pleasure.

Not knowing the waters, and knowing we would be headed into shallow territory, Yuri had decided to motor in rather than go in to the beach under sail. Tim and I were standing forward, on the lookout, keeping note of the depths as we came nearer in to shore, aware the boat's heavy keel would be a problem in shallow waters. Yuri was in the cockpit, resting one arm behind him, and the other along the length of the tiller. He, no doubt like me, was relishing the gentle calm of a south coast morning.

As the helmsman, he was relying on the signals from his two lookouts up front to let him know whether he had enough water under him. I had just turned around to give him a thumbs-up when I noticed out of the corner of my eye a small craft coming around a rocky corner of the bay, way off in the distance.

I could see how fast it was going, fast into the blinding morning sun. As it came closer, to my alarm, I could see it was heading in a straight line for *Tuska*!

'Starboard side. Two o'clock. A speedboat,' I signaled.

'Got it,' said Yuri, and started to swing *Tuska* away from the speedboat's trajectory, even though he would be going into waters Tim and I had not had a chance to assess.

Yuri could see by now how fast the other vessel was coming towards us. He knew he needed to clear a passage for it, quick smart.

Despite being a superior sailor and one who knew his boat well, clearing a passage was never going to be easy, given how fast the other boat was approaching and given how big and awkward *Tuska* was to manipulate speedily. She was a boat built to take on the biggest and roughest seas but not one that moved adroitly in shallow waters. She was a cruising yacht. And her engine was an old 20 h.p. Yanmar. She was a sailing lady. We rarely relied on the motor to get us around. Usually only when bringing her alongside or clearing a tricky harbour breakwater.

This morning, facing the predicament of an on-coming vessel, Yuri was bringing every skill he had into play to try to get his vessel out of the way of the other boat.

'God, what's it doing?' I said to Tim who was a first-time sailor and not a great deal of comfort at this stage. Tim had stunningly blue eyes in a weathery tanned face topped by a shock of curly black hair. He had the colouring of a Galway Irishman and the contagious smile that went with it. He was not smiling now, however. Neither was I. And neither was our captain.

'It's altering course! It's still heading for *Tuska*! It'll tea-bone us at this rate!' I could not believe what I was seeing. As I would later tell the Waterways authorities, it was as if the speedboat was locked onto us like an Exoset missile. No matter which way the helmsman turned *Tuska*, the other boat kept coming at it.

It was surreal; standing on deck, Tim and I waving our hands frantically, trying to attract the speeding craft's attention, and Yuri swerving *Tuska* from starboard to port and back again, desperate to avoid a collision.

I had never used the VHF radio, and had little idea how to work it, but with an accident now seeming inevitable I scurried below deck, flicked the switch and started yelling an SOS into the hand-held microphone.

I was mid-sentence when I heard the almighty thud above me, and the sound of splintering timbers. We had been hit mid-ships. Hit mightily hard.

Humpin—as we later learned was the name of the ugly twin-hulled fishing boat—had managed to t-bone us, smashing through the timber hull of the graceful old yacht we had so lovingly restored, and of which we were so proud. Miraculously no one was hurt. Only bruised, but significantly shaken. It brought the onlookers. And not long afterwards, the maritime authorities.

A middle-aged man and his younger mate had been returning from a night's fishing. Their windscreen was dirty with ocean spray and as they rode into the low-hanging sun in the east, they admitted later in court that they had been driving blind.

Driving fast and driving blind.

Not only that, but the one who had been at the wheel, the older man, explained how he had taken his eyes off the game to bend down for his sunglasses. No wonder his vessel had darted about, shifting its course so erratically. No one was at the wheel! But how random it had been that the runaway boat had managed to hone in on us, a moving target, albeit a somewhat awkwardly moving target.

I carried insurance on the boat but with Yuri's and my insistence that it be repaired in the old style, with full thirty-length timber planks and not merely patched up bits and pieces—the insurance company all-but bailed out at that point. The extra cost to bring her back into shape hit around the $25,000 mark. By the time we got to court, we believed there would be compensation from the other party's insurance company.

Wrong! The fool did not carry insurance.

And to add to our angst, it turned out the local Bateman's Bay magistrate was a drinking mate of the miscreant pilot, both were old Vietnam veterans, both long-time fishing buddies, and the man got away with a wrist slapping and a $160 fine.

We never did get to have breakfast with Carolyn and Alan that morning. John Lennon was right when he wrote that Life is what happens to you while you're busy making other plans.

~~~

For several years Yuri and I lived aboard *Tuska*—sometimes on swing moorings and other times on a marina birth.

Once he decided to sail the boat north to find shipwright work I made pilgrimages to be with him and my boat, living aboard her in Coffs Harbour, Brunswick Heads and Mackay.

Yuri was able to get reasonable, if spasmodic, ship repair work.

I still had my *Beauty & the Beast* responsibilities and so I was sometimes a fly in, fly out visitor.

I loved boat life—although I never went to sea but loved the sailing I did inside closed waters. Yuri, fine sailor that he was, made extraordinarily wild sea voyages in *Tuska*, taking her up north and back down to Sydney a couple of times, battling gale force winds and huge waves the size of tall buildings—green water—crashing over the bow and flooding the cockpit.

Single-handed sailing on wild oceans, and in a primitive, if spectacularly pretty sailing vessel is not for the faint-hearted.

It was the times during our long seasonal breaks in filming *Beauty & the Beast,* when I was able to live on the boat, that were most enjoyable. Marinas, for live-aboards, provide a cozy community. It was interesting to watch the big fishing trawlers, our neighbours, go out to sea at sunset and as the sun came up the following morning, welcome them back into harbour; to watch them unload their catch, to sit out on *Tuska's* deck eating fresh prawns for breakfast, prawns that had still been swimming in the ocean a short time before.

And there is nothing as soothing or as conducive to a good night's sleep as being in a cozy bunk on a swing mooring in a peaceful harbour. It is a primal joy. The waters lap gently against the hull. The boat enfolds you and rocks you. Romantic? Certainly. Yet there was nothing romantic about the time we set out from Mackay, heading for our Whitsundays adventure.

We got no closer than nearby St Bee's island when an unexpected storm arose and after listening on our VHF radio to the weather warnings, which were grim, we took cover in the lea of St Bees and Keswick Islands.

We dropped anchor, letting out as much chain as possible to lay on the sea bed, and for three days and nights, as the storm raged, and the winds howled, Yuri and I took two-hourly turns of standing in the centre of the cabin, looking out between the portholes on either side, finding fixed marks on the two islands and making certain the boat maintained its position. It was vital to make sure we weren't drifting.

We would later learn that a chartered yacht close by us, crewed by two American women and a Frenchman, had suffered a tragedy. Apparently, after realizing they were drifting, the man had dived to check his anchor. It was never made clear, but he went overboard and was never seen again.

We ran out of food on the third day. I salvaged a piece of dry bread, stuck it on a fishing hook, and threw the line overboard.

To my surprise, what I managed to bring in turned out—when I checked my fishing almanac—to be a whopping big barramundi. We feasted on barbecued barra all day and with what was left over, which was plenty, Yuri ceviched it by drenching small cubes in lime juice. Salt and peppered, it went down well with what was left of our vodka.

With the storm finally abating, we moved out of the protection of the twin islands and set sail north for Airlie Beach, seeing along the way many loggerhead and green turtles swimming beneath the clear waters and occasionally popping up around our boat, along with pods of dolphins that glided gracefully for nautical miles ahead of our bow.

Many times, we anchored offshore of small remote islands and went ashore to explore. For me, seeing the Whitsundays this way was a totally different experience from what I had known back in the Eighties as a visitor accompanying my Minister for Tourism spouse when he was promoting the attractions of the region to international holiday markets. Different, in that by sailing these waters in *Tuska* I felt so much closer to the real nature of the Great Barrier Reef, the quality that made it so unique and of itself. That which "... *speaks and spells.*"

At one stage my sun hat blew off. We circled around, Yuri at the helm, me poised way out on the six-foot bow sprit with my gaff ready to hook and haul in the hat.

Suddenly I saw a massive shark leap out of the water and take my lovely straw boater down to Davey Jones's Locker with him!

We had spent days diving off the transom of *Tuska*, reveling in the clear blue waters of paradise. Which only goes to show that paradise is illusory, at best a temporary madness.

All we wanted, we two gypsy souls, after all our efforts at rehabilitation and restorations, all we hoped for apart from our respective families' happiness, was for the two of us to be free to sail off into the great blue yonder, and if we were lucky, to find our tiki bar sitting on white coral sands somewhere beneath the coconut trees.

Sadly, it would never happen. Fate had other ideas.

~~~

It was 2008. Within months of returning from sailing the Whitsundays Yuri—healthy, drug-free and ready to earn money for our bigger adventure, our cruising life—was diagnosed with melanoma. Level Four. As bad as it gets.

When we were still living down in Sydney and finishing the Pittwater renovations, I had urged him to see a skin cancer specialist about what I thought was a suspicious lesion on his back. Instead, he took it to his GP in Darlinghurst who brushed it off, the nasty black thing on his back, as nothing more than a "geriatric wart".

We were living aboard *Tuska* in the Mackay harbour, Yuri working as a shipwright.

Before I left for Sydney I urged him to attend one of McKay's skin cancer clinics. The day after his visit, he received the bad news from a specialist dermatologist and was immediately admitted to the Mackay Base Hospital for surgery. I flew back up to be with him.

The surgeon, a day later, after receiving the biopsy report, phoned and said it had been a Level Two melanoma tumour he had removed. Level Two was treatable.

We breathed easy.

And then the man phoned back the following day. Sorry, he said, but there had been a mistake. The biopsy showed the tumour to be a Level Four tumour. Terminal.

I arranged an appointment for Yuri to see Professor Michael Quinn at the Sydney Melanoma Clinic. Quinn agreed with the diagnosis. Level Four. Meaning it had metastasized. Treatment for melanoma was still in its early stage, no miracle drugs were available to reverse the progress of the tumours. And Professor Quinn explained to us that neither chemotherapy nor radiotherapy was applicable to melanoma.

Our world fell apart.

I went through dark nights of the soul blaming myself. When he first visited his Taylor Street GP about the lesion and was told by the over-confident man that it was nothing to worry about I should have insisted that he seek specialist advice immediately. He had been attending that particular surgery when in Sydney because only certain GPs were licensed to prescribe the Physeptone medication he needed in the past when trying to kick his heroin habit.

I believe that the Darlinghurst doctor, knowing his patient's drug history, did not respect Yuri sufficiently. The man's misdiagnosis, and his failure to advise his patient to seek a specialist's opinion, would have a devastating effect on our lives. Yuri's, obviously, so much more than mine.

The dream ended. It seemed that all the courage and determination Yuri had shown in overcoming his addiction, the forbearance and the encouragement from the sidelines that I had been giving all these years was as nothing now. The gods were laughing.

Instead of living our pilgrim lives, instead of sitting under swaying palms and sipping Mai Tais, we were thrust into a world of anaesthetists, hospital corridors, pet scans, blood tests and the sheer gut-wrenching, life-draining awful days of waiting on biopsy results.

We returned to Sydney for his operation at the Royal Prince Alfred Hospital in Camperdown and for the on-going consultations at the Sydney Melanoma Clinic.

Yuri had thirty-six glands removed from under his left arm and drainage tubes inserted. Once he was home and I was caring for him, several times a day I would need to put a bowl beneath the end of the tube and as I had been shown by the hospital staff, push the yellowy white fluid that formed in there down the tube and into the bowl. This cleared the way for the wound to drain. To see such a big fit and handsome man having to undergo this awful procedure, for him to have to live with the anxiety of terminal cancer was cruel.

Yuri decided he would not return to the island home he had built for me on the Pittwater but would move permanently back up to Byron Bay, to live aboard *Tuska* at the Brunswick Heads marina and be close to his son and daughter and his, by now, three grandchildren, the grandchildren the daughter was still—notwithstanding that her father was so ill—withholding from him.

With his family being so cold-hearted and distant with him, I felt his emotional pain. As Zen-like as he was about his travails and his outward calm acceptance of his fate, I felt it was no time for him to be left alone. While needing to be in Sydney for work and to be close to my own family, I spent long stretches living on the boat at Brunswick Heads, putting in many travel hours in those troublesome days going backwards and forwards between my island home and Byron Bay.

If a squall is a violent gust of wind that comes up from nowhere and wreaks havoc in its path, that was what had hit us, metaphorically. We could only hope the bad winds would move on and leave us free to weigh anchor someday. Trim our sails and head out to sea.

Meanwhile, we measured time in medical appointments and the only horizon we could see was the one created by doctors' waiting rooms, surgeries, pathology departments, operating theatres and the like.

It was a limited horizon, a mighty pull-back from the one we two had aimed our sights at for so long. And yet, I never once heard Yuri curse his misfortune. He took it on the chin.

I think he believed he had been fortunate to have prevailed this long against the odds.

~~~

Working side-by-side for all those the years, sharing our lives so intensely throughout it all as we created our *Teahouse of the Splendid Moon* in Byron Bay, renovated an island home in Sydney and restored *Tuska*, was a joy and a heartache.

I had made a covenant when I promised to take an anguished man's soul back from the devil that dramatic afternoon in the old Byron Bay cemetery.

It was never going to be easy. Some might think I took too long about it, that I was slack for turning a blind eye for so long, that I was guilty of funding his addiction, being what the drug counsellor termed a co-dependent.

All I know is that I followed my intuition and have no regrets. I issued challenges, projects to engage his talents. I gave financial independence in the running of those projects. I offered encouragement. Offered praise when praise was due.

And best of all, I believe, I dreamed alongside him when he painted his enticing word pictures for me, images of the new horizons that awaited us. Our *Ultima Thule*.

Should I have done it differently? Should I have adopted the more callous zero tolerance strategy? Kicked the man out the door? Said to him, as I so often said to my *Beauty & the Beast* viewers when they complained about their misbehaving men; Here's your hat, buster, and there's the door!

I don't believe so. We muddled through. I believed his soul was redeemable, and time proved me right.

Despite the blows he suffered due to the Level Four melanoma diagnosis, despite all those terrible set-backs, sufferings and disappointments, he pulled out of his dependency, stayed clean and enjoyed a purposeful, creative life, returning to his beloved timbers and his scrimshaw work to earn a modest living.

Would I do it all again?

A thousand times yes.

Despite the heartaches, mostly my life with Yuri O'Byrne was an unalloyed joy, one great big mind-bending and thrilling adventure.

I climbed a steep learning curve during those years of living up close and personal with addiction and the view from the heights was dizzying in so many ways.

The journey took me from ignorance to understanding. From heartlessness to compassion. I lost much that can be accounted for in financial terms, but I gained insights, and for me that means everything.

I came away from the experience with the unbending belief that opioid addiction is a public-health issue and not a criminal issue. This does not mean I adopted a permissive attitude to hard drugs. But it does mean I learned to see around corners rather than being stubbornly mired in the back roads of old ideas.

Speaking to a conference in Atlanta in 2016 President Obama said, "For too long we've viewed drug addiction through the lens of criminal justice." He went on to say, "The most important thing to do is to reduce demand. And the only way to do that is to provide treatment—to see it as a public health problem and not a criminal problem."

Wise man! In the throes of their cravings a user will do anything to obtain the drug. Good people turn into cheats, become manipulative, and they lie.

They break your heart.

They can be heartless in their pursuit of what their brain receptors crave. They commit crimes for the love of heroin.

So why don't we take it off the streets and bring it into the clinics? Why not into a medical environment where there is no risk of fatal pollutants, where pharmaceutical-grade heroin is administered under the supervision of physicians. Where it can be done in tandem with a full program of psychological and social support. Who can say how many otherwise useful lives have been squandered, and how many more to come, while we ignore this approach to the problem that affects so many families?

Society has a responsibility to address the deadly issue.

Wars fought in the 1970's were responsible for the heroin plague; old men sending young men into the jaws of death. It happened in Vietnam. Soldiers who had seen the horrors of war came home with newly acquired drug habits.

It happened in Portugal when the youth of that country was drafted into Portugal's African wars, creating one of the worst drug epidemics in the world. Now, since 2001, that country treats heroin addiction as a health issue.

Canada, likewise gives therapy assistance to its addicts, with trials showing the long-term effectiveness of issuing prescriptive heroin.

Holland, often considered soft on hard drugs, is not. Holland still prosecutes large scale drug traffickers but it embraces the idea that addiction is a health issue and not one for the criminal books.

Even were it only for the effect it would have on reducing street crime, this approach to heroin addiction makes sense. But it will take a cohort of courageous politicians supported by intelligent voters to make the move towards enlightenment.

Sadly, I do not believe such a cohort exists in Australia.

I look back on the dozen or so years my gypsy and I spent together, at the way, despite our personal shortcomings—Yuri's addiction and my manic depression—we brought two neglected dwellings back to life and lovingly restored a forsaken old timber yacht so that when under full sail she would make other sailors turn to admire the beauty of her lines.

I feel grateful to the angels of Fate for giving us at least the chance, for a time, to dream, and to pursue our dreams with gusto.

For the damaged souls we were when Fate threw us together, I reckon we did not do too badly. We gave it a good shot, and by putting our creative minds to work and our backs into it, by restoring the things we believed had something that made them unique and worth the effort—call it inscape—we ourselves were brought back to life.

And to think it all started at a roundabout one afternoon as the sun was going down on that beautiful little village by the sea, Byron Bay.

EPILOGUE

What though the radiance which was once so bright
Be now forever taken from my sight,
Though nothing can bring back the hour
Of splendour in the grass, of glory in the flower;
We will grieve not, rather find
Strength in what remains behind...

William Wordsworth

It is midnight as I stand here alone on the Byron headland watching the iconic lighthouse transmit its rhythmic beam out across the ocean. I look up to the moon. A mariner's moon he would have called it; one to guide the weary sailor in to safe harbour.

I recall what Henry Miller said about the greatest adventure we can ever take in life being the one that will lead us *"...inward towards the self"*.

We were a pair of restless spirits. We lived worthy lives some of the time, but bad lives too, it must be said. All at sea, needing to find a safe harbour, that place where we could find our inner selves.

Our inscape and our true north.

I look around the wind-swept headland smothered beneath a tangle of coastal bush and I recall a night all those years ago when we climbed up here, spread our rug, laid out a picnic, got tipsy, got high, made love, fell asleep, and missed what we had come for; to be the first two people in Australia the next day to catch the sunrise.

Ever the conservationist, he had bemoaned the fact that night that the native bush around us was being wiped out by noxious weed. He told me the native vegetation was called *Lepturus repen.*

I remembered the Latin name because it sounded like "lecherous weapon" and we laughed about it and made love all over again on the strength of the inference.

He told me about the goats that night, too. Since the beginning of the century the goats had roamed these headlands. The lighthouse keeper had introduced them as food for himself. The goats were just one of the many Byron stories I loved hearing him tell in that creamy Californian accent, so like drowning in sweet caramel.

I continue to stand, face bared to the wind, scanning the dark horizon. The picture is out there, way out there, beyond the waves. Now I see it, I feel it, feel myself enfolded in the intimacy of *Tuska's* cabin, the pair of us tucked in below deck, the boat gently rocking as waves lap the hull.

Yuri sits on the double bunk, his sarong rolled down at the waist, bare feet, bare chest, his body a golden tan, and with a half-consumed White Russian close by as he picks out cords on his guitar and smiles up at me from time to time to see how his music is going down.

I'm in the galley cooking the day's catch on our tiny kerosene stove; fillets of whiting tossed with ginger, green onions, chili, a whiff of garlic, soy sauce and a squeeze of lime.

I smile as I see us making love after the supper dishes are cleared away. I hear Yuri say he will take a turn topside, keep watch while I grab some kip.

I see him climb the gangway and exit out the hatch. He will be standing up there on deck, arms folded, looking up to the skies as he studies the stars.

I can just picture it.

Then the moon dips behind a cloud and the vision vanishes. He is gone.